A Brief History of Northern Kentucky

A Brief History of Northern Kentucky

Robert D. Webster

Foreword by Paul A. Tenkotte

south limestone

Published by South Limestone Books
An imprint of the University Press of Kentucky

Editorial and Sales Offices: The University Press of Kentucky
663 South Limestone Street, Lexington, Kentucky 40508-4008
www.kentuckypress.com

Except where noted, photos are from the author's collection.

Cataloging-in-Publication data available from the Library of Congress

ISBN 978-0-8131-7787-8 (hardcover : alk. paper)
ISBN 978-0-8131-7788-5 (pdf)
ISBN 978-0-8131-7789-2 (epub)

This book is printed on acid-free paper meeting
the requirements of the American National Standard
for Permanence in Paper for Printed Library Materials.

Manufactured in the United States of America.

Contents

Foreword

A History of Northern Kentucky, by Robert D. Webster, fills an important need in providing a historical overview of Kentucky's third-largest metropolitan region. The book benefits from the research of various previous authors as well as many recent works, including *The Encyclopedia of Northern Kentucky* (2009). In addition, Webster's previous books, *The Beverly Hills Supper Club: The Untold Story behind Kentucky's Worst Tragedy* (2012), *Northern Kentucky Fires* (2006), and *The Balcony Is Closed: A History of Northern Kentucky's Long-Forgotten Neighborhood Movie Theaters* (2007), help to round out this overview. So, too, do many articles from *Northern Kentucky Heritage,* the longtime, award-winning journal dedicated to the region's history. Edited by Karl Lietzenmayer, *Northern Kentucky Heritage* has encouraged the study of the area's history and provided a forum for scholars to exchange new ideas and research.

Webster's analysis of Northern Kentucky's prehistory, as well as his coverage of early pioneers, is superb. For too long, historians have repeated errors and myths dealing with explorers such as Christopher Gist. Webster boldly explains, in detail, how some of these inaccuracies and myths occurred and diplomatically corrects them. Likewise, he succinctly captures and vividly recounts for readers important points from John Burns's unpublished multivolume manuscript on Covington, Kentucky.

Readers will enjoy Webster's overview of the Civil War period, which reflects current scholarship. The nineteenth- and twentieth-century sections of the book are seasoned with stories relating to Northern Kentucky's businesses and entertainment venues, including its notorious gambling establishments. The tragedies of the Flood of 1937, World

War II, and the Beverly Hills Supper Club fire also rightly take their place in this history of Northern Kentucky.

Webster has a gift for making history come alive. Further, he appreciates the value of illustrations in elaborating important points. This overview of Northern Kentucky history will contribute greatly to what residents of the region already appreciate. As one of the points of Kentucky's prosperous Golden Triangle, Northern Kentucky will continue to grow, occupying an increasingly significant position in the chronicles of Kentucky history.

Paul A. Tenkotte

Preface

There have certainly been many books already written about the Commonwealth of Kentucky. In fact, exciting accounts of heroic pioneers and frontiersmen have been scribed as early as John Filson's 1784 work, *The Discovery, Settlement and Present State of Kentucke.* In 1858, T. S. Arthur and W. H. Carpenter published a much-needed update, appropriately titled *The History of Kentucky,* and since then dozens of books have found their way into our public libraries, private collections, and school classrooms. As one might expect, each of these talented historians has provided readers with a slightly different perspective on Kentucky's incredible past. All, however, seem to have the same flaw: they exclude countless facts and profiles regarding the history of the northernmost part of the state.

There is little argument from those living in the region that Northern Kentucky has been slighted by historians for decades. Moreover, there is apparently a common belief that Kentucky's northern border is an imaginary line between Carrollton and Maysville and that the entire region north of that line seceded years ago and is now its own state. In Ruby Baugher and Sarah Claypool's *Kentucky: Yesterday and Today,* for example, there is no mention whatsoever of Thomas Kennedy, whose property became the city of Covington; James Taylor Jr., who founded Newport; or Jacob Fowler, the first permanent settler in the region. Even Thomas D. Clark's *History of Kentucky,* likely the most respected reference on the state, shows little regard for what many experts have now termed Kentucky's "stepchild region." In James C. and Freda Klotter's *A Concise History of Kentucky* (2008), the founding of Harrodsburg and Boonesborough is covered in earnest, but nowhere is there any mention of Banklick Creek, one of the most important travel routes for militias heading off to fight Indians in the Ohio Country; Bullittsburg Baptist Church, established near the time Kentucky was admitted into the Union and still in existence today; or the Rabbit Hash General Store, a Boone County business in continuous operation since 1831. Incredibly, even the tragic Beverly Hills Supper Club fire, which killed 169 people and remains one of the worst tragedies in United States history, is not mentioned at all. Clearly, for those interested in the history of Northern Kentucky, a new book was necessary.

There is no denying that the people, places, and events within Northern Kentucky differ greatly from those in the rest of the state and, therefore, their history is equally unique. Even novice historians and scholars are aware of Daniel Boone's epic adventures through the Cumberland Gap. Few know, however, that the early settlement of Northern Kentucky had far more to do with the Ohio River than the Wilderness Road and that Boone roamed Northern Kentucky well before founding his namesake fort.

Many unfamiliar with the region view the northernmost counties as strictly urban, as the southern suburb of neighboring Cincinnati, Ohio. However, much of the region is actually comprised of wonderful green pastures and beautiful rolling hills, with large working farms and orchards. Indeed, it may surprise many in the Central Bluegrass or Jackson Purchase regions to know there are thousands of horses roaming the upper twelve counties and an equal number of cattle, sheep, chickens, and every other type of domesticated farm animal. Many residents of Northern Kentucky are connoisseurs of Kentucky bourbon, even though that fine potion is more associated with the Bardstown area. Unlike residents in the rest of the state, however, Northern Kentuckians are quite familiar with the heritage and unique tastes of the many beers now produced or once produced there, and only Northern Kentuckians are acquainted with "goetta," as few people south of Dry Ridge have ever heard of the German-inspired breakfast staple so popular in the Greater Cincinnati area.

Certainly, many residents of Northern Kentucky see themselves as Southern Cincinnatians, and with good reason, since Kentucky's northernmost counties are officially encompassed within the Greater Cincinnati metropolitan area. But that does not mean they ignore their proud

Kentucky roots and heritage. How can they, when so many of those residents live in counties named for two of Kentucky's most famous pioneers: Daniel Boone and Simon Kenton? To paraphrase Shakespeare: "If you prick a Northern Kentuckian, do they not bleed UK blue?"

This book, long overdue, focuses on Northern Kentucky, concentrating on the state's upper twelve counties. It is in no way intended to be a complete history and is not meant to be a replacement for other works on the state, but rather a companion to them. Kentucky is a magnificent and extremely beautiful state with a long and interesting history, and I in no way intend to imply any disrespect toward other authors or other regions. It is simply time that the early explorers, settlers, businesses, and families connected to Northern Kentucky finally get their well-deserved place in the history of this fine Commonwealth.

Many previous authors and historians are to be acknowledged for their contribution, as literally hundreds of books, articles, research papers, and websites were studied over the course of four years to compile this work. Special thanks go to the dozens of contributors to *The Encyclopedia of Northern Kentucky.* A tremendous amount of new, up-to-date information was also included, of course, meticulously interlaced with the old.

Most importantly, this project could not have been completed without the support of many. I first want to thank my wonderful wife, Pam, and my son, Kevin, who, as with my previous books, endured many months with me closed off in my office or at the library. Many other family members and friends have also offered their encouragement to me and supported my goal to help archive this region's history. Finally, I feel blessed to have had the full support of the Kenton County Historical Society, the Kenton County Public Library, and many fellow local historians.

As Nick Clooney, the well-loved celebrity from this region, former news anchor, brother to singer and film star Rosemary Clooney, and father to actor George Clooney, so eloquently stated in the Kentucky Educational Television (KET) documentary *Where the River Bends,* "Northern Kentucky is a place like many others, and yet there is really no other place just like it."

1

Northern Kentucky's Prehistory

Northern Kentucky's unique history began long before the founding of Covington, Florence, or Independence—its largest cities in 2019—and long before Daniel Boone and Simon Kenton explored that landscape while dodging Indians, who often met settlers with violence. In fact, the very reason this province is now home to hundreds of thousands of "Northern Kentuckians" involves the way it was miraculously sculpted by nature millions of years ago, during this region's prehistory.[1]

It is widely accepted today that some 600 million years ago there was but one large land mass on planet Earth, known as Pangaea. Several species of dinosaur roamed Pangaea; and, over time, climate changes allowed the introduction of various forms of vegetation. Over millions of years, a series of earthquakes and volcanic eruptions caused this body of land to break into two large sections. A mass extinction took place more than 150 million years ago, the exact causes of which are still debated.[2] Afterward, the two land masses continued to drift and split apart, forming continents similar to what we have today, but in far different positions on the globe. North America, in fact, was turned some 90 degrees clockwise, with Northern Kentucky positioned near the equator. New creatures roamed the continents by this time, including the Apatosaurus, Diplodocus, and Brachiosaurus, some of the largest animals to ever walk the Earth.[3]

Sea levels rose and fell at great extremes 5 million years ago, completely covering and then receding from the continents numerous times over. The Northern Kentucky–Greater Cincinnati region permanently emerged above sea level when a large portion of the continental plate bulged upward. Today, the region still rests on the crest of that uplift, known as the Cincinnati Arch;[4] and within the limestone layers in much of the region, fossil remains of sea creatures abound.[5] The Pliocene Epoch followed, lasting until about 2.5 million years ago.[6] At this time, Northern Kentucky was abundantly filled with a variety of animals, including the ground sloth and the glyptodont, a large armadillo-type armored creature.[7] The continents continued to drift somewhat, but were very close to their present-day positions. The climate, especially during the latter part of the period, was only slightly warmer than what is currently experienced in the region.

While the Ohio River exists today as the region's major waterway, as well as the northern border of Kentucky, it did not exist as we know it 2 million years ago. Numerous rivers and creeks emptied into two ancient primary waterways, known as the Old Kentucky River and the Old Licking River. The Old Kentucky River ran a similar path to its present-day course, from the southeast to what is now Carrollton, but then turned to the northeast and followed what is now the Ohio River to the present-day Great Miami River. From there it ran north, in reverse of that river's current flow. The Old Licking River is the oldest waterway in this region.[8] It ran from deep in Kentucky to what is now southern Campbell County. There, some believe the river veered to the northeast to approximately present-day Mentor, where it turned northwest along what is now the Ohio River. The waterway continued to the Lunken Airport area of Cincinnati, where it ran the same course as today's Little Miami River, though in reverse, through Fairfax, Ohio, before turning west through St. Bernard, Ohio.[9] Others, however, believe the river continued through today's Campbell County to present-day Newport, where it veered slightly westward before turning north into the present-day Mill Creek, basically following what is now Interstate 75 through Cincinnati. Either way, these waterways became what many geologists term the Ancient Cincinnati River,[10] which emptied into a far more important ancient waterway known as the Teays River (pronounced *taze*).[11] The Teays flowed northwest from what is now West Virginia, through the central part of Ohio, Indiana, and Illinois, before turning south and joining the approximate path of the modern-day Mississippi River. An Old Ohio River existed, but not at Cincinnati. It was a much smaller tributary with headwaters at present-day Madison, Indiana, from where it ran southwestwardly toward the Mississippi.

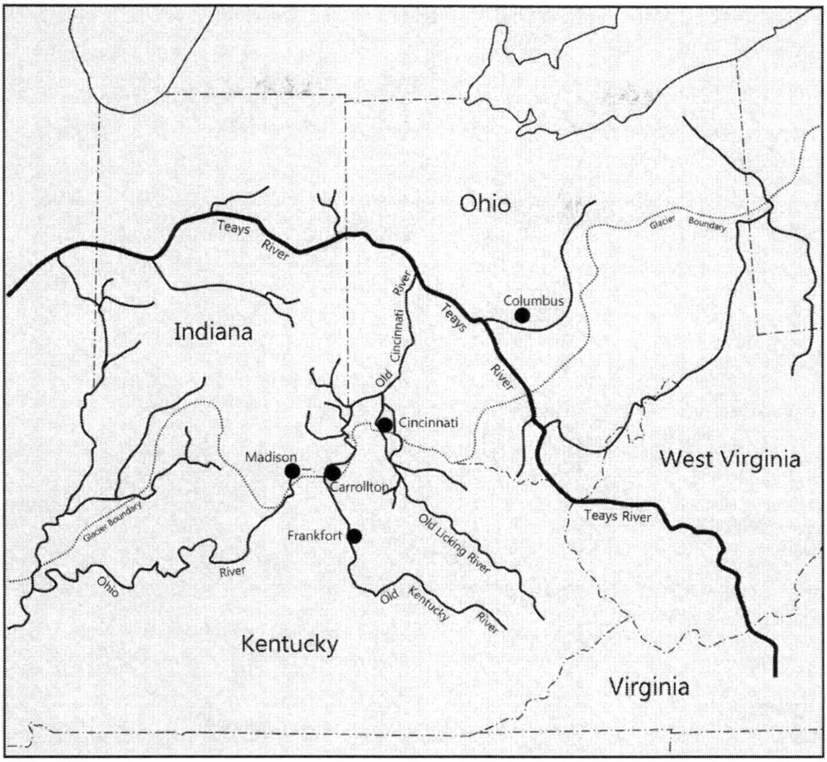

Ancient Teays river system. Map by Robert Webster.

Incredibly, the Teays River, now considered one of the great master rivers of world history, was never seen by human eyes.[12] This is due to events that occurred during the next epoch, the Pleistocene—commonly referred to as the Ice Age. That river's deep gorges and broad valleys, as well as remnants of its many tributaries, now lie hidden under mile-thick glacier deposits that were strewed throughout the region south of the Great Lakes.[13] The existence of the Teays was first studied in the 1830s, but it was not until 1983, at a meeting of the Geological Society of America, that a majority of scientists finally admitted that evidence of the Teays River's existence was overwhelming, and its study then increased in both frequency and significance. By 2019, nearly the entire course of the Teays has been accurately mapped. As mentioned, some modern-day rivers, such as the Scioto in Ohio, have completely reversed their direction of flow from the prehistoric era. While the Scioto now flows south over a deep bed of glacier material, past Columbus and Chillicothe to the Ohio River at Portsmouth, the bedrock beneath clearly shows that it once flowed north as part of the Teays system.[14]

During the Pleistocene period, or Ice Age, glaciers or ice sheets slowly moved across the landscape, accumulating sediment such as rocks, gravel, sand, and other debris. These materials became embedded in the ice and were carried along with the glaciers. Low areas were filled in and higher areas were scoured off completely, to be deposited many miles away. When the ice sheets melted, over hundreds of years, large volumes of material were left behind, mainly as outwash deposits in river and stream valleys.[15]

Experts have identified four specific glacier events that occurred in the eastern United States: the Nebraskan (the oldest), the Kansan, the Illinoisan, and the Wisconsin (the youngest).[16] All four directly or indirectly affected Northern Kentucky in some way, but remains of the Illinoisan events are far more evident and have been more widely studied. These glacier occurrences, between 200,000 and 132,000 years ago, destroyed much of the Teays River and its tributaries and transformed the entire drainage pattern, thereby assisting in the creation of the modern-day Ohio River Valley. While lands north of the new Ohio River were greatly altered, the massive ice sheets were restricted to the valley bottoms south of the river. Therefore, much of present-day Northern Kentucky offers the incredible beauty of rolling hills and meadows, while the majority of the landscape north of the Ohio River is far more level and unnoteworthy.

While glaciers are known to have carried mostly small sediment material into Northern Kentucky, massive boulders were also transplanted into this region from upper North America. One well-known feature in present-day Boone County, known as Split Rock, may date to the Illinoisan period.[17] Found at the confluence of Woolper Creek and the Ohio River, Split Rock is a wonderful example of a collection of conglomerate rock. Other large transplanted boulders in the region include the 16-ton Epworth boulder in Lewis County and the 3-ton Farmers granite boulder found in Rowan County. Microscopic studies of these specimens indicate their derivation from the area between Ottawa and Quebec City, Canada.[18]

After these incredible glacier events, an extended calm period allowed the newly formed Ohio River system time to adjust to its new course and profile. The southern shore of the new river quickly became an attractive place for post–Ice Age animals and, in short time, human inhabitants. Animals from the entire region were attracted to the suddenly abundant food supply, especially in present-day Boone County.[19] There, a series of saline springs that flowed from the floodplain of Big Bone Creek created a "lick," more commonly referred to as a "salt lick"—a deposit of minerals enjoyed by animals and used as supplements in their diet. In this case, these minerals included calcium, magnesium, sodium, and zinc. Massive woolly mammoths; mastodons, some nine feet tall and averaging 10,000 pounds; ground sloths the size of large tree trunks; giant stag moose; and beavers the size of bears all roamed the area.[20] In fact, fossil remains of over twenty-six species have been identified there.[21] The area immediately surrounding these salt springs, however, was extremely soft and marshy, and many experts believe these large animals became stuck during their visits—with no means of escape. Many were trampled or drowned.[22] Years later, when the first Europeans arrived in the region, they discovered the skeletal remains left by these enormous creatures, and the area was termed "Big Bone." Other salt licks, many of significant size, existed throughout Northern Kentucky, especially in present-day Kenton, Mason, and Robertson counties. Big Bone Lick, however, is considered Northern Kentucky's most famous geologic feature—not so much as a result of the salt lick itself, but for the extensive fossil collection found there.

So massive were the herds of these large animals, especially the mammoths and mastodons, that wide paths or "traces" were created throughout the region, marking their yearly migration habits.[23] Each year, thousands of animals traveled between the prairies of Central Ohio to grazing sites in Northern and Central Kentucky. Land between the Great Miami and Little Miami rivers in Ohio funneled these herds south, where they crossed the Ohio just west of the Licking River and then followed higher ground at present-day Greenup Street in Covington. Five miles south of the Ohio River, this trace passed by a small salt lick later known as Latonia Springs (at today's KY 17 and Highland Avenue), before continuing southwest along Banklick Creek and then west to Big Bone Lick.[24] A secondary route likely veered west from what is now Pike Street and Madison Avenue, following today's Dixie Highway to higher ground through Park Hills and Fort Mitchell, eventually extending into Central Kentucky. The major east-west trace extended from Big Bone Lick southwest along Eagle Creek, then south to Drennon Lick in Henry County before veering southeast, crossing the Kentucky River and proceeding through Stamping Ground, so named for these traveling herds. This route then headed south to what is now Great Crossing (due west of Georgetown, where a large ford across Elkhorn Creek existed), then to present-day Paris, the Blue Licks Region, Mays Lick, and eventually Maysville.[25] While initially a major highway for herds of prehistoric animals, these same trails, and their smaller tributaries, became essential means of travel for some of the earliest human civilizations.

2

Ancient Civilizations and Historic Peoples

Well before the people we know as Native Americans, and long before Europeans began their migration to the New World, Northern Kentucky was home to several ancient civilizations. In fact, human inhabitants first occupied this region as early as 12000 BC.[1] Until recently, most experts believed these early humans migrated to the Americas from Asia by way of a large strip of land now submerged beneath the Bering Strait west of Alaska.[2] New archeological studies, however, may point not only to a few alternative migration paths, including from Europe east to west, but also to an earlier date range as well, as long as 20,000 years ago. Of course, the study of when, where, and how humans first entered North America is likely never-ending. Within the past ten years, for example, new techniques to study DNA, such as polymerase chain reaction, or PCR, have enabled researchers to study even the most minute samples of human fossil evidence and are far more accurate in determining not only the age, but in many cases the actual ancestry of the sample.[3] Whatever the migration routes and the date range, these early inhabitants remained for several thousand years, and the archeological record in this region has been divided into four general phases, or periods: the Paleo (before 8000 BC), the Archaic (circa 8000 BC to 1500 BC), the Woodland (1500 BC to about AD 1000), and the Fort Ancient (AD 1000 to after AD 1600).

Paleo-period Indians entered the eastern United States after the Wisconsin glaciers.[4] They hunted the last of the large Pleistocene mammals, including the mammoth and mastodon, but evidence indicates they had a varied diet of both plants and animals. Archeology has identified both intensive and small, isolated sites from the Paleo period throughout much of the United States, although no habitation sites have been documented in Northern Kentucky.[5] Clovis-style projectile points, attributed to the Paleo, have been found throughout the region, however, especially near Big Bone Lick and in present-day Mason and Gallatin counties.

Site investigations of the Early Archaic period, around 8000 BC, indicate use of seasonal camps, often a base camp with outlying activity camps. Also, their tools indicate a more substantial use of vegetables as a food source. A wide range of Early Archaic–period sites have been discovered in Northern Kentucky, from isolated projectile points found in fields to intensive sites, generally located on river terraces.[6] Boone County has at least twenty such sites, especially in the Big Bone Lick region.

A drier, warmer climate existed for the Middle Archaic culture, from about 4500 BC. Plant and animal resources increased, and the use of stone mortars and pestles is seen for the first time. With nutting stones, grooved axes, and celts, this suggests an increased involvement in plant foraging and woodworking by the region's tribes. However, fewer Middle Archaic sites have been discovered and, as of 2019, none have been excavated.

The Late Archaic period, from about 2600 BC to 1750 BC, was marked by an increase in population. Also, clear evidence of complex trade networks over the eastern United States has been discovered. Copper from the Great Lakes, for instance, and sea shells from the Mississippian culture have been found within burial mounds, possibly indicating a status differential for the first time. The Late Archaic people hunted deer, turkey, and rabbit, and also enjoyed wild plants as a food staple. This culture also began cultivating small gardens and constructed baskets to gather food and carry other belongings. Late Archaic humans lived in one place longer than their predecessors, but still for only a few months at a time. Evidence of Late Archaic–period sites increased dramatically compared with those from earlier periods, with nearly one hundred sites researched within the region.[7]

Three main points demonstrate the difference between the Late Archaic and the Early Woodland people in Northern Kentucky. First is the presence of pottery in the Early Woodland period. Second, fewer Early Woodland sites have been discovered, indicating a decrease in population. And third, though a bit later in time, burial mounds begin to appear for the first time.[8] A total of fifty-one sites in the area contain Early Woodland–period artifacts, though none include intensive villages. Once again, most of these sites are found in present-day Boone County. The West Runway Site, for example, at the Greater Cincinnati–Northern Kentucky International Airport, was excavated and provided information on Early Woodland–period activities, including burial mounds and other earthworks. While much has been learned regarding the Early Woodland culture, in many ways their traditions are not fully understood even today. This is in part because the culture is usually discussed only in terms of its elaborate burial ceremonialism.[9] Their practice of building burial mounds, for example, often 10 to 20 feet high, resulted in their being termed the "Mound Builder" society by many nineteenth-century observers.[10]

Evidence of copper and shells are seen for the first time within the Middle Woodland period, and some of these materials were used in ornamental pieces, such as bracelets, beads, and rings. Evidence of the first use of spears for hunting and fishing is also seen during this period.[11] Numerous sites dating from 500 BC to AD 200 were excavated during the 1930s and 1940s, including Robbins Mound, Hartman Mound, and the Crigler Mounds.[12] The Hopewell Complex, centered near Chillicothe, Ohio, typically defines the Middle Woodland period. Extensive Hopewell earthworks are known and still exist in southwestern Ohio, including elaborate geometric mounds. Little evidence, however, has been found in Northern Kentucky connecting regional tribes to the Hopewell Complex. A few habitation sites, such as the Rogers Lower Village in Boone County, have produced Hopewell period artifacts, but no elaborate earthworks have been documented.[13]

During the Late Woodland period, there was an increased emphasis on domesticated plants, supplemented by hunting and intensive gathering. Late Woodland–period sites and artifacts have been documented in parts of Owen and Carroll County. Seasonal and, in some cases, year-round occupation of village sites located on terraces overlooking major stream valleys is seen in the Newtown Phase, named after a town in southwestern Ohio. The Roger's Site, including two villages and a mound and located along the river in Boone County, is one of many Newtown Phase sites in Northern Kentucky. Other sites in

Crigler Mounds, after extensive excavation. This site was located between present-day Taylorsport and Constance, Boone County. Courtesy www.nkyviews.com.

the region include at least eight in Owen County and four in Mason County.

The Fort Ancient culture existed from around AD 1000 to at least the 1600s, and was the last of the prehistoric cultures. Evidence of the first use of the bow and arrow is seen with the Fort Ancient people, who hunted deer, elk, turkey, and other small animals, as well as large birds, utilizing triangular-shaped projectile points. Fishing skills were greatly enhanced with the first use of hooks, harpoons, and nets. They also farmed beans, squash, and pumpkins as well as corn, which comprised as much as 70 percent of their diet.[14] They created hoes for gardening; and, like some of the Late Woodland–period people, they stored excess food in underground pits similar to small cellars. They tempered their pottery with shells instead of grit or limestone and produced jars, bowls, plates, and bottles, many of which included handles.

Northern Kentucky was home to several Fort Ancient–period villages, including documented sites in each of the thirteen northernmost counties. These sites are concentrated along the Ohio River Valley and major streams, and excavations indicate far more complex villages than earlier cultures. At least 300 people resided within many of these villages, with larger individual family dwellings as well. Year-round habitation continued throughout the Fort Ancient period, and typical settlements were built with houses in a circular pattern, each door facing toward the center of the compound. The middle of the complex was typically used as a community gathering space.

The Fort Ancient people buried their dead in mounds, and later in actual cemeteries within the settlements. By the early 1500s, sites overall were much smaller in size and fewer in number. Increased contact with the Mississippian people is evident by that time as well. Artifacts in Southwestern Ohio, for example, include negative-painted pottery, notched and beaded rims, and effigies, all items and styles associated with the Mississippian culture.[15] Within the late Fort Ancient period, there is also clear evidence of contact with some of the earliest European explorers and traders. Glass beads, as well as fragments of iron kettles, have been discovered at many gravesites. These likely originated from French missionaries or trappers who had traveled along the Ohio River by the early 1500s. In Boone County, sites have been located along Gunpowder Creek, Big Bone Creek, and Mud Lick Creek, as well as at Petersburg—an area rich with evidence of prehistoric civilizations. Extensive archeological research took place there from 1990 to 1992, where three previously known sites were examined in greater detail. As a result, over 1,200 schoolchildren and adults benefited from on-site visits, workshops, and classroom presentations.[16] In 2004, archeologists returned to Petersburg after the accidental discovery of human remains during construction of a home's foundation. Over ten days, thirty-five burials were excavated, representing thirty-eight individuals from the Fort Ancient period.

In Bracken County, evidence of the Fort Ancient people has been found along the Ohio River between Bracken Creek and Locust Creek. A letter from Brigadier General John Payne, an officer during the War of 1812, gives the following account of burial grounds he discovered: "From the cellar under my dwelling, sixty by seventy feet, 110 skeletons were taken. I numbered them by the skulls; skeletons were of all sizes, from seven feet to the infant. … In my garden, Indian arrowheads of flint were found and earthenware of clay and pounded mussel. A post hole near the river cannot be dug without turning up human bones, everywhere between the mouths of Bracken and Locust Creek."[17]

Fort Ancient mounds existed in what is now Kenton County as well. One notable site was located at the end of West Eleventh Street in Covington.[18] In addition, two large mounds were known to exist in the area of the old Ludlow Lagoon Amusement Park. In 1975, Kenton-Campbell Sanitation District workers all but destroyed a prehistoric campsite and burial ground while working on a project just south of Chiseled Bridge, along the 3-L Highway (Old KY 17), in a forty-seven-acre flatland at what is now Pioneer Park.[19] University of Kentucky researchers had discovered the site in 1925, a mound fifteen feet in diameter and five feet high, containing a triple-walled stone grave in the center with a number of burials surrounding.

Evidence of ancient settlements has been discovered throughout present-day Mason County as well, far too many to detail here. The most significant by far is known as the Fox Farm site, or Fox Fields. Since its discovery and first excavation in 1895, hundreds of skeletons and thousands of artifacts have been taken from the site.[20] While most excavations revealed evidence common with other sites in the region, a few extreme abnormalities were found as well. For instance, at some burial mounds only partial skeletons were found and some remains appeared as if they were just thrown into the graves in haste. Relics and symbols attributed to early Spanish explorers were also found. Certainly, when Europeans first began settling North America along the east coast and along the Mississippi River, they began trading with local natives, and some of those European goods made their way into the Fort Ancient settlements long before Europeans ever arrived in the Kentucky region.[21] It is believed, however, that no Europeans ever witnessed firsthand an occupied Fort Ancient settlement in Northern Kentucky. A site five miles south of Maysville, still visible in 2019 along the eastern side of KY 11, is also unusual. The single mound is some twelve feet high and ninety feet in diameter at the base, with an average slope of six to ten feet. While the mound is considered quite large in comparison to others, only seven remains were found there. Even more unusual, most of the bodies were buried in pairs, and each was laid on a stone bed or had a stone pillow.

One of the few remaining ancient Indian burial mounds left in Kentucky, situated along Route 11 in southern Mason County.

Evidence of the Fort Ancient people's existence disappeared fairly abruptly between 1650 and 1700. Many researchers cite the introduction of European diseases as the main cause for their extinction.[22] However, finding direct evidence to support that theory is difficult.[23] Another principal theory for their demise is warfare.[24] Evidence indicates that most later sites—those in the northeastern part of the region, for example—were clearly designed as defensive fortifications. In addition, a greater number of skeletal remains around those sites were found with arrowheads embedded in them. It also remains unclear what relationship, if any, the Fort Ancient people had to the historic-era Indian tribes such as the Shawnee, Miami, or Iroquois, who would soon be found in parts of this region. Some scholars believe that similarities within the material culture, art, and mythology of the Fort Ancient people link closely with the Shawnee tribe, making them at the very least a close relative.[25] A few historians believe that some tribes, including the Cherokee, may have actually lived in Kentucky during the mid-seventeenth century.[26] That concept has little merit, however, since there is no supporting evidence for it.[27]

At any rate, by the early 1700s, the Fort Ancient civilization was gone from the region and various groups of what we might call "American Indians" were traveling through parts of Northern Kentucky on a regular basis, generally on hunting expeditions. While commonly referred to as "Native Americans," this civilization was no more "native" to North America as the ancient civilizations who had come before, nor the European settlers who would soon follow, as each clearly migrated here from elsewhere. Specific tribes common to Northern Kentucky include the Shawnee, Miami, Delaware, Wyandot, and Mingo, whose settlements, at least by the mid-1700s, were found mainly in Central, Southeastern, and Southwestern Ohio.[28] These "Northern Kentucky Indians" utilized the abundant salt licks throughout the region, including that at Big Bone, Blue Licks (present-day Robertson County), and elsewhere. Buffalo were still quite abundant in the region at this time, as were deer and elk, and Indians who hunted and explored throughout Northern Kentucky traveled upon the ancient trails created by these animals and their ancient predecessors, such as the woolly mammoth and mastodon.

Kentucky

It is difficult to discuss the history of Northern Kentucky without attempting to tackle the question regarding the origin of the name. Researchers agree that the word *Kentucky* is from American Indian dialect, though there seems to be a great deal of confusion regarding from which tribe or tribes the term originates. One thing is very clear: "Kentucky" does not mean "dark and bloody ground," as was presented by historians and taught in school classrooms many decades ago.[29] In reality, various early European explorers—the first who traveled west of the Alleghenies—documented their English interpretations of the unusual syllables they heard the many tribes speak in reference to the region south of the Ohio River. "Kentucky," "Caintuke," "Kentucke," and "Cantucky" were the words most often transcribed in these early journals. As for meaning, however, there seems to be a mixture of definitions among the various tribes. The Wyandot translation, for example, was "fair land of tomorrow," while the Shawnee used both "land of cane" and "at the head of the river." The Mohawk and Delaware used "among the meadows," while "prairie" was used by the Catawba Indians.[30] Therefore, if asked: "What does the word *Kentucky* mean?" the most accurate reply might be: "fair land of tomorrow filled with cane, prairies, and meadows at the head of the river."

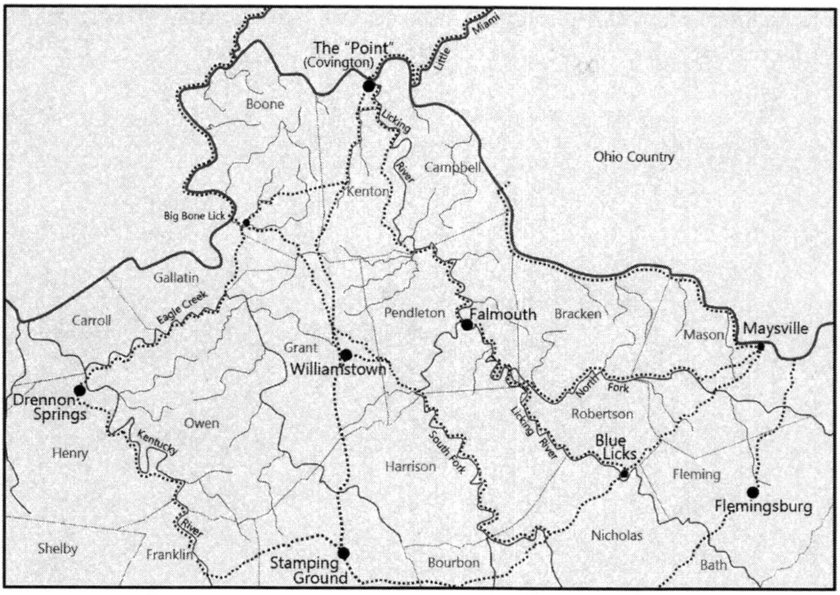

Principal buffalo/Indian trails in Northern Kentucky. Map created by Robert Webster from information gathered from several sources, including Joseph Gastright's "Buffalo Traces," in *The Encyclopedia of Northern Kentucky*, ed. Paul A. Tenkotte and James C. Claypool (Lexington: University Press of Kentucky, 2009), 128; and Willard Rouse Jillson, *Pioneer Kentucky* (Ann Arbor, MI: Standard Printing Co., 1936).

Today, virtually every major highway in Northern Kentucky is a converted Indian/animal trace. Two major arteries include the Licking River Trace and the Dry Ridge Trace. The Licking River Trace followed the western shore of the Licking River, from the Ohio River to Decoursey Creek, southwest to the ridge at present-day Marshall Road, southeast to Bowman Creek and today's Kenton Station Road, and then along what is now Decoursey Pike to Morning View. From there it continued south to Falmouth and beyond. The Dry Ridge Trace followed the "old" 3-L Highway (Madison Pike) along Banklick Creek to near present-day Independence, where it forked. One route roughly followed KY 16 to Walton and today's Dixie Highway (US 25), through Dry Ridge to near Lexington, while the other route extended west to Big Bone Lick. One important secondary trace extended from Big Bone Lick southeast to present-day Williamstown, then east to May's Lick, while others existed at several other locations along the Ohio River.

3

Early Northern Kentucky Explorers

By 1750, various tribes of American Indians were roaming what is now Northern Kentucky, generally on hunting and salt gathering expeditions. Spanish explorers had claimed present-day Florida, establishing St. Augustine in 1565, and had also laid claim to parts of what is now Mexico and the Southwest. The French had established numerous settlements in their territory of New France, extending from Quebec in the north (1608) to New Orleans in the south (1718). English settlements had been established all along the eastern seaboard, starting with Jamestown (1607) and Plymouth (1620), and including larger settlements at Boston (1630), Philadelphia (1681), Savannah (1733), and elsewhere. The population of New France was about 75,000, but more than one million people were living in the thirteen English colonies at this time, even though the French held far more territory than the English in the New World .[1] While settlements in what is now Northern Kentucky would not exist for many years, a handful of explorers had already made their way into that section of the vast western frontier, and many more would soon follow.

Many earlier histories erroneously credit Dr. Thomas Walker as the first European to explore Kentucky. Walker crossed the Alleghenies in 1750 with the Loyal Land Company, naming many of the region's topographical features during his expedition, including the Cumberland Gap. While he was never in the northernmost part of the future state, he did locate, while in the vicinity of present-day Salyersville, the source of a north-flowing waterway he named Frederick's River.[2] Referred to by Indians as Great Salt Lick Creek, we now know this major tributary, critical to the early settlement of Northern Kentucky, as the Licking

River. John Filson (1747–1788), early historian and one of the first to map the new Kentucky Territory, credits pioneer James McBride with being "the first white man we have certain accounts of who discovered this province in the year 1754."[3] McBride explored near the mouth of the Kentucky River, another extremely important waterway for the future settlement of the region, and apparently carved his initials into a tree there that same year.

Neither Walker nor McBride, however, can be credited with being the first "white man" to visit the western frontier. In fact, it is impossible to determine with any certainty exactly who was first. Several local historians, however, have mistakenly given that prestigious title to Christopher Gist. While his 1750–51 expedition, to be discussed shortly, played a vital role in the future settling of the Northern Kentucky region, Gist, contrary to local folklore, was never in the extreme northernmost part of the state, and was far from being the first to explore the West. Actually, the first explorer in the region was not even English: several French explorers predated the English by many decades.[4] René-Robert Cavelier Sieur de La Salle, for example, led an expedition down the Ohio River in 1669, reaching west of the Licking River, and most likely up parts of the Kentucky River as well.[5] In 1692, Arnout Viele, a Dutch fur trader from New York, made a successful journey down the Ohio River all the way to the Mississippi.[6] Not only had Spanish and French explorers traveled the region's waterways well before 1700, especially those in the westernmost part of the state; they had also developed extensive trade with Indians there by that time.[7] And if the journal of Hernando de Soto is accurate, he and his entourage traveled north from present-day Florida, crossing the westernmost edge of Kentucky in May 1541.[8]

Regardless of who it was, the earliest Europeans to explore what is now Northern Kentucky did not do so by horseback, nor did they scale the treacherous Appalachian Mountains or pass through the Cumberland Gap from Virginia. They arrived by means of what would soon become the main "highway" into the new West, that being the Ohio River. These explorers came first by canoe and then later by raft or flatboat, down the often treacherous waterway from such places as Maryland, New York, and Pennsylvania.[9] While most written histories on Kentucky emphasize the Cumberland Gap and the Wilderness Trail when speaking of the early settlement of the state, it is estimated that as many as 80 percent of the earliest inhabitants of Northern Kentucky actually found their new homesteads through what were known as the "river routes" rather than that highly publicized cross-country trail. As historian John Burns states, "Although the Wilderness Road played an important role in the state's early development, it remains necessary to point out the tendency of many writers to overstress its importance. Its significance never did match that of the Ohio River route. The Ohio was long the favored way into Kentucky and those who traveled it were patriots to the core."[10]

The first well-documented exploration of Northern Kentucky was in 1739, twelve years before Gist was said to have been in the region, when a detachment of French troops and allied Indians, during a campaign against the Mississippi Chickasaw, departed Canada and traveled down the Allegheny and Ohio rivers, past present-day Newport and Covington. Charles Le Moyne, second Baron de Longueuil, and his party, which included seventeen-year-old assistant engineer Joseph-Gaspard Chaussegros de Léry, discovered a marshy area and salt lick scattered with large bones they believed to be those of massive elephants. The 442-man contingent, including 319 Indians, gathered some of the bones, including a tusk, a femur, and several molars, and took them to their rendezvous point with Jean-Baptiste Le Moyne de Bienville's forces along the Mississippi River. The bones were later taken to the king of France.[11] At what is now Big Bone Lick State Historic Site in southwestern Boone County, the group was in awe at the size of the prehistoric animal bones, as well as the sulfurous springs and salt marshes.[12] In 1740, de Lery's log was used by Louisiana militiaman Philippe Mandeville to create a map of the expedition. While still not the first Europeans to explore Northern Kentucky, they are among the first to have well documented their visit.

Various other Europeans are known to have explored the region well before Gist was said to have been in the area. In 1744, for example, Robert Smith visited the area and even stopped at Big Bone Lick.[13] At the time, Smith was an Indian trader living in the Ohio Country along the Great Miami River.[14] Hugh Crawford also visited Northern Kentucky on numerous occasions before 1750. A trader from Fort Standing Stone, situated along the Juanita River in Pennsylvania, Crawford first went west in 1739. He is most renowned, however, for his later service as an interpreter for Mason and Dixon when they ran that famous line in 1767.[15]

The first explorer of major importance in what is now Northern Kentucky may be the esteemed pioneer and trader, John Finley (1722–1769). Born in Northern Ireland, Finley (also known as Findley) came to Philadelphia in the early 1730s with his parents and several other relatives. Finley had made several excursions west of the Alleghenies before 1750, evidenced by the fact that in a later, far more important visit (to be discussed shortly) he is already aware of many checkpoints and features throughout the Ohio River Valley. It is extremely important here to correct a major misconception with regard to John Finley. Many historians have confused him with Major John Finley, who is credited with discovering Blue Lick Springs, who resided in Fleming County, Kentucky, and who served in the Kentucky House of Representatives.[16] Some have considered these two men one and the same. They clearly were not. Major John Finley (1748–1837) is actually the second cousin of the elder pioneer and explorer, both being descendants of Robert Finley (1636–1712).[17]

As the British colonies became more populated, and as immigrants continued to stream to America, several efforts arose to develop lands west of the natural barrier created by the Allegheny and Appalachian Mountains.[18] Consequently, two important companies formed in colonial Virginia in the late 1740s. The Ohio Company of Virginia was chartered in 1747 and petitioned King George II for a land grant west of the Allegheny Mountains. The company received 200,000 acres on the Ohio River, with provision for an additional 300,000 acres if they built a fort and brought at least 100 settlers. Two years later, the Loyal Land Company of Virginia was chartered and received a grant of 800,000 acres west of the Appalachians. Dr. Thomas Walker was appointed that company's agent, and on March 6, 1750, he embarked on his famed exploration into present-day Kentucky. His party erected a cabin along the northern shore of the Cumberland River, near today's Barbourville, in order to establish a legal claim to the territory. Walker, however, stayed but a few days before returning to Virginia, and it would be nearly twenty years, when Daniel Boone traveled through the Cumberland Gap in 1769, before there would be any renewed interest in settling Kentucky from the southeast.[19]

4

Christopher Gist: Separating Fact from Fiction

Just seven months after Thomas Walker's disappointing expedition into what is now Kentucky, Christopher Gist (1705–1759) began his own expedition. The Ohio Company of Virginia had appointed Gist as their key explorer, and on October 31, 1750, he set out for the Ohio Country. At the time, Gist was living in the Yadkin region of western North Carolina and was focusing his attention on exploring and surveying. When hired, Gist was given specific orders by Virginia Lieutenant Governor Robert Dinwiddie:

> You are to go out as soon as possible to the westward of the great mountains, and carry with you such a number of men as you think necessary, in order to search out and discover the lands upon the river Ohio, and other adjoining branches of the Mississippi, down as low as the great Falls thereof: You are particularly to observe the ways and passes through all the mountains you cross, and take an exact account of the soil, quality, and product of the land, and the wideness and deepness of the rivers, and the several falls belonging to them, together with the courses and bearings of the rivers and mountains as near as you conveniently can. You are also to observe what nations of Indians inhabit there, their strength and numbers, who they trade with, and in what commodities they deal. When you find a large quantity of good, level land, such as you think will suit the Company, you are to measure the breadth of it, in three or four different places, and take the courses of the river and mountains on which it binds in order

> to judge the quantity. You are to fix the beginning and bounds in such a manner that they may be easily found again by your description.[1]

Gist, along with a young black companion, began his journey in Maryland, through the rugged wilderness of Pennsylvania to present-day Pittsburgh. From there, however, and contrary to popular belief, Gist did not follow the Ohio River to Northern Kentucky, but ventured due west into the heart of the Ohio Country. According to his journal, the duo visited several Indian villages, including those at what are now Coshocton, Chillicothe, and Piqua, Ohio, and eventually became guests at Shannoah Town, an Indian village near present-day Portsmouth.[2] While in the Ohio Country, Gist collected information on the various animals and vegetation, including species of trees and grass, as well as evidence of the many Indian settlements in the region. He was extremely detailed on his whereabouts, aided by several other traders and friendly Indians he met throughout that region.

After his stay at Shannoah Town, however, Gist gives far less detailed remarks regarding the names of the creeks and rivers, for the simple fact that they are unfamiliar to him. And although he clearly sees signs of other people having been in the area prior to his arrival, he meets only a couple of men while south of the Ohio River. One fact is incontrovertible: on March 13, 1751, Gist entered the future state of Kentucky opposite present-day Portsmouth, Ohio, and remained in Kentucky for about two weeks. For some unknown reason, many Northern Kentucky historians believe Gist journeyed along the Ohio River all the way to today's Campbell County, crossed the Licking River at its mouth, made a campsite at present-day Covington, and visited Big Bone Lick before continuing on to the Falls of the Ohio (present-day Louisville). Unfortunately, there is nothing within Gist's journal to even remotely suggest these things to be factual—and far more evidence to prove them to be false.

When leaving Shannoah Town on Wednesday, March 13, 1751, Gist states that he and his companion crossed to the southern shore of the Ohio and ventured "down the said river on the SE side 8 M then 10 M." In doing so, the two men entered what is now Greenup County and were most likely just west of present-day Vanceburg, Lewis County, when Gist states he "met two men belonging to Robert Smith . . . and one Hugh Crawford." Gist remarks that the men told him they were returning from an area near the Falls of the Ohio, where a large collection of bones had been found. In fact, Gist was given some of the artifacts and reportedly gave the Ohio Company a large tooth upon his return. Gist's journal entry regarding the bones found by Smith's entourage, at what we now know was Big Bone Lick in present-day Boone County, is quite fascinating:

> The teeth and bones of three large beasts, one of which was somewhat smaller than the other two, were found in a salt lick or spring upon a small creek which runs into the southern side of the Ohio, about 15 M below the mouth of the Great Miami River, and 20 above the Falls. He assured me that the rib bones of the largest of these beasts were 11 feet long and the skull bone six feet wide, the other bones in proportion; and that there were several teeth there, some of which he called horns, and they said they were upwards of five feet long, and as much as a man could well carry. The tooth which I brought to the Ohio Company was a jaw tooth of better weight than four pounds; appearing to be the furthest in the jaw. I also met four Shannoah Indians coming up the river in their canoes, who informed me there were about 60 French Indians camped at the Falls.[3]

While many give Gist credit for personally visiting Big Bone Lick, his journal entry is quite clear. The bones were discovered by Robert Smith's men and were given to Gist, who was only a few miles west of Portsmouth at the time. Gist was clearly never in the vicinity of Big Bone Lick, even though a historical marker later erected at that site commemorates such a visit.

Gist and his companion continued and, at the end of the day on Thursday, March 14, he was in the vicinity of Irwin, Mason County. The following day, Gist most likely made his camp at Cabin Creek, just east of present-day Maysville. The three-day period from Saturday, March 16, to Monday, March 18, however, is by far the most confusing stretch of Gist's entire expedition. Because Gist becomes even more vague with his descriptions after leaving the Maysville area, there has been a great deal of speculation as to any true route. Luckily, he gives enough details regarding the surrounding landscape and waterways that most researchers have agreed upon a "most probable" scenario, to be outlined shortly.[4] A portion of Monday's entry (March 18) is included here, however, in an effort to reverse still another misconception regarding Gist's Kentucky expedition: "This day we heard several guns which made me imagine the French Indians were not moved but were still hunting and firing thereabouts. We also saw some traps newly set, and the footsteps of some Indians plain on the ground as if they had been there the day before. I was now much troubled that I could not comply with my instructions, so I concluded not to go to the Falls, but traveled southward till we were over the little Cuttaway River (the Kentucky River)." While some indicate Gist visited the Falls of the Ohio, he makes it very clear he did not.

Deciphering Gist's journal during this three-day period is critical, as it is the only link between his leaving the Maysville area and his later, confirmed route from central Kentucky to Virginia. Every possibility has been examined over the years by various researchers, but the following scenario is clearly the most plausible: Christopher Gist and his companion traveled out of the Maysville area to the southwest, where they located the North Fork of the Licking River and one of many Indian trails. Following this trail, they ventured northwest into southern Bracken and Pendleton counties and most likely roamed as far north as present-day Falmouth or Butler. Turning to the southwest, they traveled through today's Grant and Owen counties, crossed Eagle Creek, and eventually located the Kentucky River. After traversing that major waterway, the duo headed southwest into central Shelby County before heading due south, where they located the Salt River at present-day Anderson County. From there, they headed southeast, following portions of the Red River and the Kentucky River on their way to Virginia.

Though Gist's route may continue to be debated for centuries, he clearly explored at least parts of present-day Northern Kentucky. It is, however, extremely unlikely that he was ever in Campbell County; he was absolutely never in Kenton or Boone counties; and he most certainly did not visit present-day Covington, Big Bone Lick, and the Falls of the Ohio, as some have suggested.[5] That being said, Gist's expedition was extremely important, not only to the future of Kentucky as a whole but even more so to Northern Kentucky specifically. While Thomas Walker reported back to the Loyal Land Company descriptions of an extremely treacherous mountain range and a rough, nearly uninhabitable countryside during his short visit to the southeastern region of what would soon be Kentucky, Gist's descriptions of what he found in the Ohio Country, as well as the central and northeastern regions of Kentucky, gave many future settlers and land speculators a vision of what was truly the "promised land." Gist said of the Ohio River Valley, "it is well watered with a great number of little streams and rivulets, and full of beautiful meadows, covered with wild rye, bluegrass and clover, and abounds with turkeys, deer, elk, and most sorts of game, particularly buffaloes, thirty or forty of which are frequently seen feeding in one meadow: in short, it wants nothing but civilization to make it a most delightful country."[6]

One year after the Gist expedition, in the autumn of 1752 and still twenty years before Boone's famous journey through the Cumberland Gap, John Finley, along with several companions, left the Piqua, Ohio, region and descended the Ohio River by canoe in his most important expedition into the West. During this journey, the group traveled to near the Falls of the Ohio and, as they returned upriver exploring various smaller creeks, they met a party of Shawnee Indians at Big Bone Lick. Either by invitation or by force, the Finley party traveled with the Indians to their camp at Eskippakithiki, in present-day Clark County. There, other traders had gathered, those returning from doing business with the Cherokee and Catawba tribes of the Carolinas. It was from the Indians and other traders that Finley learned many important facts concerning the new Kentucky, including two details in particular. First, he discovered the Indians had been utilizing an elaborate system of trails throughout the entire region; and second, he learned the specific location of a natural break in the massive Appalachian Mountain Range, which had eluded so many other explorers.[7] Initially "discovered" by Thomas Walker, Indian tribes had actually been using the so-called Cumberland Gap for decades, and many English traders had also traveled through the famous pathway well before Walker or even Daniel Boone.

During Finley's stay at Eskippakithiki, however, a dispute between some of the traders and the Indians ensued, and the Europeans were attacked. Finley and a few others escaped and were eventually able to make their way back to their settlements. Finley wasted little time spreading the word about the beautiful flatlands of Kentucky, but his plan for an immediate settlement expedition would soon be halted due to the French and Indian War (1754–1763). If not for that, Finley would certainly have enjoyed much of the fame later experienced by Daniel Boone. At any rate, the Shawnee abandoned Eskippakithiki within three months of Finley's journey.

It should be noted that, while many previous histories speak of Eskippakithiki as a full-scale Shawnee "settlement," it was much more likely a permanent winter encampment. Archeological surveys and some minor excavations have taken place throughout the region over the years, none supplying any evidence of a settlement—or even a campsite, for that matter. A French census in 1736 noted 200 Indians at what could have been Eskippakithiki.[8] However, with major development over the years, including a highway interchange at KY 974 and the Bert T. Combs Parkway about ten miles southeast of Winchester, the true location of any Indian camp will likely remain a mystery.

By this time, regional Indian tribes were becoming increasingly agitated over the further western expansion by the English. Indian attacks began taking place with greater frequency throughout the Ohio River Valley and adjacent areas. Would-be settlers traveling down the Ohio River were often ambushed and killed; Indian hunting parties also ventured well south of the Ohio in search of trespassing Europeans. In July 1755, a group of Shawnee raided a small English village, killing four settlers and taking five others captive. While the Draper's Meadow Massacre occurred in southwestern Virginia, it would soon have a significant connection to Northern Kentucky. Taken prisoner were Mary Draper Ingles; her two young sons, Tommy, age four, and George, age two; her sister-in-law, Bettie Robertson Draper; and two neighbors, James Cull and Henry Leonard. Mary's husband was nearly killed in the attack but escaped into the wilderness.

The Indians and their captives traveled for more than a month, across the mountains and up various creeks and rivers to Shannoah Town at present-day Portsmouth, Ohio. There, Cull and Leonard were killed, and the two young boys were adopted by the Shawnee. For several months, Mary was forced to work for the Indians, mainly sewing and cooking. In October 1755, she and a woman kidnapped earlier, known only as the "old Dutch woman," were taken to Big Bone Lick, where they were forced to make salt for the Indians. Mary and her fellow captive, were thus likely the first European women to ever set foot in Northern Kentucky.

On October 19, while still at Big Bone Lick, the two women escaped on foot with two blankets, wearing moccasins and carrying only a dull hatchet and a knife. They traveled northeast along the Kentucky side of the Ohio River to the mouth of the Licking at present-day Covington, where they found a small cabin with a supply of corn inside and a lone horse tied out back. The women took the horse and some food and quickly continued on their way, expecting a party of Indians to soon be on their trail. In reality, the Indians had given only a short search, assuming the women had been carried off by wild animals. The women traveled south along the Licking River, but lost their horse as they attempted to cross Dutchman's Ripple, a small creek in the vicinity of today's Visalia, Kenton County. They continued along the Licking until near Falmouth before realizing it was not a familiar path and returned to the Ohio River.

The duo proceeded east along the Ohio, traveling upstream into several creeks and tributaries along the way, eventually crossing the Kanawha and Big Sandy rivers. When their corn ran out, they survived on black walnuts, wild grapes, blackberries, pawpaws, sassafras leaves, and frogs. Near present-day Glen Lyn, Virginia, Mary wandered off alone. She found a canoe and crossed the New River at its junction with the East River, and finally made it to the home of a family friend, Adam Harmon, on December 1, 1755, an incredible forty-two days after leaving Big Bone Lick and nearly six months after being taken captive. Mary soon reunited with her husband and eventually recovered from the horrific episode. She and William had four more children: Mary, Susan, Rhoda, and John. Young George died while in Indian captivity, but Thomas was located, ransomed, and reunited with his family at age thirteen, nine years after he was taken captive. Today, several sections of KY Highway 8 in Northern Kentucky, which runs a similar course to at least part of Mary's epic journey, are named in her honor.

5

The French and Indian War, and Daniel Boone Visits Kentucky

Previous history books on Kentucky detail the expansion of the English colonies into the Indian-held western territories during the mid-1700s. Some, however, seem to minimize the fact that France had also laid claim to much of what is now North America. In an effort to force the English colonists to remain in their somewhat confined territory along the east coast, the French built a series of forts in the Ohio Country, along the Allegheny River and elsewhere. Based on England's Virginia Charter of 1609, however, the English believed these lands to be theirs. In the winter of 1754, Robert Dinwiddie, Virginia's Lieutenant Governor, sent an entourage into the Ohio Country to warn the French they were trespassing. The group consisted of a somewhat unknown twenty-one-year-old militia major named George Washington; and, on what he termed his third expedition, Christopher Gist was asked to accompany Washington as his official guide. Gist, in fact, saved young Washington's life after the younger man slipped and fell into a swollen creek during the expedition. Unfortunately, their attempt to recruit Indians along the way failed miserably: most of the natives quickly sided with the French. Furthermore, the French simply ignored the warning from the Englishmen. The trip was unsuccessful, but Washington was promoted to lieutenant colonel and was soon charged with getting rid of the French by whatever means.

Due to the newly built French forts, including Fort Duquesne at present-day Pittsburgh, Washington's plan to build an English fort in that area was impossible. He was forced to retreat to Great Meadows, about fifty miles to the southeast, where in haste he erected a small fort nicknamed Fort Necessity. Greatly outnumbered, the English easily fell to the French in a battle there on July 4, 1754. Though Washington's surrender was humiliating, many argue it was this early failure that helped form the great general and president he would soon become, as through this experience he learned much about military tactics and discipline. Shortly after the defeat, the British Parliament approved more funds to better support an expanded militia and ordered British regiments to the colonies. In January 1755, the colonists were to lead a charge against Fort Duquesne, but while en route, they were surprised by a mix of French soldiers and Indian warriors. Christopher Gist participated in that particular skirmish, as did John Finley. The result was another resounding victory for the French, as nearly 1,000 colonists and British soldiers were killed. There was, however, one extremely important event during the battle that would soon affect the future of Northern Kentucky: John Finley's chance meeting and ensuing friendship with a member of Captain Dobb's regiment from North Carolina, one Daniel Boone.[1]

Britain and France officially declared war on each other in 1756. Known as the Seven Years War in Europe, the conflict is commonly referred to as the French and Indian War in the colonies, as the primary participants were the French and their allied Indians of the Ohio Country against the English settlers in Virginia. Under the direction of new British Prime Minister Lord William Pitt (1708–1778), the tide finally turned for the British in 1758, when they began to make peace with important Indian allies and began adapting their war strategies to fit the unusual landscape of the American frontier. With numbers suddenly lopsided in favor of the British, the French collapsed, climaxing with a massive defeat at Quebec in September 1759. Great Britain thus found itself in control of the entire North American frontier, as France was forced to surrender all of her American possessions.[2]

Although the war was over, it quickly became obvious that the British government was not yet ready to settle, nor defend, their greatly expanded territory, especially the Ohio River Valley. King George III (1760–1820) issued the Royal Proclamation of 1763, which, among other things, forbade colonists from settling past a line drawn along the Appalachian Mountains. The Proclamation, however, did little to stop the migration of many pioneers who had already seen or heard about the incredibly rich soil and abundant wildlife in Kentucky.

Soon after the war, John Finley resumed his successful trading business and was visiting the Yadkin River region, where he reunited with Daniel Boone. Winter was approaching, and Boone invited Finley to spend a few weeks with him and his family. By this time, Boone had already crossed the mountains into what is now Kentucky several times, proceeding as far as present-day Floyd County, but had made no deeper penetration due to the extremely rugged terrain. It was while wintering with John Finley, however, when Boone learned of the beautiful Bluegrass Region of Kentucky and, more importantly, details of what became known as the Cumberland Gap.[3] It was John Finley's earlier Northern Kentucky expedition that gave Boone the knowledge and impetus to travel into the Kentucky frontier. While Boone was planning and recruiting for his first extended expedition, however, another pioneer would gain considerable fame while exploring lands in what would soon become Northern Kentucky.

In early 1765, George Croghan and a small party explored Big Bone Lick and other parts of present-day Boone, Kenton, and Campbell counties. While focused north of the Ohio, Croghan and his men had traded as far south as Eskippakithiki.[4] Croghan took a sizable collection of bones from Big Bone Lick and wrote in his journal: "Early in the morning, we went to the great lick, where those bones are only found, about four miles from the river, on the southeast side. . . . We found there two tusks above six feet long; we carried one, with some other bones, to our boats, and set off."[5]

Croghan returned to the area in 1766 and collected still more bones. Some of these were sent to Lord Shelburne in London, and others were given to Benjamin Franklin, who was also in London at the time. Franklin acknowledged the gift in a letter, and his words clearly indicate how unaware even the most intelligent of eighteenth-century scholars were to the concept of animal extinction. Nowhere in the world had there been any thought that the Earth was once inhabited by animals that no longer existed. The consensus of all who had witnessed the massive bones from Kentucky was that they were from extremely large elephants, as that was the only animal known to be at all similar in size.[6] Franklin wrote:

> I return you many thanks for the box of elephants' tusks and grinders. They are extremely curious on many accounts; no liv-

> ing elephants having been seen in any part of America by any of the Europeans settled there, or remembered in any tradition of the Indians. It is also puzzling to conceive what should have brought so many of them to die on the same spot. The grinders differ from those of the African and Asiatic elephant, being full of knobs, like grinders of a carnivorous animal: when those of the elephant, who eats only vegetables, are almost smooth. It is also remarkable that elephants now inhabit naturally only hot countries where there is no winter, and yet these remains are found in a winter country . . . which looks as if the earth had anciently been in another position, and the climates differently placed from what they are at present.[7]

The same year, in an effort to better define the line separating Indian territories from what the British set in 1763, the Treaty of Fort Stanwix was signed by representatives of the Six Nations (Iroquois). The British government hoped that a new boundary line might bring an end to the continuing frontier violence, while the Indians hoped that a new, permanent line might hold back British colonial expansion. There was a major problem, however, in present-day Kentucky. While the Iroquois signed the treaty, ceding all of the future state to the British, it was the Shawnee, as well as other Ohio tribes such as the Mingo, Delaware, and Wyandot, who actually claimed Kentucky, and who still hunted there. While some of these tribes became passive to the overall situation, others were extremely upset at the Iroquois for selling to the British what they believed to be their territory.

On May 11, 1769, John Finley led what would be his most important expedition since his earlier visit to Eskippakithiki. Daniel Boone, his brother-in-law John Stewart, Alexander Neeley, Joseph Holden, James Mooney, William Cool, and a few other explorers from the Yadkin region followed John Finley's lead through the rugged wilderness. During this trek, Finley showed Boone and the others several prominent topographical features, including the Wasioto Pass, Pilot Knob, old Eskippakithiki, the Kentucky Plains, and the Licking River. Boone was amazed at the fertile forests and prairies; and on June 7, 1769, he stood atop Pilot Knob in present-day Powell County, where he viewed the Bluegrass Region of Kentucky for the first time. Boone would later use many of these features as guideposts when leading settlers into Kentucky.[8]

Daniel Boone (1734–1820), accompanied by his brother, Squire Boone, and other groups of brave men, would make additional trips into the easternmost portions of present-day Kentucky over the following months. On December 22, 1769, however, he and John Stewart were captured by the Shawnee, who confiscated their bounty and held them captive for seven days, telling them to leave Kentucky and never return. Most of Boone's party quickly left the region; but Daniel, his brother, and John Stewart continued to hunt and explore Kentucky for a few weeks, ignoring the warning of the Shawnee. John Finley returned to his trading business but was unfortunately killed in the wilderness a few months later. Squire Boone eventually returned east for additional supplies, leaving Daniel and John on their own. While checking traps along the Kentucky River, Boone became separated from Stewart. When he returned to camp, his brother-in-law was nowhere to be found. After searching for days, Boone continued with his expedition, thinking Stewart had been killed by Indians, which would prove later to be a correct assumption. Alone, Boone traveled north along an old Indian trail and explored what is now the Blue Licks region.[9] There, he witnessed "thousands of buffalo, with other animals resorting there to lick the ground and drink the water."[10]

Boone then followed the Licking River north into present-day Harrison County, and journeyed along another Indian trace northeast, locating the Ohio River somewhere in today's northern Bracken County or southern Campbell County. He remained on the southern shore of the Ohio River as he proceeded to the west. Boone crossed the Licking River at its mouth, into today's Kenton County, and then continued into what is now Boone County, where he visited Big Bone Lick before continuing all the way to the Falls of the Ohio.[11] In the summer of 1770, Boone wrote "I surveyed the famous river Ohio that rolled in silent dignity, marking the western boundary of Kentucky with inconceivable grandeur."[12] After returning home, Boone began preparations in hopes to escort scores of settlers into the new Kentucky the following summer.

Like Boone, another famous frontiersman would also contribute significantly to the area now known as Northern Kentucky. Simon Kenton (1755–1836) was born in Fauquier County, Virginia, and had a somewhat uneventful childhood until 1771, when he ran away from home at the age of sixteen. Under the mistaken impression that he had killed a young man in a fistfight over the love of a young woman, Kenton fled into the wilderness of West Virginia, Ohio, and Kentucky and, for the next eighteen years went under the assumed name of Simon Butler. While on the lam, "Butler" met two frontiersmen, George Yeager and John Strader, and decided to join them on a hunting expedition into the West. The group journeyed down the Ohio River to the Falls, then backtracked to the mouth of the Licking River. While it is certain his party explored the Licking River for quite some distance, previous research makes it unclear as to exactly where the group may have disembarked. Some claim the group camped on the western shore, at present-day Covington, while others believe the group immediately proceeded up the Licking during their 1771 journey. At any rate, for the next two years, "Butler" and his companions hunted and explored the Licking River and other parts of present-day Boone, Kenton, Campbell, Bracken, and Mason counties, mainly in search of a region some Indians termed the "land of cane."[13] His best achievements, however, would come a few years later.

Meanwhile, Indian attacks on settlers continued, even after the Treaty of Fort Stanwix. By 1773, many English families were haphazardly pushing west into Kentucky in hopes to establish new homesteads, without colonial authorization. In an effort to bring some control to the chaos, Virginia governor John Murray, the Fourth Earl of Dunmore, authorized Captain Thomas Bullitt (1730–1778) to organize a party to survey what is now Northern and Eastern Kentucky. Bullitt became the first to lead an expedition into Kentucky for the primary purpose of claiming land. With Bullitt was James Harrod, John Hedges, John Floyd, Thomas Young, James Douglass, John Fitzgerald, and others; about twenty more men joined the expedition while in progress.[14] These included Hancock Taylor, who had been hired by the McAfee brothers, Robert, George, and James, to survey around present-day Frankfort and Harrodsburg.[15] The two groups met at present-day Maysville on June 22, 1773. While McAfee's group traveled cross-country through today's Mason and Bracken counties, eventually following the Licking River northward, the others continued down the Ohio River, taking short excursions up various creeks. The two groups eventually reunited at present-day Covington.[16] Bullitt's party also visited Big Bone Lick on July 4 and 5, where they made seats and tentpoles from many of the large mastodon bones they found there.[17] From Big Bone, Bullitt and a few others, including James Harrod, continued down the Ohio River to the Falls, while McAfee's group followed the Indian trail to Drennon's Lick in present-day Henry County. In the following weeks, Bullitt would lay out a town, which would later become Louisville.[18]

On September 25, 1773, Daniel Boone and his family, along with five smaller groups, about fifty people total, attempted the first true settlement of Kentucky. Before reaching their destination, however, Boone divided his party in order to gather others in the region who had planned to make the journey. These included a forty-member party led by William Bryan, who had married Daniel Boone's sister, Mary. William Bryan, along with his three brothers, Morgan, James, and Joseph, would later found Bryan Station in Central Kentucky. On October 9, a contingent of mostly Shawnee attacked the camp of the smaller group. Several were gruesomely murdered, including Boone's son, James. Backtracking, Daniel Boone and his men discovered the site of the killings, buried the dead, and returned east. Boone's first expedition to settle Kentucky was over.

In early May 1774, Virginia's governor, John Murray, the Fourth Earl of Dunmore, better known as Lord Dunmore (1730–1809), received word that fighting had increased between the Ohio Indians and the settlers and traders in the West. He asked the legislature to approve a general militia and fund a volunteer expedition into the Ohio River Valley. Dunmore favored British expansion into the West, but he was also concerned with the growing unrest in Boston and other eastern ports as a result of increased taxes and other new rules set forth against the colonists by the British government. In the end, he knew a strong militia might better secure Virginia's claim, as well as open expansion in the Ohio River Valley and Kentucky. In late 1774, a series of attacks were launched against Indian villages in what became known as Lord Dunmore's War.[19] The only major action was the Battle of Point Pleasant along the Kanawha River on October 10, 1774. The result was a victory for the colonists, as the Indians retreated back into the Ohio Country, but the casualties in the militia were devastating: 75 killed and 140 wounded, against only 40 dead Indians. The combined English forces then marched to the Indian villages at Pickaway County, Ohio, where they met with Chief Cornstalk to discuss peace negotiations. The Treaty of Camp Charlotte, on October 19, 1774, provided that the Shawnee would cease hunting south of the Ohio River, and that they would discontinue harassing travelers along that major waterway.

6

James Harrod, Richard Henderson, and the Revolutionary War

By 1773, James Harrod (1746–1779), a skilled pioneer, soldier, and hunter in the early West, had already made several excursions down the Ohio River. In May 1774, he and thirty-seven others traveled down the Ohio, past present-day Covington to the mouth of the Kentucky River. From there, they journeyed upriver into present-day Mercer County, and laid out what became Harrodsburg. The cabins Harrod's group erected there on June 16, 1774, are officially credited as the first European settlement in Kentucky.[1] The same month, however, Governor Dunmore dispatched Daniel Boone to call these settlers back from the frontier and into military service.[2] Boone traveled with Michael Stoner, retracing Harrod's route down the Ohio River through Northern Kentucky, and Harrodsburg was completely abandoned just as quickly as it had been settled.

Before the American Revolution officially began, Richard Henderson (1734–1785), a prominent judge from North Carolina, hired Daniel Boone to travel to Cherokee camps in present-day North Carolina and Tennessee and have Boone help negotiate a treaty of Henderson's own. Henderson had formed a land speculation company with a number of other prominent North Carolinians, known as the Transylvania Company, hoping to establish a British proprietary colony by purchasing from the Cherokee their interest in all lands in Kentucky.[3] He was aware of recent treaties with the Iroquois and other tribes and believed the Cherokee to be the only other Indian tribe to consult regarding that prime land. In March of 1775, Henderson met with more than 1,200

Cherokee at Sycamore Shoals (present-day Elizabethton in northeastern Tennessee). With the Treaty of Sycamore Shoals, Henderson purchased all the land between the Cumberland River, the Cumberland Mountains, the Kentucky River, and the Ohio River—roughly half of present-day Kentucky. He instructed Boone to blaze a trail from the Cumberland Gap into Central Kentucky, and granted him vast acreage there for a settlement to be named Transylvania.

While Boone made his plans for this major expedition, James Harrod was leading another group of families back to his abandoned Kentucky settlement. On March 8, 1775, they arrived at the fortification; within months the settlement had grown rapidly, and the residents found the old fort inadequate. A new village, the first permanent English settlement in Kentucky, was constructed at what is today Old Fort Harrod State Park.

Even before Boone's trailblazing through the Cumberland Gap, other families had entered Kentucky via the Ohio River route. In March of 1775, John Hinkston (often seen as Hinkson), a Pennsylvania-born Irishman, entered Northern Kentucky with about fourteen other men. They traveled down the Ohio River to the mouth of the Licking River and then up the Licking to just north of present-day Falmouth, where they camped for two days. They continued along the South Fork of the Licking River, then south along an old buffalo trace, where they erected a settlement about two miles north of the present-day village of Lair, Kentucky. Though not permanent, Hinkston's Fort—not Boonesborough—was actually the second known settlement to be established in the new Kentucky. A month later, John Haggin and others established a small settlement a few miles north of Hinkston's Fort. By the spring of 1775, the new Kentucky was slowly beginning to take shape; but, due to continued Indian violence along the Ohio River, the northernmost region of Kentucky remained without a settlement.

Meanwhile, tensions between the British government and the English colonists continued to escalate along the east coast. Events such as the passage of the Sugar Act (1764), the Townshend Acts (1767), and the Boston Tea Party (1773) brought many colonists' emotions to the edge of a revolt; and on April 19, 1775, shots rang out at Lexington, Massachusetts, an event most historians cite as the beginning of the American Revolutionary War.

In summarizing the war, most scholars can easily recall the events that took place in the original thirteen colonies, as the major battles were certainly won or lost there. The conflicts that took place in the West, however, especially those in Kentucky, are often overlooked completely. In reality, the Ohio River marked an important border between the American colonies and the Indians, who would prove to be just as much an enemy as the British soldiers. As violence erupted in Boston, Lexington, Concord, and elsewhere in the thirteen colonies, violence along the Ohio River and in Kentucky became equally aggressive. Indians, unhappy with the loss of Kentucky lands in recent treaties, saw the war as their chance to drive the colonists out and regain their prized territory. It was relatively easy, therefore, for many Indian tribes quickly to side with the British in the conflict.

Thomas Jefferson realized early on that the only way the new nation could be assured of unity and protection from foreign invasion was if it were made up of all the territory from the Atlantic to the Pacific. Recognizing the importance of winning the West, he placed George Rogers Clark (1752–1818) in a position to conquer that region. Needing provisions, Clark went to Virginia governor Patrick Henry (1736–1799), but was surprised to find that the Continental Congress was hesitant to provide what he needed. Many members of that esteemed group could not understand the reasoning behind providing such resources to a virtually uninhabited wilderness when such a greater need existed on the eastern seacoast.[4] While many are familiar with Patrick Henry's famous line, "Give me liberty or give me death," it was Clark's rebuttal that likely saved the future state of Kentucky: "If a country is not worth protecting, it is not worth claiming."[5] Virginia officials eventually realized they had to fight for the West in order to keep their new "backyard" free from all enemies in the future.

Unaware that the American Revolutionary War had begun, Simon "Butler" Kenton and Thomas Williams returned from the east, entering at present-day Maysville. They journeyed inland about two miles, where Kenton found "the richest soil I have ever seen." They cleared land with hatchets, constructed a small camp, and planted corn—some of the first of that crop by any European in what is now Kentucky. Kenton explored the surrounding area for several months, including the Blue Licks region, where he was amazed at the number of buffalo. From

Blue Licks, he followed the Licking River to the north and explored present-day Campbell and Kenton counties, and even visited Big Bone Lick on June 6, 1775.

Per Richard Henderson's orders, and along with about thirty others, Daniel Boone finally marked and widened a path from the Cumberland Gap into the interior of Kentucky, known as the Wilderness Trail. Along the Kentucky River, he founded Boonesborough on September 8, 1775, which became the second permanent settlement in the West. It was during this expedition when Boone located, within a hollowed-out tree, a powder horn bearing John Stewart's initials, as well as his skeletal remains.[6] The discovery did not halt Boone's plans, however. Within weeks, he had moved his family and many others to the new homestead in the Kentucky wilderness. In contrast to Thomas Walker's descriptions of what was found in southeastern Kentucky, a narrative by Felix Walker, one of Boone's road-cutters, well describes this group's impression of the new Kentucky:

> On leaving that river (the Rockcastle), we had to encounter and cut our way through a country of about twenty-five miles, entirely covered with dead brush, which we found a difficult and laborious task. At the end of which we arrived at the commencement of a cane country, traveled about thirty miles through thick cane and reed, and as the cane ceased, we began to discover the pleasing and rapturous appearance of the plains of Kentucky. A new sky and strange earth seemed to be presented to our view. So rich a soil we had never seen before—turkeys so numerous that it might be said they appeared but one flock, universally scattered in the woods. It appeared that nature, in the profusion of her bounty, had spread a feast for all that lives, both for the animal and for the rational world. A sight so delightful to our view and grateful to our feelings, almost inclined us an imitation of Columbus, to kiss the soil of Kentucky, as he hailed and saluted the sand on his first setting foot on the shores of America. The appearance of the country coming up to the full measure of our expectations, and seeming to exceed the fruitful source of our imaginary prospects. We felt ourselves passengers through a wilderness

> just arrived at the fields of Elysium, or the garden where was no forbidden fruit.[7]

A few months later, another group arrived in the future Kentucky, settling along the middle branch of Elkhorn Creek in present-day Fayette County. This group included brothers Francis and William McConnell, Major John Morrison, Robert Patterson, and Levi Todd. The new settlement went by the name McConnell's Station for several weeks, but when residents in the village received word that war had broken out at Lexington, Massachusetts, Patterson suggested a new name. The settlement became Lexington, and Simon Kenton, who had been visiting the village at the time, witnessed the renaming ceremony.[8]

Two days before Christmas of 1775, the first of many skirmishes between Indians and the new citizens of Boonesborough occurred.[9] Meanwhile, several other groups of pioneer settlers entered the western territory. William Bryan, with brothers Morgan, James, and Joseph, built a stockade along North Elkhorn Creek. Known as Bryan Station (often misspelled Bryant Station or Bryan's Station), the site was just northeast of present-day Lexington. Benjamin Logan (1742–1802), another Virginia-born pioneer and soldier, moved west with his family and others, building a stockade known as Logan's Fort, which eventually grew to a small village named St. Asaph's, at present-day Stanford, in Lincoln County. And John McClelland and his entourage arrived by flatboat at present-day Maysville, where Simon Kenton (still known to the settlers as Simon Butler) escorted them into present-day Scott County. There, they established a settlement known as McClelland's Station.

Simon Kenton visited each of the new settlements in their early days and met several fellow explorers, including Daniel Boone and George Rogers Clark. In a short time, he knew the Kentucky territory better than anyone, and would soon help countless families find new home sites by personally escorting them from present-day Maysville to Boonesborough, Bryan Station, McConnell's Station, and elsewhere.[10]

In the fall of 1776, Major George Stockton, his half-brother Colonel John Fleming, and Michael Cassidy descended the Ohio River by canoe and entered the future state at Salt Lick Creek in today's Lewis County, where they encountered a wide buffalo trace to the southwest.[11] They proceeded into the Kentucky countryside, where they cleared small plats of land at several locations but apparently did not immediately establish any blockhouses or stations. Stockton had been taken captive by Indians as a small child in New York and, after his release as an adult, chose the wilderness of Kentucky over what he considered the overpopulation of Virginia.[12]

Back at Boonesborough, there were great protests when Richard Henderson announced an increase in land costs and other rules for "his" new settlers.[13] While those in Boonesborough generally sided with Henderson and saw him as a great leader, settlers at Harrodsburg, Logan's Fort, and other settlements, including the newly established Boiling Springs, southeast of Harrodsburg, refused to recognize his authority. They petitioned George Rogers Clark and John Gabriel Jones to travel to Virginia and ask Governor Patrick Henry for assistance. As a direct result, Congress later ruled the entire Transylvania Purchase illegal; and, on December 31, 1776, Kentucky County, Virginia, was created, giving all the territory in present-day Kentucky to Virginia. Henderson's hard work in bringing settlers into Kentucky was not in vain, however, as he was granted vast acreage along the Ohio River west of the Falls. Today, both the city of Henderson and Henderson County are named in his honor.

7

Kentucky under Siege

Throughout the 1770s and 1780s, Indian attacks escalated in Central Kentucky and some settlers abandoned the West, returning to the eastern side of the mountains. In fact, fewer than 200 known colonists remained in Kentucky by the summer of 1776, primarily at Harrodsburg, Boonesborough, and Logan's Station.[1] It is impossible, of course, to know just how many small settlements had been established and abandoned—or annihilated completely during this time period. If there was a positive to these attacks, many of the people in the Central Kentucky settlements who successfully fought off the Indians soon became some of the earliest residents of Northern Kentucky.

Generally, the Indian warpath followed the Licking River on its western banks (what is now Covington's Eastern Avenue to Decoursey Pike), then veered slightly westward, following portions of Decoursey Creek and Bowman Creek. It then joined the Licking River near present-day Morning View and followed the South Fork of the Licking at today's Falmouth.

The settlement at McClelland's Station in present-day Scott County was attacked in late 1776. The frontier fighters defended the station well, even killing Mingo Indian Chief Pluggy in the effort. Fearing a certain retaliatory attack, however, the settlement was abandoned, and the residents took refuge at Boonesborough. In early 1777, the Indians, now well armed and supported by British lieutenant Henry Hamilton (1734–1796) at Fort Detroit, planned to do even greater damage to the remote Kentucky settlements. The Continental Army could spare no men or supplies for the defense of Kentucky County, Virginia, however, as it was so distant from the rest of the population. On April 24, 1777, the Indians attacked Boonesborough, and in the early minutes of the fight, Daniel Boone, Michael Stoner, John Todd, and Isaac Hite were injured. The hero of this skirmish was Simon "Butler" Kenton, who killed three Indians and saved the life of Boone by carrying him back to the stockade.[2] The Indians withdrew but remained in the vicinity. Three months later, Fort Boonesborough was attacked again. The settlers endured constant firing against the stockade and repeated attempts to set fire to the fort by means of flaming arrows and torches thrown over the walls. Women and girls molded bullets and reloaded extra rifles without rest. On the morning of July 6, the frustrated Indians gathered their dead and wounded, and retreated from the area.

On January 1, 1778, Daniel Boone and a small group of men in a salt-gathering expedition near Blue Licks were forced to surrender to a large scouting party of more than 100 Indian warriors, including Chief Blackfish. Boone and his men were taken to the Shawnee town of Chillicothe, where he and a few of the stronger men were adopted into the tribe.[3] Back at Boonesborough, when the group failed to return a search was initiated. Finding no signs of a fight or any bodies, the settlers assumed the men had been taken captive. Daniel's wife, Rebecca, believing her husband had been killed, took her children and returned to the eastern colonies. Soon after her departure, however, some of the men who had escaped their captors returned to Boonesborough and related Boone's surrender.

Six months later, Boone overheard plans for a massive attack on the fort. He eluded his captors and raced home to warn the settlement, covering the 160 miles in just five days. On September 7, 1778, Blackfish's forces arrived at Boonesborough with 444 Indians, as well as a dozen or so French-Canadian soldiers from Detroit, who were now fighting on behalf of the British Crown.[4] The Kentuckians, only 30 marksmen strong, created the illusion of greater numbers by having many of the women carry weapons while dressed as men. Negotiation attempts quickly failed, and gunfire was exchanged for several days. Attempts to burn the fort, as well as to dig under it, were met with the expert marksmanship of the Kentucky settlers. On September 18, 1778, the Indians and their allies separated into several groups and left the area.

Meanwhile, Pennsylvania militiamen planned their own attack against several Indian villages in the Ohio Country, another event that would have direct repercussions in Northern Kentucky. In February

1778, General Edward Hand (1744–1802) directed 500 Pennsylvania militiamen from Fort Pitt on a surprise winter expedition against Mingo towns along the Cuyahoga River. Adverse weather forced a retreat, however, and on the return march, some of Hand's men attacked peaceful Delaware Indians, killing men, women, and children and forcing that contingent to also side with the British. In addition, three of Hand's men defected to the British/Indian side. Simon Girty, Matthew Elliott, and Alexander McKee would soon leave a devastating mark on the Kentucky settlements.

Amidst the ongoing Indian attacks, other groups of settlers remarkably continued to risk their lives to enter the new western frontier. A large group led by Isaac Ruddell traveled from Pennsylvania, down the Ohio and then up the Licking River, where they followed the buffalo trail to just south of present-day Cynthiana. There they located the abandoned Hinkston Fort and claimed it as their own. Colonel Benjamin Harrison and his family settled between Hinkston's Fort and Martin's Station. His son Robert would later establish a small village nearby, named for his two daughters, Cynthia and Anna (Cynthiana). Also, Edmond Rittenhouse, a relative of the famous astronomer David Rittenhouse (1732–1796), descended the Ohio River by flatboat with his family from Pennsylvania. They ascended the Licking River with plans to establish a settlement along Banklick Creek, just west of its mouth. Realizing Indians were still in the general vicinity, the group was forced southeast and became residents at Ruddell's Station.

It was at this time that Simon "Butler" Kenton unexpectedly located his older brother John, and finally learned the young man he thought he had killed as a teenager did not die. He returned to his given name. However, while traveling along the Ohio River in September of 1778, Kenton was captured by Indians, and his captivity would prove to be long and gruesome. He is said to have endured several episodes of "running the gauntlet" as well as futile attempts to be burned at the stake.[5] Eventually, he was released at the urging of Simon Girty. He would bear the scars and pain from his captivity for the rest of his life.

Not long after the Siege of Boonesborough, while Boone was in North Carolina and Kenton was still in captivity, Colonel John Bowman of Kentucky County, Virginia, called for the mustering of a militia at "the Point" for a retaliatory strike against the Shawnee town of Chillicothe. Just when the first reference of the "Point" was made remains unclear; it describes the spot at the confluence of the Ohio River and the Licking River, specifically on the southwestern shore at what is now Covington, Kentucky. Simply called "the Point," it became a well-known meeting spot by fur traders, pioneers and explorers, Indians, the British army, and various pioneer militias. Since the Licking River was the only north-flowing waterway in the immediate area, it was easy to locate and trace to its mouth. Assembled were four companies led by Captain Benjamin Logan, Captain John Harlan, Captain John Holder, and Captain William Harrod.[6] The large group traveled north from Central Kentucky along the Dry Ridge Trace and camped at the headwaters of Banklick Creek, between present-day Walton and Nicholson. From there they followed the creek to its mouth at the Licking River and then remained on the western shore until reaching the Ohio River. Dividing their forces, Bowman and Logan attacked Chillicothe from two sides but were eventually repulsed. Blackfish successfully defended his village but was shot in the leg. He later died when the wound became infected.[7] While the Kentuckians were unable to force the Indians out of their stockade, much of the town was burned and more than 100 horses were confiscated. Although considered a defeat, Theodore Roosevelt in his work *The Winning of the West* later stated that "the expedition undoubtedly accomplished more than Clark's attack on Piqua the next year."[8]

At this time, George Rogers Clark was instructed to build three forts along the Ohio River to protect the growing Kentucky settlements.[9] One was to be built at the mouth of the Kanawha River, one at the mouth of the Big Sandy, and one at the mouth of the Licking River. The Licking garrison would be under Clark's direct command and was to be composed of 50 Kentuckians plus a regiment of 100 men to be sent from Virginia.[10] Clark, however, chose to give his attention to a possible fort at the Falls of the Ohio.

In August 1779, Captain David Rogers, a cousin of George Rogers Clark, led an expedition from Fort Pitt to New Orleans with about 30 men, to purchase gunpowder and other supplies from the Spanish.[11] On their return trip, they met another group led by Colonel John Campbell (1735–1799), for whom Campbell County would be named. The combined group of 65 men and 5 keelboats continued up the Ohio, and on October 4, 1779, they reached the sandbar at present-day Dayton, Kentucky. As they began to prepare breakfast, they noticed that several canoes of Indians had appeared from the Little Miami River and were approaching the sandbar. As they drew closer, more Indians revealed themselves from behind trees and overgrowth on the sandbar itself. Outnumbered by nearly 150, most of the Americans were killed, including Captain Rogers, and many more were taken captive in what became known as "Rogers' Defeat."[12] Campbell, a veteran of the Battle of Point Pleasant and other skirmishes, was one of the men taken prisoner.

During the spring of 1780, British officers at Detroit prepared to carry out another major offensive against settlers in the West. Captain Henry Bird (sometimes seen as Byrd), along with traitors Simon Girty and Alexander McKee, enlisted the help of hundreds of Indians as they marched through the Ohio Country from Detroit, eventually following the Great Miami River to the Ohio. From there, they traveled upriver to the mouth of the Licking on the Kentucky shore. Also gathering at the Point, their total force included 1,000 Indians and 150 soldiers.

On June 21, 1780, Bird's scouts had reached Ruddell's Station, where about 400 citizens had settled, mostly Pennsylvania Germans. The inhabitants were able to hold their own, but once Bird and his six-pound cannon arrived, they quickly surrendered. Bird had promised the village that no one would be killed if the settlers surrendered. The Indians, however, ignored those orders and rushed into the fort, killing and scalping many before plundering and pillaging the entire settlement. The old and sickly were killed outright, while babies were thrown into the fire.[13] About 25 Americans were brutally killed, with the remainder, including the Rittenhouse family, taken prisoner and marched off to Detroit.[14] According to Bird's own account, the Indians "rushed in, tore the poor children from their mothers' breasts, killed and wounded many."[15]

After the Indians had divided the prisoners and loot, they continued on to nearby Martin's Station. Bird successfully got the Indians to agree this time that any additional prisoners would be turned over to the British. At Martin's Station, settlers surrendered without hesitation, seeing the number of attackers and the cannon artillery.[16] After the two forts had been taken, the Indians mounted the settlers' horses while the prisoners, some 300 in number, were loaded down with the plunder from their own cabin homes and were driven on foot to Detroit, a distance of over 600 miles. There they were divided among their captors, and some were taken nearly 800 miles further to Mackinac and Montreal.[17] This invasion into Kentucky, ignored by many Revolutionary War historians, proved to be one of the most notorious events in the entire conflict.[18]

Word of the Indian attacks on Kentucky spread quickly throughout the western settlements. George Rogers Clark, now a general, wanted an immediate response to the savagery but was soon surprised to learn many settlers had abandoned their cabins and fortifications and were risking their lives on treacherous journeys back to the eastern colonies. He continued to muster militiamen, however, and in August 1780 led an invasion with Daniel Boone, John Todd, Simon Kenton, and others into the Ohio Country from the Falls of the Ohio. Clark's expedition destroyed five Shawnee villages.[19] However, while the invasion was intended to quell any further Indian attacks on the Kentucky settlements, it would soon prove to be of little importance.

Just before George Rogers Clark's expedition into the Ohio Country, Hubbard Taylor, a twenty-year-old deputy surveyor for Kentucky County, Virginia, departed that state to survey land for his father, Colonel James Taylor Sr., and for a family friend, Lieutenant Colonel George Muse. He descended the Ohio River, eventually disembarking just east of the mouth of the Licking River. Muse (1720–1790) had received over 5,000 acres of land for his military service, 2,700 of which comprised today's Covington, Newport, Bellevue, and Dayton.[20] He never visited the region, however, and trusted Taylor to inspect his holdings there. For whatever reason, Muse chose to sell that property to James Taylor Sr. but asked that the easternmost 1,000 acres be deeded back to his two daughters, Katy and Caroline Muse. Hubbard, who had planned to settle on the eastern side of his father's land, convinced James to deed the 200 acres on the western side of the Licking River to a fellow pioneer and friend, Lieutenant Colonel Stephen Trigg, as an enticement for him to settle there.[21] Trigg became the first person to have the 200 acres at what is now Covington surveyed, a task performed by Robert Todd Jr. The property was described as "heavily-wooded timber land, with magnificent beech, sugar maple, chestnut, oak, and others. There is an abundance of buffalo, deer, and bear. The Licking would make easy transportation of corn and other food from Central Kentucky."[22]

Trigg, however, sold the property almost immediately to his friend, Colonel John Todd, and Todd soon sold it to another early pioneer, James Welch. Todd and his two brothers, Robert and Levi, became quite famous in Kentucky. Robert rose to the rank of brigadier general, and Levi became the grandfather of Mary Todd, wife to future president Abraham Lincoln. Welch, along with his father, John Welch, was responsible for the migration of dozens of Pennsylvanians into present-day Mt. Washington, Bullitt County. In 2019, short streets in Covington's City Heights are named for Muse, Todd, and Welch. Unfortunately, not long after these property transactions, both Trigg and Todd were killed at the Battle of Blue Licks, a horrendous event that transpired at present-day Robertson County, to be discussed shortly.

Meanwhile, another brave group of pioneers safely descended the Ohio River and entered the new West. James and John Carlock, David and John Alcor, William Swango, Jacob Walters, and others traveled from Holsten Valley, Virginia, making their way down the Ohio River and up the Kentucky River. From there they ascended Eagle Creek and in 1783 established a settlement near the mouth of Two Mile Branch that eventually became the town of Sparta.[23]

Kentucky County, Virginia, was split into three new counties in 1780: Jefferson, Fayette, and Lincoln. Jefferson County was named for the nation's strong leader and future president, Thomas Jefferson (1743–1826); Fayette was named for the Marquis de Lafayette (1757–1834), who had come to America to join the rebelling English colonists; and Lincoln County was named for the American Revolutionary War general Benjamin Lincoln (1733–1810). As for Northern Kentucky, the entire region became part of Fayette County, Virginia.

The following year, George Rogers Clark planned a larger strike against Detroit, relying heavily on reinforcements from the east. Archibald Lochry was escorting about 120 men from Pennsylvania down the Ohio River to meet with Clark. A few scouts whom Lochry had sent ahead were captured, however, and a force of as many as 600 Indian warriors, including traitors Alexander McKee and Simon Girty, lay in wait on both sides of the Ohio River near Woolper Creek, in present-day Boone County. On August 21, 1781, Lochry's militia came to shore on the northern side of the river, intending to have supper. The Indians attacked without warning, killing many and taking others prisoner. Lochry, who was sitting wounded on a log immediately after the battle, was horribly mutilated by the Indians, as were others too injured for travel.[24] Clark called off his attack when the reinforcements failed to show. He would not learn of the ambush, now known as Lochry's Defeat, for many months. A historical marker stands on the Indiana side of the river, along Route 56 at the Ohio County/Dearborn County line, and a monument, erected in 1924, stands in Aurora's Riverview Cemetery, near the mouth of what is referred to as Laughery Creek (a clerk misspelled Lochry's name years ago and it has never been changed).

Meanwhile, on the east coast, British forces under Lieutenant General Lord Cornwallis, in battle against General George Washington's army at Yorktown, Virginia, found themselves in a situation that was simply hopeless. In October 1781, the American Revolutionary War was over—at least on paper. In Kentucky, word of the war's end would not be received for many months. In fact, historians who declare that the Revolutionary War ended with the surrender at Yorktown invariably overlook the fact the British Army in the West had other intentions. In addition, Indians continued to organize attacks in the region, especially against travelers along the Ohio River, as they were not going to give up their fight to reclaim the Kentucky territory. At the very least, their hope was to see the Ohio River become the northern boundary of the new United States of America.[25]

Even with continued threats, new settlers continued migrating to Kentucky, now in droves. Some of these brave families came with only the hope of acquiring land in Kentucky. Soon, however, Revolutionary War veterans arrived, those who were awarded land grants in the West as payment for their military service; the size and location of these grants were commensurate with each soldier's attained rank and/or extraordinary feat of bravery.[26] Captain Philip Buckner (1747–1820) brought his family from Caroline County, Virginia, down the Ohio to settle west of present-day Maysville. Buckner received a sizable land grant for his service, including much of present-day Fayette County and most of today's Bracken County. He also owned land on the Ohio side of the river. Buckner founded a settlement that became Augusta and built the first brick home there in 1795. He also donated land and helped construct a courthouse, the first in all of Northern Kentucky, and began selling parcels to other families that same year. Incredibly, there was a ferry across the Ohio River at Augusta as early as 1798.[27]

As colonists throughout the original thirteen colonies continued to celebrate their victory over Britain, Indian warriors in the Ohio Country were planning more raids on the lonely, unfortified Kentucky settlements. A kidnapping outside Hoy's Station, just north of present-day Richmond, and an attack on Bryan Station both brought repercussions to the Northern Kentucky region. In July 1782, 150 British rangers from Detroit, under Captain William Caldwell, and at least 1,000 Indian warriors supervised by the previously mentioned traitors, Alexander McKee, Simon Girty, and Matthew Elliott, set out for the Kentucky settlements. Their primary objective was to surprise and destroy the fort at Bryan Station. Making their way down the western shore of the Licking River, they located the abandoned Ruddell's Station, where they rested and left their canoes before continuing southwest on foot.[28] While much of the force headed directly toward Bryan Station, a large group made its way to Hoy's Station, just north of present-day Richmond, arriving on August 10, 1782. Their plan was in some way to keep the men at Hoy's Station from becoming reinforcements at Bryan Station. The group kidnapped two small children and quickly headed northeast toward Blue Licks.[29] A small group of settlers from various nearby stations immediately pursued the Indians, eventually catching up with them along the Licking River at present-day Fleming County, where, at a spot along Sap Branch in an area now named Battle Run, a skirmish took place. The settlers, greatly outnumbered, were forced to retreat, and the kidnappers made off with their captives, transporting them to their village at Piqua in the Ohio Country.[30] Five settlers were killed.

Major George Stockton, Colonel John Fleming, and Michael Cassidy were among the many settlers to assist in the clash with the Indian kidnappers. These three men had arrived in the region earlier; and, while each would soon have their own stations, they were likely staying at Strode's Station in present-day Clark County at the time. Fleming was badly injured during the battle, being shot at close range in the upper thigh. He was saved by the heroic efforts of Michael Cassidy, who rode through a barrage of gunfire, threw Fleming onto his horse saddlebag style, remounted his own horse, and quickly grabbed the reins of both animals before racing through additional gunfire as the two men forded the Licking River and escaped.[31]

Meanwhile, Captain Caldwell, the renegades Girty and McKee, about 50 loyalists and nearly 400 Indians (mostly Shawnee, Wyandot, and Mingo) were within sight of the fortification at Bryan Station. Due mainly to the terrain, the invaders could not get within 100 yards of the fort without completely exposing themselves. Meanwhile, the inhabitants of the fort realized that they had a major problem: they were almost out of water, and they knew the ensuing attack might last several days. It was decided that the women would undertake the risky chore of retrieving water from the nearby spring, some 70 yards away, and in so doing suggest to the attackers that they had not yet been seen. Led by Jemima Suggett Johnson, twelve women and sixteen young girls gathered pails and walked in the direction of the creek, all under the watchful eye of the soon-to-be-attackers. It took nearly an hour for them to fill their pails and return to the safety of the fort. The attack on the fort lasted for three days, August 15–17, 1782, but the settlers were able to prevail. Inside the fort was Jemima's infant child, a son who would grow up to become the ninth vice president of the United States, Richard Mentor Johnson.[32] The Suggett and Johnson families would soon be residents of Northern Kentucky.

8

The Battle of Blue Licks

When word of the attack on Bryan Station reached other Kentucky settlements, several groups of militiamen mustered to their neighbors' defense. On August 18, 1782, Colonel John Todd, commander of the Fayette County militia, arrived at Bryan Station with a force of 182 men, including Lieutenant Colonel Daniel Boone and about 130 men under the command of Lieutenant Colonel Stephen Trigg. Colonel Benjamin Logan of the Lincoln County militia was still gathering men, an expected 135 or so, and was still some twenty-four hours away.

Todd and his militiamen found themselves with two basic options. They could pursue the enemy immediately, though somewhat shorthanded; or they could wait for Colonel Logan to arrive with his additional forces. Major Hugh McGary, who had accompanied Boone on his second expedition into Kentucky and who had served with Clark, Boone, Kenton, and Todd in earlier skirmishes, recommended they wait for Logan and the reinforcements. Apparently, Todd shamed him for what Todd saw as his timid, almost cowardly suggestion. Todd and the other officers decided that the Kentucky militia would leave Bryan Station immediately in pursuit of the enemy, who had at least a forty-mile head start. That decision would soon prove disastrous.

The Kentucky militia, about two-thirds of them on horseback, departed Bryan Station around 10:30 a.m. on August 18. Tracking the path of their enemy, they traveled north-northwest with little in the way of obstacles or rough terrain. Just after 2:00 p.m., they arrived at Ruddell's Station, where, just as the Indians had done days earlier, they rested and watered their horses. It was at this spot that the second crucial mistake was made. Inspecting the campsite, the Kentuckians determined that the Indians numbered between 400 and 500, and they easily found their trail to the east, toward Blue Licks. What they did not see was a second trail leading out of the camp. The Indians had divided, with a much smaller contingency heading north. Had they known this, militia leaders might have trailed this smaller group, as they no longer would have been so greatly outnumbered. Instead, the Kentuckians followed the only trail they had noticed, the one leading east toward the salt licks. They traveled several hours more and camped on the banks of Stony Creek. Meanwhile, a dispatch rider was sent back to Lexington, with instructions to tell Colonel Logan to head directly to Blue Licks with his men.[1]

On August 19, 1782, the Kentuckians arose, ate breakfast, and gathered to again pursue the enemy. They continued along the buffalo trace toward Blue Licks, and at 8:00 a.m. the group reached the southern bank of the Licking River. A small scouting group forded the river and made a quick inspection, witnessing only a few Indians, who were fleeing up the hill away from the bank.[2] Colonel Todd then called a conference of his officers to prepare a plan.

The Licking River where the men were located forms a large loop, and the militiamen faced a hill surrounded by many steep ravines. Daniel Boone, the most experienced woodsman of the group, was extremely leery about continuing any farther. He had been perplexed the entire journey by the obvious trail that British Captain William Caldwell's Indian forces had left, and remarked to Colonel Todd that it appeared to him that the Indians in fact had made no attempt whatsoever to hide their tracks. Boone, as well as the majority of the officers, suggested they wait for Logan's men.[3] McGary, however, likely wanting to dispel earlier suggestions that he was a coward, urged an immediate attack on what seemed to be just a small Indian party. When no one listened, he is said to have mounted his horse, forded the river and yelled, "Them that ain't cowards, follow me and I'll show you the Indians!"[4] The Kentuckians immediately headed across the narrow ford, in single file. Boone, Todd, and Trigg followed, hoping to restore order on the other side of the river. Boone, however, is said to have remarked as he crossed the waters, "We are all slaughtered men."[5]

On the other side of the Licking, most of the men dismounted and formed battle lines several rows deep. An advance column of the militia then proceeded up the hill where the Indians had been spotted, immediately followed by the main force. While Colonel John Todd was in overall charge, the militiamen, now in three divisions, were commanded by McGary and Major Silas Harlan in the center, Lieutenant Colonel Stephen Trigg and Major Edward Bulger on the right, and Lieutenant Colonel Daniel Boone and Captain Robert Patterson on the left. With Boone were his son, Israel; his nephews, Thomas, Squire, and Samuel Boone; and his cousins, Abraham, Joseph, and Peter Scholl.

It remains unclear as to whose division first engaged the enemy. What became immediately obvious, however, was that Daniel Boone's intuition was right. It was an ambush. Caldwell's forces—some 450 strong—were waiting, poised above the major ravine and hiding behind trees. As the Kentuckians neared the summit, the British soldiers and Indian fighters opened fire at close range with devastating accuracy. Boone had some initial success on the left flank, being able to push the enemy back some 100 yards, but the center group was doing little more than holding their own against the well-armed Indians. On the right side, however, everything went wrong. In fewer than ninety seconds Trigg, an easy target atop his tall horse, was shot dead. Total chaos ensued; and, before order could be restored, the entire right flank broke down, and enemy forces were suddenly surrounding the entire militia. Todd, seeing the problem to his right, quickly rode in that direction and was just as quickly shot dead. In only four minutes, Bulger ordered the right division to retreat. Seeing the enemy beginning to surround the entire group, McGary gave the same order to the center division. On the left, however, Boone and Patterson had no idea that the entire battle had already been lost. Once Boone realized he and his force were alone in the fight, he gave the order to retreat as well; and his men, most of whom had already dismounted, grabbed the nearest horse and quickly fled down the hillside. Boone retrieved a riderless horse and instructed his son, Israel, to mount and escape as quickly as possible. Just as he turned to locate a horse for himself, Israel fell to the ground, having been shot through the lower neck. Knowing the wound would be fatal, Daniel mounted Israel's horse and joined in the retreat, having no choice but to leave his dying son on the battlefield.

The Kentuckians ran, fighting hand-to-hand with Indians who had since flanked them from the east. In fewer than fifteen minutes, the Battle of Blue Licks was over. The militiamen continued running and were chased by their attackers for nearly two miles. Afterward, the Indians returned to the battlefield, where they scalped and mutilated many of the dead. While only 10 men from the enemy's ranks were reportedly killed, the death toll for the Kentuckians numbered 60, nearly one-third of the gathered militia. Once they were no longer being chased, the Kentuckians slowly headed toward Bryan Station, mostly on foot. Incredibly, Colonel Logan's reinforcements, some 500 strong, met them within five miles of the battle site. Logan's party assisted the badly injured and returned to Bryan Station, choosing to gather even more troops before continuing any further toward Caldwell and the Indians. Four days later, a reorganized militia left in search of their enemy, only to find that Caldwell and the Indians were long gone. At Blue Licks, they buried what remained of the mutilated bodies. Daniel Boone participated in this expedition and later wrote: "Being reinforced, we returned to bury the dead and found their bodies strewed everywhere, cut and mangled in a dreadful manner. This mournful scene exhibited a horror almost unparalleled: some torn and eaten by wild beasts; those in the river eaten by fishes; all in such a putrefied condition, that no one could be distinguished from another." He added that several of those killed had first been taken prisoner, as they had clearly been tied up and tortured before "being killed in the most barbaric manner as training for the youngest warriors."[6] Only 43 of the 60 bodies were located; these were placed in a common grave just north of the battlefield, where they remain today.[7]

Many published histories describe the Battle of Blue Licks as the last conflict of the American Revolutionary War. It clearly was not. Other skirmishes and several outright battles took place throughout the thirteen colonies for many months, including several more Indian raids in Kentucky. On September 2, two weeks after Blue Licks, Indians attacked Kincheloe Station near Bardstown, killing or capturing 37; and in midsummer 1783, McAfee Station (just west of Harrodsburg) was attacked, resulting in several more dead. By the fall of 1783, four more stations in Kentucky had been captured by Indians or abandoned because of threatened attacks, including Grant's (near today's Nicholasville), Lee's (southeast of present-day Maysville), and Painted Stone (Squire Boone's settlement at present-day Shelbyville). While Blue Licks has received the most notoriety, the inhabitants of Kentucky suffered far more losses after that battle than during it. In the five-year period immediately following, Indians, especially along the Ohio River between present-day Portsmouth and Louisville, killed, injured, or captured more than 1,000 men, women, and children who were on their way to establish new settlements in Kentucky.[8]

Little time passed before the Kentucky militia, as well as the dwindling population of the western settlements, began placing blame for the embarrassing defeat at Blue Licks. Many focused on McGary, Todd, and the other officers, but far more accusations were directed against George Rogers Clark for failing to establish forts along the Ohio River as suggested. Many believe that with a fort at the Point, Indian raids in Kentucky would have ceased completely. Many brave men were killed at Blue Licks; and some, including John Todd and Stephen Trigg, were later immortalized when new Kentucky counties were established and named for them.

Clark soon took the initiative to amass troops for a retaliatory invasion into the Ohio Country. By mobilizing the men of Virginia's three western counties, he hoped he could collect about 950 troops and, with the help of the Virginia regulars, defeat the British and their Indian allies once and for all. His plan proved far too optimistic. Initially his call was met with only a half-hearted response, as with such a humiliating defeat at Blue Licks few men wanted to face the Indians again. Clark, however, showing why he is now considered one of the most effective generals of the Revolutionary War, eventually mustered 39 militia companies and in early November 1782 organized an army of over 1,100 men—once again meeting at the Point. The invasion into the Ohio Country eventually destroyed Chillicothe and five other Indian towns. No Indians were killed, however, as they fled their villages and ran away just as quickly as the Kentuckians had run from Blue Licks.

While many historians cite Clark's invasion as the key to opening Northern Kentucky for settlement, it was in fact a failure.[9] Clark was revered for his earlier victories at Vincennes and Kaskaskia in the Illinois Territory, and in 1779 Virginia statesman George Mason (1725–1792) even termed Clark the "Conqueror of the Northwest," since the Indians later ceded the entire region to the United States with the Treaty of Paris. Other historians, however, state that Clark's conquest was little more than a temporary occupation of that future state. In the end, the

Ohio Indians continued to wreak havoc in the region for another twelve years.

The Traveling Church

Shortly before the infamous Battle of Blue Licks, an event took place in Virginia that would have a lasting impact on the future settlement of Northern Kentucky. In September 1791, a large group of Baptists, nearly 600 strong, left more than a dozen churches in the Spotsylvania County area on a journey west. Well organized, these men, women, children, slaves, pack horses, cattle, and loaded wagons formed a convoy several miles long as they passed through the Cumberland Gap and into Central Kentucky. In a movement known as the "Traveling Church," they left the safety of colonial Virginia and risked their lives relocating to Kentucky with the purpose of establishing new settlements where they could spread the gospel west of the Allegheny and Appalachian mountain ranges.

Captain William Ellis was one of the main organizers. He and Peter Durrett, the slave of neighbor Lewis Craig, had explored present-day Kentucky on multiple occasions before 1780, and had even accompanied Colonel John Grant when he established his fort between Bryan Station and Boonesborough in 1778. Lewis Craig, son of Tolliver Craig Sr., was the coleader of the group. The Craigs, with their many relatives, are certainly among the most important settlers to enter the future state.

The Traveling Church first came to the Dix River region of present-day Lincoln and Garrard counties, where Lewis Craig established Craig's Station. In December 1781, with Craig serving as minister, the group held the first organized religious services in the West, at Gilbert's Creek Church, just south of today's Lancaster. Two years later, Craig established a church at Elkhorn Creek and remained there nine years before moving his family to Dover, Mason County. There, in 1793, the old Bracken Church at Minerva was formed. Craig not only served as pastor there, but is also considered the father of the Bracken Baptist Association. He traveled throughout much of the state, helping to organize churches in every corner of the Commonwealth. Lewis Craig died in Bracken County in 1825.

Lewis's brother Benjamin Craig and his family soon settled at McCoull's Bottoms (now Ghent) in Carroll County. The home he built there is among the first brick homes in the West. Another brother, Elijah Craig, established a settlement at what is now Georgetown in Scott County. Great Crossing Baptist Church was organized there by Elijah, the Suggett and Johnson families, and others. The Suggetts are listed among the brave residents of Bryan Station during its siege. Jemima Suggett married Colonel Robert "Robin" Johnson, who would soon found the town of Warsaw, in Gallatin County. Their son, Richard M. Johnson, later served as vice president of the United States. Robert Johnson was the son of William Johnson and Elizabeth Cave; and, like the Craig and Suggett families, the Caves became quite prominent in Northern Kentucky. Elizabeth Cave was the daughter of Benjamin Cave and Hannah Bledsoe—the Bledsoes being another important family in the early West. Elizabeth's brother William Cave and his family, with several others, were instrumental in organizing the Bullittsburg Baptist Church at present-day Boone County. Prominent names from that congregation include the Gaines, Cloud, Conner, Ryle, Mosby, and Graves families.

Soon other Northern Kentucky Baptist churches had been established, all as a result of the Traveling Church members and their descendants: Alexandria Baptist (1820), organized by members of Licking Baptist, with the help of the Stevens and Gosney families; Bank Lick Baptist (1801), founded by Thomas Griffin and Jeremiah Riggs, with help from the Stephens and McCollum families; Bethel Baptist (1812), near Union, established by Presley Peak, Asa Peak, Elijah Anderson, and Cornelius McLaughlin; Big Bone Baptist; East Bend Baptist (1798), about five miles south of Rabbit Hash; Flagg Spring Baptist (1833); Forks of Gunpowder Baptist (1812); Middle Creek Baptist (1803), which became Belleview Baptist; Mouth of the Licking Baptist (1794), later Licking Baptist, organized at the home of William Decoursey; Mud Lick Baptist (1804), near today's US 42 and KY 338; Oak Ridge Baptist (1844), founded at the home of John Lipscomb along Decoursey Creek; Sand Run Baptist (1819), about twelve miles south of Bullittsburg; West Creek Baptist (1808), near the Licking in today's Bracken County; Wilmington Baptist (1804), organized by William Stephens,

Samuel Bryant, Thomas Griffin, and William Gosney, on the Licking River near present-day Demossville (later moved to near Fiskburg, Kenton County); and Woolper Creek (1801), organized with the help of Cave Johnson and John Conner.

9

Permanent Northern Kentucky Settlers

The new Kentucky settlers were able to score a minor victory over the Indians with George Rogers Clark's raid in November 1782. Unfortunately, this attack would not be the last time a Kentucky militia crossed the mighty Ohio to engage the Indians.

Jacob Fowler (1764–1850) was one of the many men who mustered for Clark, and it was Fowler who escorted the Kentucky militia, including Benjamin Logan and Daniel Boone, in their march from Central Kentucky to the Point. Fowler had come to Kentucky earlier with his parents, Edward Fowler and Rachel Piatt, and resided at Lexington. Other relatives, Joseph and John Fowler, resided at Bryan Station and are listed among those who bravely defended that fort during the famous siege. After the raid, Jacob Fowler built a cabin in Northern Kentucky, undoubtedly becoming the first European to permanently settle in the region. The exact location of this cabin, however, continues to be debated. The earliest reference would not come for many years, when brothers Hubbard and James Taylor Jr. first arrived at what would become Newport. According to this source, "when (Hubbard) Taylor first arrived, he found that Jacob Fowler was already living in the vicinity." For some reason, it has been assumed that Fowler's cabin was located right at present-day Newport when "in the vicinity" could define any spot within several miles. Even a half day's journey could be considered "in the vicinity" in 1783. Other historians, including Mary Keturah Jones, a direct descendant of James Taylor Jr., state that Fowler's cabin was located at the Point.[1] Given Jones's statement, and knowing that Fowler had passed through present-day Kenton County and not Campbell County on previous excursions, it is this author's belief that Fowler's first cabin was on the western side of the Licking River, and that he moved to the eastern side of the Licking River after James Taylor Jr. arrived and as Newport was being established.

Edmond Rittenhouse and his family, who had been taken captive during the Ruddell's Station massacre, were released by the Indians in late 1782. They returned to the region the following spring and established a settlement along the western bank of the Licking River, in the vicinity of what is now the twelfth fairway at Twin Oaks Golf and Plantation Club, Latonia.[2] Brackett Owen also arrived with his family that same year, founding Owen's Station four miles from present-day Shelbyville. There were nine sons and three daughters in the Owen family, and several played important roles in the region's history. Many of Brackett's sons became military officers, including Colonel Abraham Owen (1769–1811), who was later killed at the Battle of Tippecanoe. Both Owen County and the city of Owensboro are named for him.

Also in 1783, George Mefford and his family descended the Ohio River from Pennsylvania and disembarked at Cabin Creek, just east of present-day Maysville. Like many families in this period, Mefford built his home from the actual boards of the flatboat the family used on their journey down the Ohio. His cabin was located on the East Fork of Cabin Creek, about two miles due south from today's Maysville. That structure, now fully restored and relocated to Washington, Kentucky, is one of the only original structures remaining of the Revolutionary War era in the state, and is the last of the "flatboat houses" in Kentucky.[3]

A few months later, in early 1784, Prettyman Merry (1742–1817) and his family arrived in Northern Kentucky. Prettyman had married Catherine Suggett in 1769 and was later granted about 2,500 acres along the Ohio River, a few miles west of the mouth of the Licking. There he built a large four-room home of fieldstone, with two-foot-thick walls. Giant hand-hewn black walnut logs were used as joists in the cellar to hold up the superstructure of more than 2,000 stones.[4] In 2019, the Merrys' "Landmark" remains the oldest structure still standing in Kenton County, located at the western end of Shelby Street in Bromley.

The Suggett family was headed by John and Mary Davis Suggett, who had come from New York after relocating from Virginia. John brought his family west in 1779, descending the Ohio River to the Falls,

The Prettyman Merry home, Bromley, Kentucky, 2018.

then on to Boonesborough. The Suggetts were related to another pioneer family in early Kentucky, headed by Robert "Robin" Johnson (1745–1815), who had married Jemima Suggett. The Johnsons had come to Kentucky with the Traveling Church and had first settled at Bryan Station with several siblings and many other relatives. Jemima Suggett, as mentioned earlier, was the woman who led the girls at Bryan Station on their mission of gathering water just before the Indian siege. In 1783, Robin and Jemima Johnson, along with others, established a settlement about five miles west of present-day Georgetown. First named Johnson Station, it was renamed Great Crossing due to the large ford over Elkhorn Creek used by massive herds of buffalo.

Brothers Edward and John Waller also arrived in Kentucky at about this time. John had received a grant of some 2,300 acres in the new Kentucky, 800 at present-day Mason County and the remainder in today's Pendleton County. The brothers erected a double log cabin and blockhouse at Limestone Creek around 1784, later known as the Maysville Blockhouse.

Colonel John Grant returned to Kentucky with his family, having been ousted by Indians from the fort he had established earlier near Bryan Station. In 1784, he and a small group entered present-day Campbell County, establishing a settlement at what is now Grant's Lick. His brother, Squire Grant, one of the survivors of the Battle of Blue Licks, relocated there as well, and would operate a general store by 1800.[5] John and Squire were sons of William Grant and Elizabeth Boone Grant, sister of Daniel Boone.[6] Mary Boone Bryan (1736–1819), another sister of Daniel Boone, had married William Bryan, cofounder of Bryan Station. After repeated Indian attacks there and the loss of her husband and three sons, Mary moved back to Virginia but later returned to the West, settling at Grant's Lick with John and Squire Grant and another son, Samuel.[7] By around 1805 Samuel Bryan was operating a tavern from his home, and a ferry was also established crossing the nearby Licking River. Within a decade, John and Samuel Bryan, along with Charles Morgan, began a salt-making operation. James Taylor Jr. would later become a business partner in that endeavor. John Grant also owned vast acreage a few miles to the north, on the western side of the Licking River, in present-day Kenton County, at a spot easily identifiable on a map as the "big loop," at what became known as Grant's Bend.[8]

Elijah Craig, a major participant in the Traveling Church movement and a former resident at Bryan Station, founded a settlement of his own in today's Scott County. He named this village Lebanon, but in 1790 it was renamed "George Town" in honor of the country's first president. Brothers George, John, and William May, with partner Samuel Beall, had surveyed and laid claim to over 765,000 acres for themselves immediately following the American Revolutionary War.[9] John May (1737–1790) was the first teacher at McAfee Station in the neighborhood of Harrodsburg and was likely the first person in that profession in all of Kentucky. He journeyed often between Virginia, Limestone, Boonesborough, and Harrodsburg. Later he purchased from Simon Kenton the 100 acres that became the city of Maysville. Unfortunately, John May never lived in the city named for him, as he was killed by Indians in 1790 while traveling on the Ohio River at present-day Portsmouth.[10]

The first substantial migration into Northern Kentucky began in 1785. While some entered the new West via the Cumberland Gap and Daniel Boone's Wilderness Road, scores of settlers departed such places as Pennsylvania, Maryland, upper Virginia, and the New England region, traveling across land and stream to present-day Pittsburgh, where they descended the Ohio River. Many families disembarked at present-day Maysville, where by 1789 thirty flatboats per day were landing.[11] Others continued down the Ohio River in search of their new homesteads. Some found their way into the state's interior by means of the Kentucky River; many others at present-day Louisville; and some in the Salt River region and further points west.[12] Many, however, found that ascending the Licking River from the Point was the best highway into what would soon become the fifteenth state of the Union.

Ellison B. Williams Sr. (1766–1850), along with a brother, built a home near the mouth of the Licking River at present-day Covington in 1785.[13] These men had arrived in Kentucky with their father, Allison Williams, and first resided at Bryan Station. They were present during the 1782 attack. Ellison also briefly resided at Higgin's Blockhouse, just north of today's Cynthiana, where he became good friends with Daniel Boone and accompanied the famous frontiersman on several excursions.[14] Later Ellison helped clear many roads, including the first from the mouth of the Licking to Lexington, and was a frequent escort to and from those two points.

Robert McKay and his family arrived from Frederick County, Virginia, settling on property that encompassed most of present-day Villa Hills, Fort Mitchell, Lakeside Park, and Crescent Springs.[15] Large parcels of his land were later deeded to the four McKay girls when they married. Alice married John Allen and they lived near present-day Buttermilk Pike, owning most of today's Crescent Springs. Rachel married Captain Levi Cleveland, brother of Moses Cleveland, for whom the Ohio city is named. This family resided on today's Amsterdam Road. Anna married Samuel Bell Kyle, son of Robert and Sallie Kyle, whose family eventually ran a successful farm and orchard at what is now Kyle's Lane and Interstates 71/75, Fort Wright.[16] Still another daughter married a Sanford, residing along what is now Madison Pike and Highland Avenue, in an area known well into the 1950s as Sanfordtown.[17]

David Leitch (1753–1794) was born in Scotland and came to Kentucky during the early 1780s, residing at Lexington. There he married Keturah Moss, one of the brave young girls who helped gather water during the siege at Bryan Station. Leitch was granted 13,800 acres in

1785, which included much of what is now Wilder, Cold Spring, and Alexandria, as well as parts of eastern Kenton County.[18] He later deeded 4,600 of those acres to William Kennedy, who arrived in the region by 1789. Leitch, with several others, moved to the Northern Kentucky property and erected a settlement known as Leitch's Station, situated at present-day Wilder. Edward and Rachel Piatt Fowler, parents of Jacob Fowler, were among the first settlers there, as was Thomas Lindsey Sr.[19] Lindsey had spent two years at Limestone, followed by a short stint at Lexington, before relocating to Leitch's Station.[20] In early 1794, while on a cold and bitter excursion to meet another group to whom he had sold land, Major David Leitch became very ill and died a week after returning to his station along the Licking. A historical marker commemorating Leitch's Station sits alongside the AA Highway in Wilder, directly across from the Waffle House and McDonald's restaurants.

William Wood, a Baptist preacher from New York, and Arthur Fox Sr., a young surveyor from Virginia, were among the first pioneers Simon Kenton welcomed at Limestone. The two men purchased land from Kenton, and in 1785 laid out what would become the town of Washington, the first of many such named towns in the new United States of America. Arthur Fox Sr. surveyed and acquired land in the area but died in 1794. Before his death, he had amassed more than 29,000 acres. Five children were born to the Fox couple, including Arthur Fox Jr., who later founded a settlement several miles downriver from Maysville. This village's name was taken from his father's hometown of Dover, England.[21] The junior Fox received his father's entire parcel, except for land already sold to Jeremiah Washburn. Washburn and his family constructed a log house in 1786 at the mouth of Lee's Creek. After the senior Fox's death, his widow married Henry Lee, and this couple became one of the largest landowners in the region. Lee (1757–1845) first came to the area in 1775 and founded Lee's Station two miles from present-day Maysville, at what became Washington. He opened the first branch bank in the region and served in the Kentucky legislature. Several others arrived with Lee: Edmund Phillips; his father, Moses Phillips; sons John, Gabriel, and Moses; sons-in-law Peter and William Bryan; Chestnut Theobalds; many wives; and a family of African Americans. Other early arrivals at present-day Mason County were Francis McDermed Sr. and George Sheppard.

Street scene in Old Washington, Kentucky, 2016.

Many historic structures remain at "Old Washington"—a town later annexed by the city of Maysville. An incomplete list includes the Bayless-Foreman-Taylor House, built in 1802; the Marshall Key Home, built in 1800 (Harriet Beecher Stowe was visiting there when she witnessed a slave auction at the old courthouse, basing *Uncle Tom's Cabin* on her experience); the birthplace of Civil War general Albert Sidney Johnston, a house built in 1797; the old courthouse, built of native stone by Lewis Craig in 1794; Federal Hill, built in 1795 by Thomas Marshall, brother of the first Chief Justice of the United States; the Arthur Fox home, built in 1795 by one of the town's founding fathers; Mefford Station, built in 1793 by George Mefford; the Paxton Inn, built in 1810 by James Paxton; and the Old Baptist Cemetery, established in 1797.

Also in 1785, Samuel Strode (1754–1842) established a small settlement along what he named Strode's Creek, at present-day Lewisburg, in Mason County. Within a few months, a small group headed by Richard Masterson erected cabins in the same general vicinity. The Strode family was extremely important to pioneer Kentucky history, beginning with Edward Strode and wife Susannah Hatchett. The offspring of three of their four children would leave lasting impressions here. Edward and Susannah's son, another Edward Strode, produced a son, John, who founded Strode's Station in present-day Clark County. Another son, Samuel, had a son also named Samuel, who founded Strode's Station in present-day Mason County. Daughter Martha Strode, married Morgan Bryan and bore William, Joseph, and Morgan Bryan, who, with William Grant, founded Bryan Station near present-day Lexington.[22] William Bryan and William Grant had married sisters of Daniel Boone, Mary and Rebecca, respectively.

Robert "Robin" and Jemima Johnson left Great Crossing (present-day Scott County) in 1785, relocating to present-day Gallatin County. Robin soon operated a grist mill there, and the new settlement became known as Johnson's Landing.[23] In 1790 Robin, along with Henry Yates and Henry Ellis, laid out a town they named Fredericksburg, after Fredericksburg, Virginia, from where these families had originally come. This town was eventually renamed Warsaw, according to the *Warsaw Independent* of May 1880, in honor of the great struggle for Polish independence in Russian-held Warsaw, Poland. Robin Johnson, as well as the other early settlers, took advantage of the old buffalo trace through the region. Daniel Boone had utilized that same passageway when he explored the area. Parts of that same trail are named Boone Road and Johnson Road. The original trace followed much of what is now KY 16 out of Boone County, to the north of Glencoe, then 465 (Boone Road) to near Sparta. From there, it followed present-day KY 467 toward Worthville, then south to Drennon's Lick.[24]

Over 2,000 acres at present-day Elsmere were granted to John Watkins and Robert "Robin" Johnson in 1785. The first home there was situated at today's Shaw Avenue. Bartlett Graves and John Stansifer purchased land from Watkins and Johnson, and these two men were later instrumental in developing what is now Erlanger. William Thornton Timberlake built one of the first homes there, which still stands, though somewhat altered. The home, along with its historical marker, is situated on the north side of Stevenson Road just east of Dixie Highway.

Revolutionary War veteran Colonel Abner Gaines, along with his family, settled on a ridge along a former buffalo trail in present-day Boone County and erected a log cabin. The property was sold by

Abner Gaines house, Walton, Kentucky, 2017.

Archibald Reid, an earlier settler. A magnificent brick home replaced the cabin, and in 2019 it serves as the Gaines Tavern History Center.[25] The Gaines Settlement became widely known as Gaines Crossroads before the area was later incorporated as the city of Walton in 1841.

By 1785, several new counties had been added to western Virginia. As for the northernmost section of Kentucky, areas west of the Licking River remained in Fayette County while areas east of the Licking became part of Bourbon County, Virginia. Major George Stockton, who would later become a state senator, established a station at present-day Flemingsburg around 1785, on what is now (2019) the ridge behind the Ford dealership. Colonel John Fleming, who first settled at Strode's Station at present-day Clark County, founded Fleming Station along Fleming Creek, about five miles west of today's Flemingsburg, around 1787.[26] Michael Cassidy, who had accompanied Fleming and Stockton into Kentucky a few years earlier, founded his own station about two and a half miles west of Stockton's Station.[27] Cassidy was the first senator from the region in 1806 and served several terms as a state representative. Other early arrivals at present-day Fleming County include the Benjamin Threlkeld family, along with a family friend, Henry Bruce, all from Frederick County, Virginia. Many in this group settled along Johnson's Creek in what is now northwest Fleming County.[28] William Kennan arrived a few years later, settling along Fleming Creek.

10

Northwest Territory and Fort Washington

In July 1787, the Continental Congress officially organized the land north of the Ohio River and west to the Mississippi River as the Northwest Territory. A year later, Mathias Denman, Colonel Robert Patterson, and Israel Ludlow landed on the north bank of the Ohio, opposite the mouth of the Licking River, and began a settlement there. The original surveyor, John Filson, named the settlement "Losantiville"—which simply translates as "city opposite the mouth of the Licking."[1] The same year, John Cleves Symmes, a congressman from New Jersey, purchased from the government over 300,000 acres situated between the Great Miami and Little Miami rivers in the new Northwest Territory. Soon small settlements formed at Columbia, just downriver from today's Lunken Airport, and at North Bend, at Ohio's present-day border with Indiana.

Back on the southern side of the Ohio River, Mason County was formed in 1788. Taken from part of Bourbon County, Virginia, it is doubtful any other county in Kentucky has a more intricate and celebrated pioneer history. While today's Bell County can boast of its Cumberland Gap and the many families who entered the future state through that famous route, far more families found their new Kentucky homesteads by entering what is now Mason County. The county was named for George Mason, who by 1752 had served as treasurer of the Ohio Company and, along with George Rogers Clark and others, supported the Continental Congress and the defeat of the British. He wrote the Virginia Bill of Rights and was Thomas Jefferson's law professor, certainly influencing Jefferson's later penning of the Declaration of Independence.[2]

Several other forts were established in the immediate area around this time. Daniel Feagan built his station just east of present-day Germantown; Bailey's Station, built in 1791, was situated two and a half miles south of Maysville and one mile from Washington; Bosley's Station, also established in 1791, was located along Wells Creek just southeast of Washington; Colonel Thomas Waring built his station one mile southwest of town; and James McKinley built his station in 1785, located along the main trace, southwest of present-day Washington.

A group of Pennsylvania Dutch settled in Mason County in 1788, at what was called Buchannan Station. The first home there was built at present-day Asbury Road and KY 10. The name of the town was later changed to Germantown after an influx of German immigrants in the early 1800s. Daniel Drake (1785–1852) came to Maysville in 1788. A renowned physician, lecturer, and author, he eventually founded the Medical College of Ohio, which became the University of Cincinnati College of Medicine in 1819. He also founded what later became Cincinnati's University Hospital.[3]

In early 1789, Francis Kennedy left the safe haven of Pennsylvania and traveled down the Ohio River into the western frontier. With his wife, Rebecca, and their seven children, the group landed at Losantiville on February 8, 1789.[4] At that time, Losantiville consisted of only a couple of log homes housing the families of Colonel Robert Patterson, William McMillan, and Israel Ludlow.[5] Soon, Francis Kennedy became the first ferryman in the area, operating a flatboat ferry from the end of what is now Sycamore Street in Cincinnati, just west of Yeatman's Cove, to the Point.

Meanwhile, John Tanner and his brother, David, had arrived in Central Kentucky as early as 1775.[6] David erected a cabin there in about 1784, along the Licking River at what is now the northwestern tip of Nicholas County. Restored, and in 2019 part of the Blue Licks Battlefield State Resort Park, the cabin is situated on the southern side of US 68 just west of the park's main entrance. His brother John relocated along the Ohio River in 1789, opposite present-day Lawrenceburg, Indiana.[7] A year later, a group of Pennsylvanians came down the Ohio River to join him, clearing 30–40 acres there, and this became the first settlement in present-day Boone County. Although a blockhouse was built, it would be several years before the site was settled in any significant numbers. John Tanner's life, however, is a great example of the dangers of early Kentucky settlement. In his first year at present-day Boone County, before Tanner completed his blockhouse, his nine-year-old son, John, was taken captive by Indians. The young boy remained with his kidnappers for more than twenty years before being ransomed.[8] He later worked for the United States government as an interpreter.[9] A year after that boy was taken, another son, Edward, nearly fifteen years old at the time, was also taken hostage by Indians. Unlike his younger sibling, however, Edward was able to escape his captors and return home. The elder Tanner did not remain at Tanner's Station very long. He moved to Missouri in 1798 and died there within a few years of his relocation.

James Ryle left North Carolina with his wife and children, arriving at Tanner's Station in 1789. Polly Ann Ryle was born there in December 1790, the first European child born in what is now Boone County. A devout Baptist, Ryle later settled several miles to the southwest. William Underhill and his family arrived in 1790. Residing in the Gunpowder Creek area, Underhill became the preacher at Gunpowder Creek Baptist Church, a position he held for fifty years.

The great influx of settlers into Northern Kentucky, which began in 1785, continued for several years. However, the paramount need—protection—remained, as settlements on both sides of the Ohio were still completely isolated from the rest of the country. Attacks along the Ohio River continued, and many would-be settlers were killed or taken captive in this period. The Kentucky militia continued to plead for assistance, realizing they could not protect the territory on their own. President George Washington eventually responded with an order that a fortification be erected within the Northwest Territory's new Symmes Purchase, and in 1789 the army erected a fort on the north side of the Ohio River, opposite the mouth of the Licking River. Named for the country's first president, Fort Washington housed 1,500 persons and was protected by cannon mounted at the blockhouses built at each of the four corners. It included a hospital, military quarters, and a powder magazine, as well as working facilities for such craftsmen as a blacksmith, clothier, carpenter, and wheelwright.[10] The fort stood between what is now Fourth Street, Pike Street, Broadway, and the Ohio River. A historical marker recognizing the importance of Fort Washington stands at the southern edge of Lytle Park in downtown Cincinnati.

That same year, William Kennedy (1728–1799) and his family—no known relation to the aforementioned Francis Kennedy—erected a small settlement at present-day Flagg Springs, Campbell County.[11] He and his son, James, quickly became valued surveyors, and the Kennedys soon owned vast acreage in what is now southern Campbell County. A daughter, Jeanette Kennedy, married Benjamin Beall, and they were also able to acquire large land tracts in the region. Benjamin Beall (1750–1809) settled at what he called Beallmont, at present-day Mentor, where he and his wife raised nine children, including Benjamin Duke Beall, who built a two-story frame house that stood for decades just east of the old courthouse in Alexandria.[12]

Colonel William Peachey (1729–1802; also known as Peachy) had served in the French and Indian War and received 2,000 acres at the mouth of the Kentucky River in exchange for his service. In 1789, he settled on that land, along the eastern shore.[13] General Charles Scott (1739–1813) arrived with Peachey and built a blockhouse nearby, not only for protection but also as preparation for future expeditions against the Indians. John Guill relocated from Caroline County, Virginia, in 1790 and built a cabin on a stream that emptied into Big Eagle Creek, a location he named Guill's Branch. His settlement, three miles west of the point where Owen, Grant, and Harrison Counties meet today, became known as New Columbus.[14]

In late summer 1790, Thomas Kennedy Jr. arrived in the area, having followed his brother, Francis, who had settled at Losantiville. With Thomas was his wife, the widow Dinah (Davis) Piersel Kennedy; three children from her previous marriage, Mrs. Mary Scott, Zaccheus Piersel, and Mrs. Sallie Kyle; and Sallie's husband, Robert Samuel Kyle.[15] This group made their way down the Ohio River by flatboat and disembarked at the Point. Soon, Thomas was operating the Kentucky side of the ferry between the Point and Losantiville, while his brother continued operations on the Ohio side. In 1791, Thomas began construction of a stone house on the property and began farming the land.[16] The walls of his new home were three feet thick, and there was a large porch across the entire front of the building, which faced the Ohio River. In short time, a flourishing tavern and inn were in operation at the home, and the Kennedys would play host to hundreds of emigrants who descended the Ohio River by flatboat. There, they rested, replenished their supplies, and learned of any available land for settling. Even in those days, the government saw fit to fix and regulate prices of certain goods and services. Kennedy was allowed to charge, "for breakfast or supper, one shilling; for a night's lodging in a good feather bed with clean sheets, one shilling."[17] Kennedy's estate also boasted a barn, a springhouse, a henhouse, an icehouse, and a smokehouse, all made of stone. Soon there were far fewer references to the "Point" and far more to "Kennedy's Ferry." A stone monument and plaque now stand near the site of the old home, which was on the southern side of the alley within George Rogers Clark Park, at Covington's Riverside Drive and Greenup Street.

William Thompson had surveyed an area about nine miles south of present-day Maysville, and Robert Patterson, who with others had founded the city of Lexington, explored the same area in 1775. A group of related families eventually purchased about 1,400 acres from William May and settled there in 1789. These families included brothers Abraham, Cornelius, and Isaac Drake; David Morris; and John Shotwell, who named the village May's Lick (now Mayslick) in honor of John May, William's brother. The same year George Lewis, for whom Lewis County would later be named, reestablished the small fort abandoned by Samuel Strode in today's southern Mason County. That settlement was officially established as Lewisburg on December 17, 1795; and by 1800, Lewis had built a mill, a dam, and a canal to bring water to the mill.

By this time, another county was added to the region, and the population of western Virginia had reached over 73,000. Most of what is now Carroll, Owen, Gallatin, Boone, Kenton, and Grant counties became Woodford County, Virginia, while what is now Campbell, Pendleton, Bracken, Fleming, Robertson, and Mason counties were all part of Mason County, Virginia.

Colonel Joshua Baker (1765–1816), from Rowan County, North Carolina, relocated to what is now Owen County. There he built a large home about two miles south of Owenton. A historical marker is located at the present-day intersection of Route 227 and Highway 330. Baker had married Mary North Calloway, who was related to Richard Calloway of Boonesborough, before their move to Owen County. A Mr. Rowlett built and operated a trading post at what became Rowlett's

Landing in Owen County. A few years later, James and Alexander Williams opened their post at Williamsburg, which was later named Monterey.

The Waller brothers, who had assisted in the formation of Kenton Station, both relocated around this time. Edward moved to Paris, Bourbon County, while John founded Forks of the Licking, which in 1793 became the city of Falmouth, Pendleton County. Falmouth was established on property owned by Waller, John Cook, William McDowell, and John Grant, and the first court was held in the home of Alvin Mountjoy.[18] To the west, a group led by Elders Lewis Corban and John Conner established a Baptist church in present-day Grant County in 1791. Squire Boone preached at what was known as the Old Baptist Church on the Dry Ridge in 1798. Founders included the Childers, Conrad, Conyers, Franks, Lawless, and Skirvin families.

North of the Ohio River, the name of the Losantiville settlement was changed by Arthur St. Clair (circa 1737–1818), governor of the Northwest Territory. The new name became Cincinnati, in honor of the Society of the Cincinnati, made up of Revolutionary War veterans, of which St. Clair was a member. Many Indian tribes, however, continued their refusal to recognize the boundaries of the new United States, especially the Miami, led by Chief Little Turtle, and the Shawnee, now led by Chief Blue Jacket. Therefore, attacks against European settlers continued, almost exclusively along the Ohio River rather than deep within the wilderness. President Washington had little choice but to order a massive attack on those tribes. He soon authorized General St. Clair to organize a militia, and more than 1,400 men mustered. Those from Kentucky met at Kennedy's Ferry. The army then marched into present-day Fort Wayne, Indiana, under the leadership of Josiah Harmar, commander of the United States Army in the Northwest Territory. Scouts for Little Turtle spotted the approaching militia, however, and warriors purposely drew the enemy deeper and deeper into the woods by advancing, then retreating further, over and over again. Once the gathered militia was in the desired position, the Indians attacked.[19] In what is known as Harmar's Defeat, in October 1790, 223 settlers were killed or wounded. Meanwhile, General Charles Scott (1739–1812) had a more favorable outcome in a raid he had commanded. His 800-man militia from Central Kentucky crossed the Ohio River at present-day

Carrollton and destroyed several villages, including a major settlement at Lafayette, Indiana.[20]

Washington then ordered a more vigorous attack. St. Clair organized nearly 2,000 men, but before his plan commenced, scores of his men deserted. His ranks had been filled with many new, untrained soldiers, and their promised pay had apparently been severely cut. By the time St. Clair's group reached the mouth of the Wabash River, his numbers had dwindled to about 950, while the Indian contingency totaled as many as 2,000. At dawn on November 4, 1791, the Indians surrounded St. Clair's campsite and simply waited for the soldiers to march off for breakfast. They attacked quickly, catching the Army completely off guard. Many ran, leaving their weapons behind, while others fought the tribe hand to hand. The Army's artillery force, which was situated on a nearby bluff, wheeled their weapons around to take position, but those men were killed or captured before firing a single cannon shot. The casualty rate was the highest ever suffered by a United States Army unit. Of the officers, 88 percent were either killed or wounded in the ambush; among the soldiers, the figure was over 97 percent. In all, 832 Americans were killed, nearly one-fourth of the entire United States Army at the time.[21]

11

Kentucky Becomes a State

On June 1, 1792, Kentucky was granted statehood, becoming the first state west of the Appalachian Mountains. Isaac Shelby, who had fought in Lord Dunmore's War as well as at Point Pleasant, became the state's first governor. Shelby was an early resident at Boonesborough and was a strong advocate for Kentucky's separation from Virginia. New counties were formed at this time, and the Northern Kentucky region was split into three large tracts. Land east of the Licking remained as Mason County, while parts of today's Carroll and Owen counties remained in Woodford County. What is now Boone and Kenton counties, as well as sections of Owen, Grant, and Pendleton counties, became Scott County, named for General Charles Scott, who would serve as Kentucky's governor from 1808 to 1812.

A few months after Kentucky became a state, Presley Peak Sr. (also seen as Peake) entered the region with his family. He constructed a log home along the Licking River, a short distance below present-day East Thirteenth Street, in Covington.[1] Many members of his family later resided in today's Boone County. General Thomas Sandford (1762–1808) came to Kentucky with his family at around the same time. He had married Sara Redman in Virginia and had two children, then married Peggy Bell and had another son.[2] Many records indicate that the family settled "on the hills back of Covington," but some historians may have confused this family with that of Benjamin Franklin Sanford, who would arrive a few years later and reside along what is now Madison Pike (KY 17).[3] The area known as Sanfordtown was named for Benjamin Franklin Sanford.[4] In 2019, a short street near the bottom of Dudley Pike is the only remaining reference to the old town, which was obliterated when Interstate 275 was constructed. Unfortunately, the modern sign mistakenly includes a *d* in the first syllable: Sandfordtown Street.

General Thomas Sandford (with the *d*) owned a large estate at present-day Ludlow, which was later sold to Thomas D. Carneal, who built Elmwood Hall there.[5] Thomas Sandford was elected to congress in 1806, and in 1808 was elected senator. Tragically, he drowned at age forty-six in the Ohio River near Cincinnati, just months before taking office. His sons, Alexander Pope Sandford and Cassius Sandford, remained in Northern Kentucky and raised families of their own. For many years, Alexander owned a home along Dixie Highway, technically on "the hills south of Covington." The home, since razed, was on the eastern side of the highway, just north of today's Highland Cemetery.[6] John Leathers Sandford, son of Cassius, married Kate Marshall and later served as mayor of Covington. He was killed in a shootout with later Governor William Goebel (1856–1900) in 1895.[7] A cousin of General Thomas Sandford, Richard Sandford, also traveled to Kentucky. Unfortunately, Richard died during the long trip and was buried at Great Crossing, near present-day Georgetown.[8] Richard (1755–1795) had married Winifred Redman, sister to Thomas's wife, and had six children, including Lawrence and Thomas, who both raised families in Northern Kentucky. To add to the confusion with these two families, a street in downtown Covington was named for the family of General Thomas Sandford, but the spelling on the street sign omits the *d*—Sanford Street.[9]

In the mid-1790s, Raleigh Colston purchased from his brother-in-law William Peachey a 5,000-acre tract along the Ohio River that today includes much of the western suburbs of Covington.[10] Colston married Elizabeth Marshall and became a prominent Covington attorney. Descendants of this couple intermarried with the Beall family and other early settlers of what is now eastern Campbell County. James Taylor Jr. donated two acres for public use, and a short time later a school board was formed at Newport, including many names very familiar in the region's history: William Kennedy, Washington Berry, Charles Morgan, John Grant, Thomas Kennedy, Thomas Sandford, Thomas Carneal, Richard Southgate, Daniel Mayo, John Crittenden, Robert Stubbs, and James Taylor Jr.

Lewis Craig had come to Kentucky earlier with the Traveling Church. In 1793, he relocated to present-day Mason County and helped form the Bracken Baptist Church at Minerva, now known as the

Lewis Craig Memorial Church. Minerva was named for the first European woman known to reside in the area, Minerva Green. The same year, Joseph Desha came from Pennsylvania, first to Tennessee then to Mason County, Kentucky. He served with William Henry Harrison and later with "Mad" Anthony Wayne (1745–1796) in campaigns against the Indians, before becoming governor of Kentucky in 1824.[11] Brothers Miles Withers Conway and John Conway also settled at Washington.[12]

After two horrendous defeats in warfare against Indians in the Northwest Territory, President Washington reorganized his army and called retired Brigadier General Anthony Wayne away from civilian life. Wayne had served well in the American Revolutionary War and because of his fiery personality and military exploits was nicknamed "Mad" Anthony Wayne. He soon established the first basic training program for incoming soldiers and, while volunteers were at first slow in coming, they soon arrived at Pittsburgh in heavier numbers. One of the new soldiers was a young lieutenant in the cavalry named Leonard Wales Covington (1768–1813). Soon the soldiers had built river craft, and in April 1793 a long train of flatboats descended the Ohio River to Fort Washington. Wayne's new army arrived on May 8, 1793, but immediately found Fort Washington too small to adequately train the men.[13] Wayne selected an area just west of the fort and east of Mill Creek for a drilling ground; but, dissatisfied with that property as well, he sent a team to the southern side of the Ohio River in search of better grounds, appointing Lieutenant Covington as detail commander. Within days, soldiers began training exercises at Kennedy's Ferry, and the ferry became an important means of transportation for General Wayne and his men. In early 1794, however, Francis Kennedy overloaded his ferry with the soldiers' cattle, was crowded off the vessel, and drowned.[14] His son, David, took charge temporarily, but the Cincinnati side of the ferry services was eventually transferred to Pliny Bliss, another early settler, around 1800.

It was quickly evident that Anthony Wayne's group was far different than those mustered by Arthur St. Clair, as Wayne's group enjoyed true military leadership. Once his troops were ready, Wayne dispatched a force to establish Fort Recovery on the very site of St. Clair's Defeat and then established Fort Defiance in northwestern Ohio. In August 1794, Wayne mounted a massive expedition into the Ohio Country.

As the men headed north toward the Maumee River, an Indian force of Shawnee, Delaware, Miami, Mingo, and others met the Americans at an area known by the Indians as Fallen Timbers—so named because an earlier tornado had knocked down many trees.[15] Although the Indians were able to use the fallen trees for cover, "Mad" Anthony Wayne's men quickly drove them out into the open. The Battle of Fallen Timbers was a decisive victory for the Americans; and the Treaty of Greenville, signed many months later, gave most of what is now Ohio to the United States, clearing the way for that territory to be admitted to the Union in 1803. Indian attacks against the Kentucky settlements diminished tremendously after this battle, but they would not cease completely for another twenty years.[16] One of the many heroes of the battle was young Leonard Covington, who would later hold the rank of general. Theodore Roosevelt, in his *Winning of the West,* wrote that the success of the battle was owed to Covington, who "led forward the troops and, the dragoons burst among the savages at full speed and routed them in a moment. Covington cut down two Indians with his own hand."[17]

Major Jacob Fowler participated in the victorious Fallen Timbers battle.[18] In fact, Fowler had fought with George Rogers Clark against the Shawnee and against Little Turtle's confederacy at Harmar's Defeat. Ellison B. Williams, Sr., also played an important role during Wayne's expedition, as he was contracted as a supplier of venison and wild game for the troops.[19] After the battle, Ellison and his wife, Mary Johnston, relocated to a home along Banklick Creek, about eight miles south of the Ohio River, and had nine children, including sons Ellison, Nathan, Isaac, John, and Peter. A small tributary of Banklick Creek and a nearby street along Old Madison Pike behind Pioneer Park are named for this early pioneer.

Simon Kenton also served with Wayne in the Northwest Indian War and later moved from Kentucky to Urbana, Ohio, with his family. His name, however, can be found all over Northern Kentucky, as well as throughout present-day Virginia, Ohio, and Indiana. Locally, Kenton County is named for him, of course, as is Kenton Elementary School and Simon Kenton High School, both in Independence. A statue of him on Covington's Riverside Drive overlooks the Ohio River at the Point. Simon Kenton is credited by historians as doing more to help open Kentucky for settlement than any other man, including the far more publicized Daniel Boone, who was twice saved from certain death by an alert Kenton. And unlike Boone, Kenton was almost constantly engaged in warfare with Indians, helping to protect the new West, from the time of his arrival on the frontier to the signing of the Greenville Treaty.[20]

Daniel Boone had settled at Maysville, where he operated a tavern and worked as a land speculator. He was already a celebrity, however, as on his fiftieth birthday in 1784 historian John Filson published *The Discovery, Settlement, and Present State of Kentucke,* a book that included a chronicle of Boone's adventures. In 1788, Boone relocated to Point Pleasant (now in West Virginia) but came back to Nicholas County, Kentucky, in 1795. He eventually lost all of his Kentucky land holdings after failing to properly register them, however. Disgruntled with the state he had worked so hard to help settle, he and his wife relocated to Missouri around 1799.

Immediately after "Mad" Anthony Wayne's successful mission, more groups of settlers came to Northern Kentucky. One such party, in 1794, journeyed from present-day Woodford and Scott counties to present-day Boone County, where they formed Bullittsburg Baptist Church, upriver from Tanner's Station. Lewis Deweese, John and Elizabeth Hall, Chichester and Agnes Matthew, and Joseph and Leannah Smith had first settled at Bullitt's Bottom (North Bend). Led by Joseph Redding and William Cave, and accompanied by Elder John Taylor, they formed what was the first church of any denomination in the northernmost counties of Kentucky.[21] It remains the longest continuously active church in the region, still holding worship services in an 1819 sanctuary.[22]

Revolutionary War veteran William Decoursey, Sr. (1756–1841), had received land for his service with the militia of Rowan County, North Carolina.[23] In 1794, he ascended the Licking River and settled on its western shore at present-day Decoursey Creek, about two miles south of the mouth of Banklick Creek.[24] He married Elizabeth Irvin and had one son, William Decoursey Jr. (1786–1858), who married Martha Frances Spilman, daughter of Frank Spilman and Rebecca Erskine. Decoursey was instrumental in the founding of Mouth of the Licking Baptist Church (later Cold Spring Baptist), and several famous Northern Kentucky surnames exist among the three descendants of Martha

Spilman and William Decoursey Jr. Francis Decoursey married Mary Ann Holmes, sister of Daniel Henry Holmes of Holmes High School (Covington) fame; Oliver Decoursey married Elizabeth Shaw, daughter of Robert Shaw, whose family helped incorporate the city of Independence; and Joel Decoursey married Mary Ann Pierce.[25] Frank Spilman was among a group who in 1790 came down the Ohio River, landing at present-day Maysville. This group eventually migrated to today's Campbell County, establishing a settlement there.[26] Others who settled in that region were the Baker, Beal, Movin, Reiley, Steven, Thatcher, and White families. Spilman had served with George Rogers Clark; and it is said that, while at war, he came upon a dying soldier who asked him to look after his wife, Rebecca Mumford. Francis Spilman and Rebecca Mumford were married in 1786, and the couple had eight children.[27] In 1819, Frank Spilman donated land for a courthouse and began selling lots for a town he named after his hometown of Alexandria, Virginia.[28]

Captain John Bartle (1745–1839) established Bartle's Ridge (now Cold Spring) in 1794. Bartle came from New York in 1789 with a flatboat of merchandise and established a store in Maysville before relocating to Lexington.[29] In 1790, he opened a store at Losantiville, built that town's first shingled house, and sold provisions to the soldiers at Fort Washington. He purchased lots in Newport and built a home on Second Street before eventually establishing his own settlement at present-day Cold Spring.

Whitfield Craig founded a settlement along Bracken Creek in Campbell County in about 1794. A small village on the western side of the county was also settled about the same time. First named Pleasant Ridge, that village was known by 1859 as Hagensville in honor of the Hagens family. Later, after a migration of German settlers, the town was renamed Berlin.[30] The nearby village of Lenoxburg was named in honor of an early storekeeper, Samuel B. Lenox.

In the same time period, John Martin and his family from Pennsylvania stopped shortly at Limestone before continuing down the Ohio to the Licking, where they ascended and settled between present-day Meinken Field and Holmes High School.[31] John married Sara Rittenhouse, possibly the sister of Edmond, and in 1805 purchased the old Presley Peak home, at what is now Thirteenth and Eastern, Covington. John's son, William Martin, married Margaret Rittenhouse, daughter of

Edmond, the first marriage between residents of what is now Kenton County. The couple's first son, Isaac Martin, was the first European to be born in the county. Isaac and his family would later settle along the Banklick Turnpike (now Madison Pike) between present-day Dudley Road and Horse Branch Road.

In the early 1790s, Colonel William Peachey sold some of his acreage at the mouth of the Kentucky River to Benjamin Craig and James Hawkins. Craig would eventually own more than 4,000 acres in present-day Carroll, Campbell, and Madison counties.[32] With Thomas Montague, Cave Johnson, and Jeremiah Craig as trustees, the town of Port William was laid out in 1792, likely named for Colonel William Peachey. Forty-six years later, the town would be officially incorporated as the city of Carrollton. Not long after Port William had been established, Richard and Sarah Shore Masterson built a magnificent brick home, which remains as one of the oldest two-story brick structures along the entire Ohio River.[33] By 1795, Craig's nephew, Elijah Craig Jr., was running a flatboat service from the mouth of the Kentucky River to various settlements inland. Captain James Wharton English and his family settled six miles southwest of Port William at about the same time. He built a log cabin along Mill Creek, and this settlement was later named English in his honor.[34] Joshua Hunter settled along the Ohio River between Locust Creek and Catnip Creek, just west of present-day Carrollton. He built a single cabin at what was called Hunter's Bottoms but apparently did not remain in the area. Cornelius Hoagland soon claimed that spot. Another early settlement existed to the south known as Coonskin, since local merchants willingly accepted animal skins in place of standard currency as payment for merchandise. That town was eventually renamed Worthville after Mexican War hero General William Worth.[35]

Campbell County was created in 1794 from parts of Scott, Harrison, and Mason counties, with the town of Wilmington (now in Kenton County) named as the county seat. The first session of court was held in the home of John Grant, and Jacob Fowler was named sheriff.[36] All of what is now Boone, Kenton, and Campbell counties, as well as most of Grant and Pendleton counties, became the new Campbell County.

12

Newport Established

In 1795 Hubbard Taylor returned to his father's holdings in Northern Kentucky and platted lots for a town on the eastern side of the Licking River at its confluence with the Ohio. He named the new settlement Newport after Christopher Newport, captain of the first ship that had arrived at Jamestown.[1] His brother, James Taylor Jr., was given 500 acres by their father, James Taylor Sr., in exchange for managing the property. James Taylor Jr. arrived and began selling the individual lots.[2] Newport was established on December 14, 1795.[3]

James Taylor Jr. immediately brought other settlers to Newport, including his sister Alice and her husband, Washington Berry. Washington's brother John Berry, John Buckner, and a handful of slaves and servants also arrived. Later, the Muse sisters sold the rights to their land to Washington Berry. James Taylor Jr. married Keturah Moss Leitch, the young widow of his friend David Leitch, consolidating two of the state's largest landholdings. Taylor built a large brick home, which still stands in 2019, at 335 East Third Street.

One of the earliest settlements in present-day Owen County was that organized by William Jones and named for his father-in-law, Samuel Cobb. Cobb's Station, later known as Cobb's Mills, was established in 1795 along Eagle Creek at today's Lusby's Mill. A small village in Grant County was first settled as the Wells, where the focal point was a tavern operated at the home of Archibald Reid (Reed) as early as 1795. Reid became very active in the government of Campbell County. Just to the west of his tavern was the Lebanon Presbyterian Church, founded in 1796.[4] The Wells was also known as Pin Hook, but the town name changed in 1834 to honor a Kentucky surveyor, statesman, and future governor, John J. Crittenden (1787–1863). Thomas Clark settled in the area the same year and operated a tavern halfway between Lexington and Kennedy's Ferry. His village became known as Hardscrabble and then Cherry Grove, just a few miles south of today's Williamstown.

John Kenton, brother to Simon, established a town called Newtown in 1795. This hamlet, at present-day US 62 and KY 617 in Robertson County, was later renamed Kentontown in honor of Simon Kenton.[5] Richard Southgate (1774–1857) also arrived in Northern Kentucky in 1795. A distinguished attorney in the region, Southgate accumulated vast real estate in Kentucky and was considered one of the wealthiest men in the state.[6] His home, built later by prisoners of the War of 1812 who were housed at the Newport Barracks, still stands at 24 East Third Street in Newport, though it has been greatly modified.

Wilmington was settled by Squire Grant and others on the western side of the Licking River opposite Grant's Lick.[7] Brothers Bryan, Phillip, John, and Daniel Senour (Seignour) also arrived in the region in 1795.[8] Two of the men married into land-wealthy families nearby: John married Rhonda Wayman, and Bryan married Ann McCollum. Rhonda was the daughter of William Wayman, who operated one of the first taverns in what became Kenton County. Ann was the daughter of John McCollum, who donated land for the first Kenton County courthouse. Though clearly shown with an *o* in early histories, the spelling of the McCollum family name changed over time to McCullum. These three families are each honored with street names in central Kenton County.

Quakers from Maryland, brothers Stephen and Thomas Rich, came to the area by flatboat around 1795.[9] Thomas settled in what is now Boone County, where many of his descendants remain. Stephen Rich married Jane Blackburn and settled in present-day Kenton County. This couple had nine children, including John, who married Susan Ross and settled near what is now the intersection of Old State Road and Sleepy Hollow Road. Sarah married John Leathers, who was twice elected as Kenton County Sheriff. Joseph married several times, first to Sallie Kyle, sister to Jacob Kyle, who operated a successful orchard (Kyle's Lane). Stephen Jr. married Nancy Drucker, settling east of present-day Piner (Rich Road). Alfred married Nancy Helm, their offspring remaining in the Sleepy Hollow Road area. And Samuel married Sarah Rittenhouse, their descendants settling throughout southeastern Kenton County.[10]

Bracken County was formed from parts of Mason and Campbell counties on June 1, 1797.[11] Within months, Augusta became a major shipping center for Central Kentucky. The county was named for William Bracken, who had first visited Northern Kentucky in 1773 with a group of explorers, including the McAfee brothers. As they descended the Ohio River, they met another party led by Captain Thomas Bullitt. Two members of the party, John Hedges and Captain Thomas Young, cleared land and erected a cabin, but did not remain there very long. West of Limestone Creek (Maysville), the group discovered two smaller creeks, the Big Bracken and Little Bracken. William later left the expedition and settled along these creeks, at present-day Augusta, but was killed by Indians sometime before 1800; his place of burial is unknown.[12]

Israel Foster settled along the Ohio River several miles downstream from Augusta and had control of a large tract of land. First known as Foster's Landing and now simply Foster, this remained an important trade town until the railroad was completed. William Pepper initially came to Fleming County, then relocated to Mason County before settling at Fairview, Bracken County. There he built a schoolhouse and became the area's first teacher. Other early settlers include the Jordan, Pearl, and Cooper families.

Captain Abner Howell (1744–1779) came from Pennsylvania with his daughter Rebecca Stout and several grandchildren. William and Joel Woodward arrived around 1800 and built cabins, and later brick homes, in the region. (One still stands at the corner of Miami Street and KY 19 in Brooksville.)[13] Their settlement was known as Woodward's Crossing until 1839 when resident David Brooks spearheaded a change of the county seat from Augusta to the more centrally located Woodward's Crossing. In his honor, Woodward's Crossing became Brooksville.[14]

Major John Finley was a pioneer surveyor who came from Pennsylvania to Kentucky in 1773 with a group led by Captain William Thompson. Finley surveyed a large tract at what is now Lower Blue Licks; and, once Indian hostilities ceased in the region around 1796, he settled at Hill Top, Fleming County.[15] He later operated a ferry across the Licking near that spot, as well as a tavern for travelers along the river. Finley is one of the county's most honored citizens, serving as a state representative from 1800 to 1804 and as a justice of the peace from 1801 to 1805.[16]

General Percival Butler (1760–1821) also arrived in Kentucky in 1796 along with his family, which included three sons: Thomas L., General William O., and Percival Jr. The Butler family would prove important throughout the state in the following years. The elder Percival Butler was the first adjutant general of the United States. In 1796 the family moved to Port William in Carroll County. There Percival built a two-story log home three miles from the river. His son, William Orlando Butler (1791–1880), served in the War of 1812, achieving the rank of general. He married Eliza Todd, daughter of General Robert Todd. General Butler State Resort Park at Carrollton is named in his honor, and his home still stands at Carrollton.[17]

Several settlements were born in Pendleton County in the late 1790s as well. Boston Station, now known simply as Boston, was founded by Gabriel Mullins. There the Harris School, one of the first in the county, was erected, as was United Boston Church, one of the first churches in the region.[18] William Caldwell founded Caldwell Station on the Licking River between present-day Demossville and Butler. William Littell erected Littell's Station and that settlement was renamed Collinsville after resident Jonathan Collins in the early 1800s.[19] Robert Samuel Kyle purchased 100 acres adjoining the land of Thomas and Dinah Kennedy, and in 1806 bought 50 more acres. The Kyle home once stood near today's Pike and Madison streets, where a small country lane eventually served as a public road connecting Kennedy's Ferry to Banklick Road and to Lexington.[20]

In 1797, Cave Johnson (1760–1850) relocated to Northern Kentucky, making his home along the Ohio River at North Bend Bottoms. Johnson first came to Kentucky in 1779 with his brother, Robert "Robin" Johnson, as well as William Tomlinson. The group joined the Bryans, first settling at Boonesborough. Later, Cave Johnson and William Tomlinson helped erect the fort at Bryan Station. Robert and Cave Johnson were back in Virginia during the Battle at Blue Licks but rendezvoused with George Rogers Clark for his retaliatory expedition in 1782. Cave would eventually own more than 8,000 acres at various places in the state. At North Bend, he built an impressive brick home, which still stands in 2019, just west of KY 237 along KY 8, River Road, at the northernmost point of Boone County. A family friend, William Henry Harrison, lived directly across the river at North Bend, Ohio.

Cave Johnson's daughter, Nancy, married William McKirtley, who built a brick home overlooking the Ohio River, where one could see Ohio, Kentucky, and Indiana. This home, situated near the westernmost end of KY 8 in Boone County, remains one of the most historically significant Greek Revival structures in Boone County.[21]

Colonel William Preston, one of Kentucky's initial land grant recipients, surveyed much of Kentucky, including present-day Carroll County. Though he never settled in the area, the town of Prestonsburg was named for him in 1797. A few years later, Rislerville, named for a local merchant, was established along Eagle Creek in the southeastern corner of the current county's borders. In 1816, when Nathaniel Sanders established a mill there, the town name was changed to Sander's Mill, but is now known as Sanders, Kentucky. Nathaniel had run away and lived with the Cherokee for seven years, after which time he worked as a spy during the American Revolutionary War, receiving this acreage for his brave service.[22] Neil and Ann McCoull founded McCoull's (also seen as McCool's) Bottoms along the Ohio River in the northeastern section of present-day Carroll County. Benjamin Craig (1751–1822) had come to the region with several brothers and dozens of other pioneers, including his cousin, James Hawkins, as part of the Traveling Church.[23] He and Hawkins settled at McCoull's Bottoms, on land he purchased from Ann McCoull, Neil's widow.[24] Lewis Sanders (1781–1861) also arrived in the area with his parents as part of the Traveling Church, also settling at McCoull's Creek. After his father's death, however, Lewis was raised in Lexington.

More counties were established in the state of Kentucky in 1798. Gallatin County was formed from parts of Franklin and Shelby counties and was named for Albert Gallatin, a Swiss native and US Representative. Gallatin also served as treasury secretary for two US presidents, Thomas Jefferson and James Madison. Pendleton County was formed from parts of Campbell and Bracken counties and was named for Edmund Pendleton (1721–1803), a well-known politician, lawyer, and judge. Boone County was formed from part of Campbell County and was named for Kentucky's most famous pioneer-explorer, Daniel Boone. The first county court there was held at the home of William Cave at North Bend Bottoms. At that meeting, it was decided to relocate the county seat to land donated by Robert Johnson and John

Hawkins Craig, situated in the north-central part of the county.[25] That settlement, originally known as Craig's Camp, was eventually renamed Burlington in 1816. The first courthouse there was a log structure facing Jefferson Street, completed in 1817. Fleming County was also created in 1798, with Flemingsburg as the county seat. That town had been laid out two years earlier by Major George Stockton and named for his late half-brother, Colonel John Fleming. Fleming, who never fully recovered from being shot during the Battle Run skirmish in 1782, died at his station four years before his namesake town was established.

In 1798, Jacob Fowler purchased 5,000 acres of land in Northern Kentucky: half in present-day Kenton County, where Fowler Creek empties into Banklick Creek; the remainder in Boone County, where Fowler's Branch of Gunpowder Creek exists today.[26] Fowler's son, Benjamin Piatt Fowler, later resided on the Boone County property, building a stone home there that still stands, on the eastern side of Old Union Road near Clarkston Lane. He also built a home in Burlington, later known as the Renaker House, which stood behind the courthouse.[27] Other family names in the area include Lassing, Stansifer, Scott, and Rice.

Nathaniel Vice Jr. settled along the western shore of the Licking River around 1799, and the small town of Visalia was later named for him. Vice eventually relocated to the Pacific Coast; Visalia, California, about thirty miles south of Fresno, is also named in his honor. While now a part of Kenton County, Visalia was actually the Campbell County seat in 1823–1824.

At present-day Owen County, a family by the name of Dallas founded Dallasburg sometime before 1800. While the Dallasburg Baptist Church remains, the town has been renamed in honor of a well-respected local citizen, Reverend George W. Wheatley. Another early Owen County settlement went by the name Nosuch until seven families by the name of Jones moved to the area. This town, on the eastern side of the county, is known today as Jonesville. Mountain Island is a 110-acre tract within Eagle Creek in northern Owen County. First settled in 1792, it at one time was occupied exclusively by African Americans.[28]

In present-day Grant County, the town of Philadelphia was settled around 1800. Learning that name had already been used in Kentucky, the village was renamed to honor one of its founders, William

William Arnold cabin, Williamstown, Kentucky.

Arnold. Williamstown, however, was not officially established until 1820. Arnold eventually owned property in Pendleton, Grant, Bourbon, Campbell, Fayette, and Mason counties. He was the first sheriff of Grant County, donated land for the first courthouse, and helped found Grant Seminary. The original William Arnold log cabin has been saved over the years and relocated. In 2019 the cabin sits on the western side of Dixie Highway (US 25), one block south of the courthouse.[29]

Just before the start of the nineteenth century, Robert Piatt (1769–1857) founded Piatt's Landing at an area now known as East Bend Bottoms, Boone County. The Piatt family would operate three ferries in the area as early as 1800: one from Piatt's Landing to Lawrenceburg; one from Rabbit Hash to Rising Sun; and one from East Bend to North's Landing, Indiana.[30] Benjamin and John Piatt ran flatboats of their produce and that of several neighbors down the Ohio to the Mississippi and to New Orleans, where they not only sold the produce

Historic image of the Anderson Ferry. Courtesy www.nkyviews.com.

but the boat itself. They would then follow the Natchez Trail through the wilderness and back home to repeat the procedure the following season.[31] They would bring back with them supplies of sugar, molasses, coffee, and other commodities that could not be produced back home.[32] Two other Piatts were active in Cincinnati business. They helped form the city's first park, Piatt Park, at present-day Garfield Square, in downtown Cincinnati. Another descendant, Elizabeth Piatt, married Israel T. Canby; their son, Edward Canby (1817–1873), would become a Union general during the Civil War.[33] The two main Piatt homesteads, Winnfield Cottage and Federal Hall, are long gone, replaced in the 1970s by the $750 million East Bend Power Station.[34]

Other early settlements in present-day Boone County include several founded mostly by German immigrants. These include Hebron, as well as Constance, named for the Rhine River town of Konstanz. There, the Anderson family operated a ferry from as early as 1800. In 1817, George Anderson bought 107 acres and an additional ferryboat from local property owner Raleigh Colston.[35] After many decades, the Anderson family eventually sold the ferry service, and it exchanged hands many more times before being sold to Charles Kottmeyer.

Charles's grandsons continued operation after his death; and in 2019 the business, still known as the Anderson Ferry, continues to take passengers and automobiles across the Ohio, from a spot just west of Kenton County's border with Boone County to the intersection of River Road and Anderson Ferry Road in Cincinnati's western suburbs.

The Mann family arrived in the region at about this time, including Benjamin Mann (1770–1826) and his wife, Mildred. The family resided in the area of Cruise Creek in present-day Kenton County. Bartlett Graves purchased land in the same region from John Grant in 1808. Other new arrivals in the area included Jesse Bracking, William Stephen, and C. B. Armstrong. Colonel Maurice Langhorne opened the Eagle Tavern and Hotel on the southeast corner of Front and Market streets in Maysville. His son, John T. Langhorne, ran the business before selling it to Judith Goddard, who renamed the place the Goddard House in the 1830s.[36]

The tiny town of Beaverlick, Boone County, was thriving even before 1800. Founded in the 1780s, the town's unusual name was the result of hunters bringing their catches there to sell to traders, as the settlement was located on Beaver Branch of Big Bone Creek. At its peak, the town included a hotel, three churches, a flour mill, a blacksmith, a carriage maker, a general store, and two physicians.[37] Nearby Richwood was first settled as Richwood Station, a fortified settlement on the site of a previous Fort Ancient Indian village. In the early 1800s, settlers included the Southgate, Menzie, Hudson, Hughes, Bedinger, Clarkson, and Gaines families.[38]

13

Northern Kentucky in the Early 1800s

By 1800, the population of Kentucky was just under 221,000.[1] The most populous settlements remained in the central part of the state, but Northern Kentucky was progressing. Settlements at Port William, Kennedy's Ferry, Newport, Augusta, and Maysville were growing rapidly, but were still considered to be in their infancy. While some property owners were happy to remain somewhat isolated from their new neighbors, others, including James Taylor Jr., in particular, sought ways to draw even more families into the region. Taylor's dream was to create cities that would eventually rival those on the east coast.

In early 1803, Taylor learned that the US government planned to build an arsenal somewhere in Kentucky and that General Charles Scott (1739–1813) had been appointed to investigate the most suitable location. Taylor wanted that location to be Newport. He contacted Scott and also solicited the help of his cousin in Washington, DC, James Madison, who was then US secretary of state. Taylor had ceded land to the town of Newport for use as a public common and soon offered the War Department a plot at the confluence of the Ohio and Licking rivers. Not only was Taylor's generous offer accepted; he was also hired as the superintendent of construction of what became the Newport Barracks. Taylor knew that the attention drawn to Newport as a result of the new army installation, which would provide added protection to citizens throughout the region, might bring hundreds of new families into the area, and many of those new arrivals would be purchasing lots in his town.

Newport Barracks

In 1803 John Metcalf of Fleming County and Daniel Mayo of Newport were contracted for the brick and stone work of what would become Newport Barracks, at $7.00 per thousand bricks and 75 cents per perch of stone. In the early years, poor food, poor housing, and little to do caused many troops to desert. Upon Colonel William Boyd's arrival in 1811, however, the Newport Barracks became the recruiting center for Ohio and Kentucky and was responsible for furnishing equipment and soldiers for the newly acquired Louisiana Territory.

By the start of the War of 1812, there were about 12,000 men at the barracks. Most of the soldiers, guns, and equipment of the Western Theater came from the Newport Barracks. Later in the war, the barracks were used to house prisoners. Afterward, the post was used once again for recruiting.

In 1832, floodwaters overpowered the installation, and sickness and decay followed the receding waters. The same year, a cholera epidemic hit the region, killing 4 percent of the population of the area. Between disease and desertion, by January 1837 there were only 46 recruits at the Newport Barracks.

Major improvements took place in 1842, including the construction of a hospital and officers' quarters. Additional land was purchased as well. During the Civil War, wounded Union soldiers were brought to the barracks, as were Confederate prisoners.

After the Civil War, the Newport Barracks lost its usefulness. Floods in 1882, 1883, and 1884 brought destruction, making several of the buildings uninhabitable. The Secretary of War purchased 112 acres on a hilltop three miles to the east, and by November 1894, all personnel and equipment had been transferred to the new Fort Thomas. General James Taylor Park sits on the very spot of the old Newport Barracks.[2]

As work on the Newport Barracks began, one small, remote section of the Northern Kentucky landscape would soon be known worldwide. Thomas Jefferson had known about Big Bone Lick in present-day Boone County for decades and was extremely interested in receiving a collection of bones from that unique site. He had recently become president of the American Philosophical Society and was on the committee "to collect information respecting the past and present state of this country." The group had published a circular recommending various topics of inquiry to its members. First on this list was "to procure one or more entire skeletons of the so-called Mammoth, and other such unknown animals that either have been or hereafter may be discovered in America." By this time, hundreds of bones had been taken from the historic site; and in early 1803 Dr. William Goforth, a Cincinnati physician, collected and shipped five tons of specimens to Pittsburgh with the intention that they eventually reach Philadelphia, where they would be sold for use in scientific investigations. A traveler, Thomas Ashe, met Goforth and offered to be his agent for a percentage of the profits. Ashe eventually sold the bones in England for around $20,000, but kept the money for himself.[3]

Meanwhile, Meriwether Lewis (1774–1809) had agreed to lead Thomas Jefferson's western exploration of the vast new territory claimed with the Louisiana Purchase in May 1803. Looking for, among other things, the best land route to the Pacific Ocean, Lewis invited Kentuckian William Clark (1770–1838), brother of George Rogers Clark, to join in what became known as the Lewis and Clark Expedition. In August 1803, Lewis enlisted men and gathered supplies; and in Cincinnati, on his way to meet William Clark, President Jefferson instructed Lewis to meet with Dr. William Goforth and to examine more bones Goforth had recently unearthed at Big Bone Lick. Soon Clark had hired ten men to assist in the endeavor and sent three crates filled with artifacts to the White House.[4] It is from this early investigation that tiny Big Bone Lick, Kentucky, is now known as the birthplace of American vertebrate paleontology.

In 1804, a rough census was taken at Kennedy's Ferry and environs on the western side of the Licking River as a direct result of a smallpox epidemic. That disease was raging in Cincinnati and spreading across the river to Kentucky, where there were no doctors.[5] Cincinnati physicians treated the sick on the southern side of the Ohio, and Covingtonian Captain William Martin was placed in charge of the Kentucky residents. He reported that the population south and west of the Ohio and Licking rivers was 76, including both blacks and whites.[6] The number of smallpox deaths in Northern Kentucky, if any, was not recorded.

By 1810, several other families became neighbors to Thomas Kennedy at Kennedy's Ferry. Besides the Kyle, Fowler, Martin, Craig, and Rittenhouse families, there were the Leonard, Harris, Hardin, Fleming, Johnson, and Robertson families.[7] More settlers entered today's Gallatin County as well, including Samuel Conners, who, with others, founded what later became the town of Napoleon.[8] Around 1803, Achilles Webster and his family, including several siblings and their families, relocated from Lexington to north of Crittenden. The property, purchased from John Fowler, was situated on the eastern side of the Dry Ridge Trace (Dixie Highway), just south of present-day York Street, about one mile south of Walton. The Webster family had traveled first from England to Caroline County, Virginia; according to a March 30, 1872, article in the *Covington Journal,* "The Webster family forms about one-eighth of the total population of Grant County." This family expanded into other parts of Northern Kentucky; and today, parts of Grant, Owen, and Kenton counties continue to be saturated by this early pioneer family.

Isaac Chamberlain, a schoolteacher from Piqua, Ohio, arrived in the early 1800s and founded the small town of Piqua, Kentucky, in what is now south-central Robertson County. (Piqua seems to have two pronunciations based on local traditions. In Ohio it's "pick-wah," while "pick-way" is used in Kentucky.) Nearby Mount Olivet, first known as Hell's Half Acre, was settled around 1820.

Major George Michael Bedinger (1756–1843) was one of the first Europeans in Kentucky, and one of the first to volunteer in Lord Dunmore's War. He fought in several battles, including many alongside Daniel Boone. Bedinger arrived at Boonesborough in time to help defend it from the Indians and remained there seven months, serving as an Indian spy, scout, hunter, surveyor, and soldier, before returning to Maryland, where he married.[9] After the death of his first wife, he moved back to Kentucky and worked as a surveyor for many who were granted land in the new state, accumulating vast acreage for himself in the process. After being commissioned a major by George Washington, Bedinger resigned from the Army and eloped on horseback with sixteen-year-old Henrietta Clay (1776–1853), cousin to the famous statesman Henry Clay.[10] Bedinger built three houses on his property near Blue Licks: first a log home, then a stone house, and finally a large, thirty-room frame structure. He donated acreage for the first school and church in the area and served as a state legislator and congressman. When he died in 1843, he was buried in the family plot along the Licking River at Blue Licks.[11] He and Henrietta had ten children, many of whom stayed in Kentucky.

John Tanner's heirs sold 750 acres in northern Boone County to Daniel Boone's nephew, John Grant, around 1805, and Grant began operating a ferry service there.[12] Grant's son-in-law, John J. Flourney, later inherited the property, plated a town, and named it Petersburg in 1818. A historical marker showing the location of Tanner's Station stands at Third and Tanner streets, near the Petersburg Community Center (formerly Petersburg Elementary School). Up until the Civil War, Petersburg was the largest community in Boone County.

George Plummer and his family arrived in Fleming County in the early 1800s, establishing a mill in the area of Sand Lick and Big Run creeks. His son, Benjamin, named the small hamlets of Plummer's Landing and Plummer's Mill.[13] The Foudray family settled in northeastern Fleming County, and a village there was known as Foudraysville until the name was changed to Hillsboro. Several families settled at a spot several miles southeast of Flemingsburg as well. This town was eventually named in honor of a veteran of the American Revolutionary War, Joseph Goddard. By 1807, Robert Andrews was operating a grist mill, and in 1815 his son, John, founded the town of Sherburne Mills, named for their hometown of Sherburne, New York. Today, this town is simply known as Sherburne. Another grist mill operation was located along Fox Creek in the southeastern part of the county. A settlement there was named Muse's Mill in honor of George Muse Sr., another American Revolutionary War hero and local resident, who died there in 1827.[14] His descendants remained in this area of Fleming County well into the late 1800s.

Richard Bell and others arrived in the area of Bedford, Trimble County, in the early 1800s. A large brick home, built around 1807, once stood at present-day US 42 and KY 421. The Bell family came by flatboat to the mouth of Corn Creek, where they unloaded and proceeded inland. Bell returned to Virginia to lend his services during the War of 1812, and afterward he returned to this settlement and helped establish a town, using his son's middle name, Bedford, as the village's name.

Camp Springs in southern Campbell County was settled in the

One of the many stone houses in rural Campbell County, this one was once utilized as the Camp Springs House, a bed and breakfast (shown here in 2018).

early 1800s, on an ancient Indian village. A predominantly German settlement, these residents began a distinctive architectural heritage with their handcrafted stone homes, barns, smokehouses, and other outbuildings.[15] Also, many Camp Springs families harvested grapes for wine production. In fact, in the early 1800s, Kentucky had become the third largest producer of wine in the United States.[16]

William Smith and Jacob Foster operated a grist mill on Banklick Creek sometime before September 7, 1795; on that date Foster petitioned the Campbell County court for approval of his "already-existing" milldam, claiming land ownership on both sides of Banklick Creek. William Wilson lived at the mill from about 1799 to about 1811, at which time James Taylor Jr. purchased the property. Years later, a town sprung up around the mill, first known as Taylor's Mill and now simply Taylor Mill. According to court documents, the actual mill was situated on the north side of Banklick Creek where present-day Reidlin Road intersects Grand Avenue, at the southern end of present-day Victory Avenue.

In 1805, a large group of German Lutherans from Madison County, Virginia, relocated to Northern Kentucky. Settling at what was known as Hopeful, they formed Hopeful Lutheran Church in an area that now lies within the city limits of Florence. One of the last Indian raids and massacres in the entire state of Kentucky occurred at the log cabin of Andrew Bran and his family, situated along Bullock Pen Creek just west of present-day Crittenden. The attack in 1807 left Bran and several children dead. Andrew's wife, who had been scalped, was the only survivor. She relocated to Harrison County.[17] A historical marker stands near the site of their home, along KY 491 just west of Interstate 75.

In 1806, Thomas Kennedy and others were appointed to build a log jail on the public square at Newport, which was completed by 1810. Kennedy was also licensed to operate a ferry across the Licking River at its mouth. Rates for service were: foot passenger, 6¼ cents; passenger with horse, 12½ cents; horned cattle, 6¼ cents; and for wagon and team, 50 cents. He was also permitted one hand (slave) to attend the ferry.[18] While the town of Newport was growing rapidly, residents on the western side of the Licking River were happy to keep their area as private homesteads.

General Leonard Stephens (1791–1873) left Orange County, Virginia, in 1806 and settled along present-day Dixie Highway in southern Kenton County. He married Katherine Sanford, daughter of Richard Sanford and Winifred Redmon, in 1813. Stephens held several offices in Boone and Kenton counties, including that of sheriff, and later became a brigadier general during the War of 1812. He operated a farm until age seventy-five, and in 1855 helped organize Florence Baptist Church.[19]

In 1810 John and Samuel Sanders bought 300 acres at McCoull's Bottoms from Benjamin Craig and laid out a town now known as Ghent.[20] It is said the name of the town was suggested by Henry Clay, who was one of the signers of the Treaty of Ghent. A few years earlier, Craig had held worship services there in connection with the Great Awakening, and that pioneer congregation eventually became Ghent Baptist Church.

Captain James Riddle settled southwest of Kennedy's Ferry around 1810, on property that bordered what is now Craig Street, Willow Run Creek, Ninth Street (named Riddle Street for many years), and the Ohio River. Riddle operated a ferry service across the Ohio from the foot of what is now Main Street as early as 1821. He envisioned his own town at that location, at what is now Main Strasse, to be named Hibernia. His 580 acres were foreclosed on in 1827, however, and subdivided by the bank. Thomas Bakewell and William Johnson acquired much of that property and now have streets named for them in that community.

14

Earthquakes and the War of 1812

From December 1811 to April 1812, more than 100 earthquakes struck the Midwest; and, while the Richter scale had not yet been devised, seismologists from the US Geological Survey and elsewhere have since rated the largest of these tremors as high as a 9.2, with more than a dozen aftershocks registering over 7.5.[1] In fact, for the lower forty-eight states, the most intense quake in this series ranks as the worst earthquake in US history.

The first quake occurred at 2:00 a.m. on December 16, 1811. The epicenter is listed as New Madrid, Missouri, only because that was the largest town in the region at the time. Before sunrise, a total of twenty-seven quakes transpired, the more intense being felt as far away as Savannah, Georgia, and Concord, New Hampshire.[2] On February 7, 1812, an estimated 8.8 quake not only permanently altered the course of the Mississippi River; it actually caused that massive waterway to flow backward for several hours.[3] With this quake, President James Madison was reportedly jolted out of his bed in Washington, DC, and church bells randomly rang in Boston. Incredibly, reports from people who experienced this particular quake were printed in newspapers as far away as Havana, Cuba, and Ontario, Canada.

Locally, bricks fell from houses, dishes fell from cabinets, and people fell to the ground, having been tossed like rag dolls. While a few of the well educated had read about earthquakes, no one in the United States had ever lived through one. Therefore, the majority of those affected had no idea what they were experiencing. Entries written in personal diaries and reports published in local newspapers are heart-wrenching. A resident of Louisville recorded the following:

December 16, 1811: There was a great shaking of the earth this morning. Tables and chairs turned over and knocked around. All of us knocked out of bed. The roar I thought would leave us def if we lived. It was not a storm. When you could hear anything, it was the screams of people and animals. You could not hold onto nothing—neither man nor woman strong enough. The shaking would knock you lose like hickory nuts out of a tree. When it got daybreak, you could see the damage done. We still had our home—had some damage, some people that the home was not built to strong did not. I made my mind to one thing, if this did not happen in the Territory of Indiana then me and my family is moving as soon as I find my animals.

January 23, 1812: What are we gonna do? You cannot fight it cause you don't know how. If it was a storm, you could see the dark clouds and know you might get strong winds but this you cannot see anything but a house that just lays in a pile on the ground and trees that just fall over with the roots still attached. We lost our Amandy Jane in this one—a log fell on her. We still have not found animals to pull the wagons, and you cannot find any to buy or trade.

April 14, 1812: We lived to make it to Pigeon Roost. We did not lose any more lives but we had plenty troubles. As much as I love my place in Kentucky—I never want to go back. From December to April no man—woman or animal, if they could talk, would dare to believe what we lived through. From what people say, it wasn't as bad here. They felt the ground move and shake, but it did not destroy cabins and trees like it did in Kentucky.[4]

Northern Kentuckians Witness Their First Steamboat

Just before the first quake hit, an incredible sight intrigued the newest citizens in the region as they witnessed the first steamboat on western waters, sailing down the Ohio River. Captained by Nicholas Roosevelt, the *New Orleans* left Pittsburgh in late September 1811, with a small crew and Roosevelt's pregnant wife, Lydia Latrobe Roosevelt.

They docked at Cincinnati, where it seemed the entire town came out to greet them. The people were fascinated to inspect the new ship on its way downriver, but thought it absurd to expect such a huge vessel to be able to return upriver. The vessel reached the Falls of the Ohio (Louisville) during a full moon; and the roar of escaping steam, heard for the first time, roused the entire population there. Since the river's depth was too shallow to attempt the falls, Roosevelt took full advantage to convince the incredulous Cincinnatians and Northern Kentuckians of the viability of steam and forged the *New Orleans* upriver, where it was received by an even more enthusiastic crowd than before. No longer was there any doubt that steamboats would replace keelboats on the waterways. On the steamboat's return to Louisville, Lydia gave birth to a son, Henry. The following day the river rose sufficiently for the boat to vault the falls under full steam; but as they lay at anchor downstream, the first jolt of the Great Quake was felt. As the *New Orleans* continued on, the tremors continued, changing the river in such ways that the ship's experienced pilots could no longer recognize the river's landmarks. Frightened Indians along the river blamed the quake on Roosevelt's "fireboat." With much difficulty, the *New Orleans* found its way through new channels created by the continuing quakes and finally made it successfully to the city of New Orleans.[5]

Before Kentuckians could rest and find any bit of normality after the Great Quake, the War of 1812 began, once again calling men from near and far into military service. Sometimes referred to by historians as America's "forgotten war," this major conflict would prove devastating to the new Kentucky settlers.[6]

Of all the causes for the United States to declare war against Britain, many historians see the impressment of American sailors as the most important.[7] Under British law, their navy had the right to sweep through the streets of Great Britain, essentially arresting men and placing them into the Royal Navy.[8] It was also common for these press gangs to board ships at sea, literally kidnapping tens of thousands of men and pressing them into military service. American merchant vessels became a common target, and by 1812 the British had impressed more than 15,000 US sailors to supplement their navy.

As a result of these actions by the British, Kentucky congressman

Richard Mentor Johnson (1780–1850), nephew to early Boone County pioneer Cave Johnson, called for an immediate attack on Canada, at that time a British colony. Far more than their fellow citizens back east, Kentuckians were well aware that the British were arming the Indians in the northwest and prodding them into war with American outposts, and that England had never given up its intent to have a kind of "Indian buffer state" that might serve as an effective barrier to any further western expansion by its former colonies.[9] The United States declared war on Great Britain on June 18; but in contrast to many people in the original thirteen colonies, Kentuckians saw the War of 1812 as "their" battle, as control of the Ohio and Mississippi rivers was at stake.

President Madison ordered William Hull (1753–1825), territorial governor of Michigan, to take charge of the 2,000 Ohio militiamen at Dayton, Ohio. Hull's suggestion, however, that the Great Lakes be secured first, was ignored by those in Washington.[10] Meanwhile, Newport's James Taylor Jr. also took the field, as a brigadier general. He assembled a small staff, including Thomas Carneal and other prominent Northern Kentuckians, and quickly joined with Hull. Taylor was soon appointed the quartermaster general and paymaster general of the Northwestern Army. Hull's army reached Detroit quickly, crossing into Canada with the intent to attack British installations there. By this time, however, Hull had received word of major British victories elsewhere, so he canceled his plans and withdrew to Detroit. A small contingent of British soldiers followed the Americans and on August 15 demanded that Hull surrender, which he did the following day without any shots being fired.

Before Hull's surrender, reinforcements had been requested from officials in Frankfort, and a strong force mustered from throughout Kentucky with orders to meet at the Point. By the time they reached Kennedy's Ferry on August 24, 1812, they had been traveling through heavy rain for several days. When word was received that Hull had already surrendered, the troops' morale plummeted. Still, they gathered their arms and supplies and marched northward. During the journey, the militia learned of a pro-British confederation of Indians led by Chief Tecumseh, who planned to attack Fort Wayne. By this time, Brigadier General James Winchester had arrived in the region with his army. He took charge of the Kentucky reinforcements, and the combined forces marched to Fort Wayne, which was quickly made secure.

Afterward, General William Henry Harrison, now in charge of all the Northwestern forces, ordered Winchester to move his men toward Detroit. In early January 1813, Winchester's army, including the Kentucky reinforcements, reached a small American village at present-day Monroe, Michigan, and was alerted that British-led Indians were within miles with a plan to attack. Winchester quickly dispatched a force of nearly 700 men, mostly Kentuckians. A battle ensued, and the Americans quickly drove the Indian and British forces back over the Raisin River, where the Kentuckians barricaded themselves within the strong walls of a fortification there. At the same time, they requested additional forces. Soon a force of 250 regulars arrived, but rather than placing them within the fortress, they were ordered to camp outside the walls. On the morning of January 22, more than 2,000 British and Indians commanded by General Henry Proctor struck the fort. Those inside the stockade managed to inflict a heavy loss on the enemy. Those outside, however, were sitting ducks, and quickly fled in panic. While the British soldiers continued their fight against the fortress, most of the Indians pursued the fleeing troops and slaughtered them without mercy. Two entire companies of Kentuckians left the stockade in a futile attempt to save their comrades. They, too, were massacred. By the end of the day, nearly 400 Americans died and more than 500, including General Winchester and Port William's William Orlando Butler, were taken prisoner. Forces inside the stockade continued to fight until Proctor enlisted the captured Winchester to order a full surrender. The Americans eventually put down their weapons, but only after insisting that General Proctor promise full protection from any further Indian massacre. Proctor marched all who were uninjured to safe confinement, leaving those who were too sick or injured. The following morning, more than 200 Indian warriors returned to the scene. They mutilated every one of the defenseless men. Some were scalped, some were tomahawked, and many were piled and burned.[11]

In the coming months, other lopsided defeats were experienced by American forces, especially by Kentucky volunteers, including nearly 60 killed under the command of Captain Leslie Combs. It was not until

American authorities realized the significance of securing Lake Erie that any headway was made against the British in the war. Under Commodore Oliver Hazard Perry (1785–1819), a crushing defeat was levied against the British in September 1813.

Just before Perry's victory, another cry for help was sent to Kentucky Governor Isaac Shelby by William Henry Harrison. Shelby ordered the mustering of 2,000 troops; but, true to the brave reputation of the new Kentucky pioneers, more than twice that number answered the call. Word had spread quickly of the massacre at Raisin River, and the newly gathered men at Kennedy's Ferry were eager to avenge the murder of those American prisoners of war. A battle cry of "Remember the Raisin" was soon shouted throughout the land.[12] As the 4,000 Kentuckians marched through Ohio, they found themselves near Urbana; knowing that Simon Kenton now made that place his home, they detoured from their mission to meet the famous pioneer. As they stood in awe of the former Kentuckian, some men begged him to join their cause. Kenton gathered his arms and ammunition and, against the wishes of his wife, the fifty-seven-year-old agreed to join the men in battle.

Meanwhile, General Harrison was pursuing the British near the Thames River, eighty miles from Detroit. On October 4, they caught up with the enemy, and a battle ensued the following day. Mounted riflemen, under the charge of Colonel Richard Mentor Johnson, quickly swept through the enemy lines, killing many. Proctor fled immediately and was never seen again on the battlefield. While most of the British soldiers retreated, the massive Indian force, under the powerful command of Chief Tecumseh, remained in the fight. Johnson dismounted his men as the battle continued, joined by Isaac Shelby and his force. While no fewer than twenty-four men have claimed to be Chief Tecumseh's killer, most historians believe that feat was accomplished by none other than Colonel Johnson.[13] Over 500 prisoners were taken by the Americans in this fight; these prisoners were eventually led to the Newport Barracks, after which some—mostly officers—were sent to a penitentiary at Frankfort, Kentucky.[14] According to Colonel Joseph Donnelly in his book on the Barracks, "Newport was still a village with unpaved streets and less than 500 souls when the population doubled with Indian lovers, who spoke an outlandish sort of English."

While little is known about each individual prisoner of war, the roster included James Alford, a drummer boy from England who was just ten years old.[15]

During Harrison's victory at the Battle of the Thames, another major conflict was taking place in the eastern theater. It was during this battle that General Leonard Covington was killed. On the afternoon of November 11, American forces engaged the enemy at Chrysler's Field on the Canadian side of the St. Lawrence River. With no way of retreat, the Americans crossed the river and attacked; Covington suffered what would become a fatal wound. Buried briefly at French Mills just outside the New York border, his remains were later moved to Sackett's Harbor, Jefferson County, New York, at a spot now named Mount Covington in his honor.

Meanwhile, the US Navy had been able to score several victories over the Royal Navy; but Britain soon turned its full attention to the war effort in North America.[16] Large numbers of troops arrived, and British forces moved in on the US capital, capturing Washington, DC, on August 24, 1814, and burning government buildings, including the Capitol and the White House. On September 13, 1814, Baltimore's Fort McHenry withstood twenty-five hours of bombardment. The following morning an enormous but battered American flag still flew over the fort, a sight that inspired Francis Scott Key to write a poem that later became "The Star-Spangled Banner."

By this time, both sides wanted an end to the war. The United States was nearly bankrupt and Britain was war-weary from its battles in North America and in Europe with Napoleon.[17] Peace talks began at Ghent (in modern-day Belgium); and on December 24, 1814, the Treaty of Ghent was signed, though it would not be ratified until the following February. On January 8, 1815, unaware that peace had been achieved and they had lost the war, the British sent a force of 8,000 men for a major attack on New Orleans.

Kentucky's interest in the war had diminished by this time, as no financial support was coming from the legislature for resupplying ammunition and firearms. When Louisiana and Tennessee governors requested Kentucky's help against the British at New Orleans, Governor Shelby called up another 2,500 militiamen, but could only find

254 guns. While some brought their own, fewer than one in thirty men mustered were armed.[18] James Taylor Jr. supplied boats to transport the volunteers, mortgaging his property in Newport to do so.

On January 8, 1815, the Battle of New Orleans was waged at an abandoned sugar plantation just outside the city limits. General John Adair (1757–1840) was placed in charge of the Kentucky troops and immediately requested from city officials a supply of rifles and ammunition. He had planned to place his men as reinforcements behind the Tennessee militia under Colonel William Carroll. Unfortunately, Andrew Jackson was unaware of Adair's plans and ordered many of the unarmed Kentuckians, about 400 men under Colonel John Davis, to the west bank of the Mississippi River to assist the Louisiana regiment.[19] When they arrived, Davis was able to secure about 200 guns, but they were mostly older muskets in various stages of disrepair.[20] Luckily, the British relied on tactics used in the Napoleonic wars, marching in open formation in their bright red coats, and were slaughtered by the Americans firing long rifles from behind earthworks. In addition, the higher-ranking British officers generally led their troops, and many were picked off early in the battle by the Kentucky sharpshooters, causing even more chaos within the British ranks. However, those Kentuckians situated on the west bank, poorly equipped and without barricades, were forced to retreat. Fortunately, enough damage had been done in the main attack, including by Adair's Kentucky reinforcements, that the victory had been won. In less than thirty minutes, the British lost 2,034 men while the Americans lost somewhere between 13 and 43.[21] Future president James Monroe would later praise Jackson by saying, "History records no example of so glorious a victory obtained with so little bloodshed on the part of the victorious."[22]

While the War of 1812 receives little importance with historians nationwide, the conflict put volunteers from Kentucky in the forefront. More than 64 percent of the Americans killed were Kentuckians, representing 1,200 of the 1,876 dead. In 1821, Samuel Woodworth wrote the song "The Hunters of Kentucky," which glorified the Kentucky volunteers (though it somewhat exaggerated their role at New Orleans). Andrew Jackson adopted the tune as his campaign song on his road to the White House in 1828.[23] Fighting with makeshift weapons or no weapons at all, some believe the Kentucky volunteers had little impact on the fight. Andrew Jackson even asserted that many "fled the battlefield unceremoniously."[24] However, few argue that it was the massive initial attack against the British—in which many Kentuckians participated—that decided the battle, and that the quick retreat by some soldiers on the west bank was irrelevant. In the final analysis, the War of 1812 ended in a stalemate, as the Treaty of Ghent returned all territorial conquests made by the two sides and did not at all address the issue of impressment. The War of 1812 did, however, allow the United States to break free from its colonial past and told the nations of Europe that a new player had emerged on the world stage.[25]

Choctaw Academy

In the early 1800s, Native American tribes east of the Mississippi were forced to cede millions of acres to the federal government for white settlers. The Kentucky Baptist Mission Society opened a school for Native Americans in 1818, on the property of Richard Mentor Johnson just outside Georgetown, but due to lack of funding it closed after two years. The school was revived in 1825 after Choctaws in Mississippi asked that part of the money they had received be used to educate young men from their more elite families.

Johnson was a Kentucky congressman and militia colonel in the War of 1812, whose political career took off after he was credited with the killing of Indian chief Tecumseh. He would eventually hold the office of vice president under Martin Van Buren (1837–1841). His personal life, however, was scandalous. His common-law wife, Julia Chinn, was a mixed-race woman he legally owned. She bore him two daughters who were raised as white. He was perpetually in debt, and Choctaw Academy became an important source of income for him.

The school was so successful that some local white families sent their sons there. Johnson insisted that the headmaster privately instruct his daughters. Amid reports that their sons were being hired out as forced labor, however, tribal leaders contested Johnson's financial management of the school.

Meanwhile, white politicians realized that educated tribes were harder to manipulate and control. The school changed from academics to vocational training, and enrollment declined. Six hundred Native American young men and boys from seventeen tribes, along with a few whites, received formal education there, but the Choctaw Academy closed in 1848. Most of the buildings on the property soon fell into disrepair and were eventually razed. In 2019, two of the buildings were saved and were in the process of being restored.[26]

15

Covington Is Established, and Roads Become Turnpikes

The War of 1812 had finally ended, and back in Northern Kentucky things were about to change drastically at Kennedy's Ferry. In December 1814, Thomas Kennedy publicly offered his land for sale, and within weeks a partnership was formed by three men with the intent to purchase the property and lay out a new town.[1] The corporation included Richard Montgomery Gano (1775–1815), who was one of the commanders at the Battle of the Thames; his brother, General John Stites Gano (1766–1821); and Thomas David Carneal (1786–1860). The Gano brothers had been among the first families to settle at Columbia, Ohio, arriving in 1788. Today this area is best known as Columbia Parkway between Torrance and Delta avenues in Cincinnati. Earlier, John Gano formed a partnership with Major William Stanley (Stanley Avenue) as merchants in that same area. Stanley died in 1814, and his widow, Salley Howell Stanley, married Thomas David Carneal.[2] Carneal already owned a significant amount of land in Northern Kentucky.

On March 2, 1815, Thomas and Dinah Kennedy sold land to the Gano brothers and Thomas D. Carneal. The property bordered the Ohio River on the north, the Licking River on the east, what is now Washington Street to the west, and the northern edge of Sixth Street to the south.[3] The Kennedys were able to acquire three lots for their children in the transaction. In May, Carneal sold all his interest in the town to the Gano brothers for $4,000 cash and about ten acres of land valued at $5,000. Although Thomas Kennedy is often referred to as the "founder" of Covington, it was only after the sale of his property that the concept to incorporate a new town emerged. The new town was officially established on August 31, 1815, and was named for Brigadier General

Leonard Covington, who had once trained troops for "Mad" Anthony Wayne on the site.[4]

Before Richard Gano's death on October 22, 1815, he had contracted with Benjamin Bakewell, Benjamin Page, and Thomas Bakewell of Pittsburgh for the sale of his share of the lots and other property. Joseph A. Keen, another earlier settler, purchased about six acres to the southwest of the new town, upon which he built the first brick home in the area and operated a brickyard for many years. His land bordered what is now Main, Philadelphia, Pike, and Ninth streets. The Gano's Covington Company never paid the loan in full, however, and eventually the old stone tavern reverted back to the Kennedy family. Thomas's son Samuel occupied the structure and continued to run the ferry business for many years while new homes were being constructed around them. In 1816, Thomas and Dinah built what would be known as the Cooper Home, at Sixth and Greenup streets, where he and his wife died in 1820. That home was razed in 1904. Due to its historical significance, the original stone house was later offered to the City of Covington by descendant Louise K. Southgate, but unfortunately it was razed in 1909.

Meanwhile, Benjamin Elliston and his family had settled on Ten-Mile Creek in Grant County in 1813. With eleven children, the Elliston family grew their settlement well into the late 1800s. Similarly, the Lawrence family settled Lawrenceburg a few miles to the south, at an area now known as Folsom. The same year, four Culbertson brothers, James, William, Allen, and Robert, settled about one mile south of William Decoursey's property along the Licking River in present-day Kenton County.[5] The Culbertson boys were four of eight children born to James and Margaret Culbertson of Ireland. Their four sisters accompanied the men and married into the Kyle, Taylor, and Youtsey families. Several other families settled on the nearby ridge between Fowler Creek and Decoursey Creek, and this area became known as Oak Ridge.[6] A few retail establishments and two churches remain at the eastern end of Hand's Pike, a reminder of the small village that once stood there. William and Nancy Lipscomb settled in the area of what is now Claryville, Campbell County, but many in the family soon migrated into present-day Kenton County and elsewhere.[7] A descendant, John Lipscomb, later founded Oak Ridge Baptist Church along Decoursey Creek in 1844. John Frederick Kleete, who married Jane Field, arrived around the same time, and children from this union married with other early settlers whose surnames ring familiar in the immediate area, including the McCollum and Marshall families.[8] Robert Samuel Kyle relocated to the ridge above present-day Covington, where he and his descendants operated a successful orchard.[9] The Kyle children married into several prominent area families, including Rich and McKay. Kyles Lane, a major thoroughfare running from Dixie Highway on the west to Madison Pike on the east, is named for this family.

Prettyman Merry's son, John Merry, took ownership of his father's property and magnificent stone home, and in 1818 it was transferred to John's daughter, Nancy, and her husband, William Moore. Their daughter, Lucinda Moore, later married Charles Collins, and that couple took ownership of the home in 1848. Charles platted a new town to surround the large home, naming the new village after his birthplace of Bromley, England.[10]

James G. Arnold (1792–1876) moved to Covington in 1817 and established himself in the tobacco business. Arnold was born near present-day Paris, Kentucky, and spent his childhood at North Bend in Boone County. He and his brother, Willis, then moved to Washington, Mason County, where they founded the Washington Male Academy. At Covington, James also served as a teacher at the log schoolhouse at the public square and ran a successful hotel. He was involved heavily in local politics and later established the Covington Female Academy. Arnold's Covington home was at the west end of Seventh Street, between Philadelphia Street and Willow Run Creek. Out in Boone County, Erastus Tousey purchased a lot just outside of Burlington in 1817 and built a fine brick residence there in 1822.[11] That structure remains as the Tousey House Tavern, a fine dining establishment.

In 1818 James Taylor Jr., along with Jacob Fowler and others, began clearing what would be the first "improved" road in the region. At this time, the old buffalo traces were the only method of land transportation, but they were crude trails, barely wide enough in some places for two horsemen to pass side by side, let alone a small carriage or wagon. Of course, an "improved" road in 1818 meant something far different than it does today. Macadamized roads (layers of crushed stone over a bed of larger stones, developed by John McAdam) became the standard several years later; Taylor's new road and the other early turnpikes were

Tousey House Tavern in 2018.

unpaved dirt roads, which often turned into muddy rivers after a heavy rain. Still, strict guidelines were given to those men who were given the task of building the roads. Some charters, for instance, required the roadway to be a minimum of sixty feet wide and allowed tree stumps to protrude no more than eight inches. Once completed, it became the responsibility of property owners to maintain the road directly in front of their place, and in many cases they collected tolls to defray the costs of doing so. Toll gates were allowed every few miles, with an additional toll required to cross some specific bridges.

Taylor's Newport and Cynthiana Turnpike became the main artery for several years, following much of what is now US 27 from Newport to Cynthiana and eventually to Paris, where it connected with the Maysville and Lexington Turnpike after its completion in 1827.[12] Following the most accessible route, however, the finished roadway bypassed the main business districts of some towns, such as Alexandria and Butler.[13]

The Covington and Lexington Turnpike (what is now Dixie Highway US 25) later became the preferred route for travelers from Central Kentucky to Covington, Newport, and Cincinnati, as it was several miles shorter than the old route. From Covington the turnpike ran to the southwest, through Crossroads (Florence), and then south to Dry Ridge, Williamstown, and Georgetown before reaching Lexington. Another popular route was the Florence and Union Turnpike (US 42), which headed southwest from Florence to Union, then west to the Ohio River where it extended to Warsaw, Carrollton, and eventually Louisville.

Soon other turnpikes were chartered, and the entire region was crisscrossed by improved roadways. However, nearly all of these were constructed over the already existing buffalo traces. Other turnpikes in Campbell County included the Licking Turnpike (from Newport, present-day KY 9, 915, and 27 to Claryville); Jamestown Pike (Dayton Pike and North Fort Thomas Avenue); Covert Run Turnpike; and Reservoir Road (now Waterworks Road). In Kenton County, other important turnpikes included the Covington and Decoursey Turnpike (Decoursey Pike, Marshall Road, Staffordsburg Road, and Kenton Station Road); Taylor's Mill Road; the Banklick Turnpike (Old KY 17 from Covington to approximately Hands Pike); and the Independence Turnpike (Old KY 17 from Hands Pike south through Independence to Falmouth). Other major Boone County turnpikes were the Petersburg and Burlington Turnpike (KY 20) and the Florence and Burlington Turnpike—and its extension, the Burlington and Belleview Turnpike (KY 18). Two important arteries were constructed in Gallatin County before 1800. One extended from Port William (present-day Carrollton), taking "the nearest and best way possible" in the direction of Frankfort; and a second, ordered by Percival Butler, Martin Hawkins, Richard Masterson, Benjamin Craig, and others, ran from Port William to the Boone County line—what became US 42.[14]

So-called "mass transit" began on such roads around the same time. Abner Gaines, for example, operated the first stagecoach line between Covington and Lexington in 1818, making one round trip weekly.[15] The trip took over twenty-four hours, and his Gaines Tavern became one of many rest stops along the way. (While today a "tavern" is generally understood to be a bar or restaurant, in pioneer Kentucky a tavern also included rooms for one to stay overnight.) Another frequent stop on this line was the Sherman Tavern, operated by Louis Cason into

Toll gate on the turnpike near Constance. Courtesy www.nkyviews.com.

the mid-1800s, about four miles north of present-day Dry Ridge. Both of these structures have been restored and are still standing. Another busy stagecoach route was along the Maysville and Lexington Turnpike. Built by Irish workers under Irish contractors, the Maysville and Lexington Turnpike was the first macadamized road in all of Kentucky, and it quickly became the main artery from the Ohio River to Central Kentucky.[16]

As travel across numerous creeks and rivers was necessary along these improved routes, various bridges were erected, including several wonderful covered bridges. Covered bridges replaced standard wooden bridges, especially at important crossings, in an effort to better protect the bridge floor and supports, thereby prolonging the life of the span. Most of these impressive structures have since been replaced—by iron after the Civil War and later by steel structures. Many have been completely destroyed, usually by fire. In 2019, only eight covered bridges remain in the region. In Bracken County, the Walcott Bridge, circa 1880, is easily visible from the AA Highway at KY 1159. Located just four miles northeast of Brooksville, this 74-foot-long, king- and queen-post truss-designed bridge is no longer in use and is preserved as a historic site. The Johnson Creek Bridge stretches across Johnson Creek northeast of Blue Licks State Park in Robertson County, on what was once a crossing for KY 1029. Built in 1874, the Smith truss-designed bridge has a span of 131 feet and is also no longer being used by passenger vehicles. In the northwestern part of Lewis County, the Cabin Creek–Rectorville Bridge stands near KY 984, about a quarter-mile east of KY 1443. This 114-foot, single-span Burr truss-style bridge was built in 1873 but was closed from 1983 to 2014. With repairs, it has since reopened to automobile traffic.

Three covered bridges remain in Fleming County in 2019. The Goddard-White Bridge, circa 1880, crosses Sand Lick Creek just off of KY 32, about eight miles south of Flemingsburg. The 90-foot-long lattice truss design is the last of its kind in Kentucky. At Ringo's Mill, a double-posted, 81-foot-long bridge was built in 1869 across Fox Creek. It is located three miles west of KY 32 along Rawlings Road in the southern part of the county. While it originally carried what is now KY 158, it is currently closed to traffic. The Grange City Bridge connects Hillsboro and the village of Grange City across Fox Creek along KY 111, about thirteen miles south of Flemingsburg. This bridge, also closed to traffic, is an 86-foot-long, double-post-and-brace design originally built in 1865. In 1998, the Kentucky General Assembly designated Fleming County as the Covered Bridge Capital of Kentucky.

In 1835, a 61-foot-long covered bridge was built at Dover in northeastern Mason County.[17] The double-queen post trusses on each side are the original design, but iron beams were installed later for support due to weight limitations. It is one of the oldest surviving covered bridges in Kentucky and remains open to pedestrian traffic.[18] The Valley Pike Covered Bridge, located along Valley Pike about two miles north of Germantown Road, also remains, but is privately owned.

Covered bridges once stood in Kentucky's northernmost counties as well. In fact, a bridge across the Licking River at Butler was the longest span ever erected in the state.[19] Built in 1870, the Burr Arch–style bridge was 456 feet long and was razed in 1937. Covered bridges also stood in Falmouth, Morgan, and Grassy Creek in Pendleton County, as well as over Banklick Creek at Taylor's Mill Road in Kenton County.

Owen County was formed from parts of Franklin, Gallatin, Pendleton, and Scott counties in 1819; its first county seat was a settlement founded by Jacob Hesler named Heslerville. When a portion of Galla-

Johnson Creek covered bridge.

Cabin Creek covered bridge. Kimberly Welch.

tin County was added to Owen County in 1821, the county seat was moved to the more centrally located town of Owenton.[20] Another early resident in the area was John Gayle, who, with a group of slaves, built a ten-room cabin in 1806.[21] Arriving around the same time was Reuben Adams, whose settlement was known as Adamstown for several years before being changed to Twins or Twinsville, in reference to the Big Twin and Little Twin creeks, which flow nearby. In the early 1800s, the Baptist Church of the Twins was organized there. In 1827, however, the town was renamed again, this time to New Liberty.

Grant County was formed a year later, in 1820, from part of Pendleton County. The Grant family name is widely scattered throughout Northern Kentucky, of course, and most of the descendants can be traced to William and Margery Verner Grant, who came to the New World from Scotland in 1725. The Grant family eventually found themselves in the Yadkin River Valley near the Boone and Bryan families. William Grant II married Elizabeth Boone, daughter of Squire and Sarah and sister to Daniel Boone. In 1777, William and Elizabeth came to Kentucky and resided with Daniel at Boonesborough. Their son, Samuel, for whom Grant County is named, married Lydia Craig, daughter of Captain Elijah Craig of Traveling Church fame.

In 1821, the US Army hired Northern Kentucky's own Jacob Fowler as a surveyor to accompany Colonel Hugh Glenn up the Arkansas River to the northern Rio Grande.[22] At age fifty-seven, Fowler crossed the plains with a slave named Paul. The Glenn and Fowler Expedition was among the earliest groups to discover and route what would become the Santa Fe Trail. Fowler was also assigned by the Army to build a habitable house and corral, which was completed at modern-day Pueblo, Colorado. Incredibly, this famed Northern Kentucky pioneer is just as well known to historians of that state. In fact, the city of Fowler, Colorado, and Fowler Junior High School, just southeast of Pueblo, are named in his honor. Jacob Fowler returned to Covington on July 27, 1822, after thirteen months and thirteen days in the west, and resided there until his death on October 16, 1849.

William Bullock (1773–1849) was born in England and came to Northern Kentucky in the early 1820s. He purchased 1,000 acres from Thomas D. Carneal, including the homestead Carneal had named Elmwood Estate, with a plan to lay out a new town called Hygeia. His plans, however, fell through for financial reasons. The property was sold in 1831 to Israel L. Ludlow, son of one of the cofounders of Losantiville, who then founded the town of his namesake.[23]

There was a small village in eastern Boone County known as "Polecat," apparently because of an earlier Indian trade with furs and pelts. It was later known as Crossroads due to the intersection of the Dry Ridge Trace and the path to Burlington. In 1821 the town became known as Maddensville, as Covington attorney Thomas Madden owned a farm along Burlington Pike. When he moved from the area in 1828, Jacob Conner assumed responsibility for the town and named it Connersville, but since that name was already being used in Harrison County, he renamed the town after his wife, Florence.[24]

The year 1823 marks the first reference to a burying ground in the region.[25] Later termed the Craig Street Burying Ground, it was bounded by what is now Craig, Kentucky, Pershing, and Johnson streets in Covington. Until this time, the deceased were typically laid to rest in plots on the family farm or within rural church cemeteries. As the population of the urban centers developed, larger space was needed. By 1872, however, Covington's Craig Street Burying Ground was obsolete, and Linden Grove Cemetery was established upon land owned by the Western Baptist Theological Institute. The residents of Newport and its surrounding towns were also in need of a proper burial ground, and in 1847 Evergreen Cemetery was established along the Alexandria Pike at today's Southgate, Kentucky. Highland Cemetery at present-day Fort Mitchell was established in 1869. Over time, those buried at Craig Street were eventually reinterred; about 1,700 went to Highland Cemetery, many others were reinterred at Linden Grove, and dozens more went to other places chosen by the relatives of the deceased.[26] As there were no public parks in the entire region, these beautiful cemeteries became popular picnic spots for many families on Sunday afternoons.

16

Northern Kentucky Welcomes Industry

By 1830, Covington and Newport trailed only Louisville, Lexington, and Maysville in population. Most commerce in Northern Kentucky was connected with the Ohio River and its many tributaries, such as the Licking and Kentucky rivers. However, because of the variance in depth of the northern and southern shores of the Ohio, Covington and Newport were not as successful at welcoming steamboats, which instead moored at Cincinnati. Several steamboat-building facilities had been established on the Ohio side of the river, causing the population to grow much more rapidly there than in Northern Kentucky. Covington, in fact, scarcely grew until 1828, when the Covington Cotton Factory was established on the western half of the block of Front, Second, Scott, and Greenup streets. Three years later, John McNickel purchased lots between Madison and Scott streets along the Ohio River and established a rolling mill and nail factory, employing 120 and manufacturing 1,800 tons of iron and nails a year.[1] Covington's first center of commercial activity grew around the public square, located between Third and Fourth streets and Scott and Greenup streets. A market house was established in 1831, and a public well was dug about one block from the square.[2] By the end of the decade retail stores, business offices, and other commercial establishments flourished in the area. Sidney Sherman, a resident of Newport, opened a sheet-lead manufacturing plant, producing, among other things, ammunition; and the first machine-operated cotton bagging plant also opened at Covington.[3] On the eastern side of the Licking, a powerful shift took place at Newport as well with the construction of the town's first steam-driven sawmill. While water-powered mills had been in the vicinity since 1797, this mill, located along the Licking River, soon made the others obsolete and brought about Newport's rise as a major source of lumber production. A silk manufacturing plant opened a few years later, also bringing more revenue and population into the city. Industrial growth was not confined to Covington and Newport, of course. Maysville and many of the more rural cities experienced the same growth industrially.

Hydrotherapy, or "taking the waters," was a widely prescribed medical treatment by 1825, and by 1830 Kentucky was extremely well known for its mineral water spas.[4] Rich southerners, often with their slaves, fled the heat, yellow fever, malaria, and—worst of all—cholera, for the dozens of Kentucky spas. Dr. Daniel Drake, who first settled at Maysville and was later Cincinnati's most prominent physician, published a review of Kentucky's many mineral water spas in 1828.[5] Drake's publication featured several locations, including one in Montgomery County, two near Harrodsburg, and one in Estill County, as well as Bedford Springs in Trimble County and Drennon Springs at Henry County. Locally, the well-to-do from many states flocked to three main sites. At Big Bone Lick, tourism boomed at the Clay Hotel, built just after 1800. Bathhouses lined the major creek there, and bathers would modestly emerge from those shelters and enter the "healing waters" of the creek.[6] Blue Lick Springs, in present-day Nicholas County on the Robertson County border, began with only moderate success during the 1830s, but when John and L. P. Holladay took control in the 1840s, a three-story hotel 670 feet in length was built with a spacious 100-by-36-foot dining room and a 26-by-80-foot ballroom. Located directly on the stagecoach line between Maysville and Lexington, Blue Lick Springs became a favorite stop for vacationers and travelers alike.[7] Five miles south of the Ohio River, along Banklick Creek at what is now KY 17 and Highland Avenue in Fort Wright, Ralph Letton constructed a small hotel near the existing natural spring there. In 1832, however, he sold the Latonia Springs and fifty-seven acres to Elisha Morgan for $8,000. Morgan then built a fifty-room hotel three stories high, with 100-foot piazzas running the full length of the building and a massive ballroom in the rear. In the 1840s, Dr. Stephen Mosher purchased the Latonia Springs, and the place continued to thrive up until the Civil War. The springs were sold again in 1866 and suffered financially after the war, as did the other area spas, until they all eventually closed.

The Latonia name lived on, however: in 1882 the Latonia Agricultural Association developed fairgrounds a mile or so northeast of the springs, and soon after, a world-renowned horse racing track was built at that site, named the Latonia Racetrack. A town, initially known as Milldale, emerged in the vicinity and also took the Latonia name, though it is now encompassed within the city limits of Covington. A United Dairy Farmers stands at the actual site of the old Latonia Springs Hotel; and the Latonia Shopping Center, situated on the western side of Winston Avenue south of Thirty-Eighth Street, eventually replaced the racetrack, which closed in 1939.[8] Dry Ridge housed another popular Northern Kentucky mineral spa, the Carlsbad Springs Hotel. That hotel, however, was not established until early 1912 and will be discussed later, as will the Latonia Racetrack.

Cholera Epidemics

Among the several feared diseases during the nineteenth century, cholera was considered king, and its visitation to a city was cause for dread.[9] Three times the Northern Kentucky region was hit by this terrible malady, in 1832, 1849, and 1873. While rural residents were generally spared, residents of Covington and Newport were hard hit. A person infected could show no sign of the sickness in the morning and be dead by evening. Entire families were often destroyed in a matter of days.[10] Early on, ignorance of the true cause of the disease brought many bizarre recommendations, from purging and aggressive hydration to opium and lead acetate (a toxic compound). One physician ordered that "green vegetables should be strictly avoided," and another believed that "watermelon was a cholera bomb." Incredibly, the most common suggestion was simply to "stay calm and do not speak about the illness in front of others."[11]

In the first epidemic, Cincinnati lost 732 residents. Since Northern Kentucky had no health department, the exact mortality rate of the first epidemic there remains unknown. At Maysville, however, 67 deaths were reported.[12] There is no reason to believe that Covington and Newport were affected any less seriously than its neighbors to the north and east. Sadly, a planned fifty-year anniversary, called by Simon Kenton and other soldiers who had gathered at the Point in

November 1782, was canceled as a result of this 1832 epidemic. The second wave hit in 1849 and was not confined to the big cities. The *Louisville Daily Courier* reported that 58 people had died within a two-mile radius of the Grassy Creek community in Pendleton County.[13] As mentioned, these epidemics helped secure the success of the region's mineral water spas, as hundreds flocked to the "pure" water there. Many believed that the 1849 epidemic was caused by soldiers returning from the Mexican War. Once again, because of few records and no health department, the exact number of deaths within the two cities is unknown. By the third wave, in 1873, much more was known about the disease and how it was spread. Still, Newport and Covington witnessed many casualties.

In a small corner of present-day Boone County, a general store opened in 1831 that continues to be historically significant to the entire region. The tiny hamlet of Rabbit Hash had been visited by steamboat traffic since at least 1813.[14] Soon after, several area farmers built a warehouse to hold goods for shipment until the next steamboat arrived, and that business became known as the Rabbit Hash General Store. The business temporarily relocated a few times over the years due to flooding, but in each instance quickly reopened. For more than 180 years, locals and out-of-town visitors have enjoyed the nostalgic look of the store as well as its unusual contents. The structure, as well as the small town surrounding it, was placed on the National Register of Historic Places in the 1970s, and the store has been designated a Kentucky Landmark.[15] Rabbit Hash has also received national attention for the fact that for many years, citizens have voted a canine as mayor. Tragically, the general store suffered a devastating fire in February 2016. Immediately, plans were made to rebuild; but, because of its being listed on the National Register, only period materials and construction were permitted to be used. Several historic structures were dismantled by hand to supply material, and the new "old" general store reopened on April 1, 2017. The entire building looks exactly like the original—inside and out.

Around 1832, a settlement was organized just north of the mouth of Big Bone Creek in Boone County and was soon an important stop for river travelers. Joel Hamilton and George McGlasson founded the vil-

Rabbit Hash General Store, circa 1930. Courtesy Kenton County Public Library, KY.

Grand opening of the rebuilt Rabbit Hash General Store, April 1, 2017.

lage of Hamilton Landing in 1835. The McGlasson descendants, as well as other area families in the vicinity, would operate successful orchards for many decades. Residents from the entire tri-state area still eagerly await the annual harvest season in order to purchase various types of home-grown produce as well as to pick their own apples, peaches, and other items from farms along KY 8—from KY 237 on the west to KY 20 on the east.

Around 1845, William Shotwell built a cotton mill at Maysville, and that company became one of the longest-lasting businesses in all of Northern Kentucky, closing around 2008. Cotton was grown in the Deep South and shipped by steamboat to Maysville from markets in New Orleans and Memphis.[16] Richard Henry Lee (son of General Henry Lee) purchased the mill in 1844 and built a four-story building on Second Street. By 1851, Andrew January and Benjamin Wood owned the business, and the company name became January and Wood.

Trimble County was formed from parts of Gallatin, Oldham, and Henry counties in 1836 and was named for Robert Trimble, attorney, judge, and justice of the US Supreme Court. Trimble first settled at Boonesborough before later practicing law at Paris, Kentucky. Carroll County was formed from part of Gallatin County in 1838 and was named for Charles Carroll of Carrollton, Maryland, the only Roman Catholic signer of the Declaration of Independence. Isaac Everett settled at Everett's Creek in what is now southern Kenton County in the 1830s, but by 1838 the small waterway was renamed Crew's Creek to honor the Crew family (it is now known as Cruise Creek). Robert and Elizabeth Bagby arrived in the vicinity in 1839; and to the north, Colonel Thomas Buckner and his wife, Mildred Washington (Berry) Buckner, built what they called the Beechwood Home on a plantation of over 1,500 acres. This house, built in 1839, still stands on Heritage Lane in Edgewood.[17] At about the same time, the Caleb Manley Home was erected on the eastern side of present-day Dixie Highway in Erlanger. This site, now home to Forest Lawn Cemetery, remains as one of the most picturesque areas in the entire region. A post office was established at Verona, Boone County, in 1834, not long after the area was settled by Zadock and Delphia Stephenson, among other families. The New Bethel Baptist Church was established at what is now the intersection of KY 14, 16, and 491. Arthur Stephenson ran a mill on nearby McCoy's fork, and a school stood in the vicinity as well.[18]

As the population on the western side of the Licking River continued to grow in numbers and influence, there came a growing demand for that area to be recognized as a separate political unit. While many within the inner city of Covington opposed such an idea, including such influential men as Mortimer Benton, William Southgate, Herman Groesbeck, James G. Arnold, and Moses Grant, residents further out in the county favored such a move. Kenton County was formed in 1840 from part of Campbell County and is named, of course, for the famous frontiersman Simon Kenton. The new county seat was named Independence, as an indication of the rural citizens' joy to have won their "independence" from Campbell County. The immediate area had been known earlier by several other names, including Crewett's Creek and Bagby.[19] An unusual situation existed in both Kenton and neighboring Campbell counties, however, as the county seats of Independence and Alexandria were both sparsely populated and situated more than ten miles away from each county's population centers, that being Covington and Newport. The residents and lawyers of the thriving urban areas found it far more convenient to transact official business at the Covington and Newport courthouses. Recognizing the problem, the Kentucky legislature enacted laws authorizing Kenton and Campbell counties to each have *two* county seats, and these remain the only counties in the entire state to have dual offices.[20]

In 1842 James and Martha Dinsmore, transplants from Louisiana, established a fine home and farm in western Boone County. From harvesting grapes to growing willow trees used in basket weaving to raising bees, the farm thrived through several generations. The Dinsmore Homestead remains as a museum, filled with artifacts on the history of the family and their association with a wide array of individuals prominent on the national scene.[21] The estate is situated along the north side of KY 18, six miles west of Burlington.

Before the 1840s, the majority of Northern Kentucky's residents were farmers. After that time, however, neighborhoods in Covington and Newport became far more compact, and urban dwellers no longer had the space or the time to produce their own food. An increasing number of people earned their living through various forms of manufacturing. While industries such as cotton factories and sawmills were rapidly growing, hundreds of local workers were soon employed within two other long-lasting occupations: meatpacking and brewing.

Cincinnati proudly held the nickname "porkopolis" in the late 1800s and early 1900s, slaughtering of as many as 500,000 hogs a year; but Covington's meatpacking plants were equally respected, being able to process as many as 100,000 per season.[22] Cattle drovers herded their stock, mainly hogs, from central and eastern Kentucky to Covington and Cincinnati, where the animals were slaughtered, dressed, packed, sold locally, and shipped to distant markets.[23] Before the railroad, these herds traveled the Covington and Lexington Turnpike (US 25), spending the night in pens alongside hotels along the way, with the animals fed and watered at each layover. A primary stop for many was Drover's Inn, where the Fort Mitchell Garage now stands, along Dixie Highway in Park Hills.[24] Some of these hotels could house as many as 100 herders and for decades were also the sites of various political rallies. If no immediate deal was made with local buyers, the hogs were herded to Lewisburg, along present-day Dixie Highway and Interstate 75, where Covington's stockyards were first located. Once the railroad arrived, Covington's stockyards relocated near the rail line at Twenty-Second Street, between present-day Donaldson Avenue and the tracks. Later still, when refrigeration was available, the major producers moved to Chicago. Incredibly, from November to December 1844, a total of 41,287 hogs, cattle, and sheep were processed in Covington, mainly at a 100-by-58-foot plant along Willow Run Creek just west of the city limits, and at the two-acre Milward and Oldershaw company along the Licking River, which was the largest pork processor in the United States in 1850.[25] While meat was the main commodity derived from the animals, lard and leather were profitable side products. Meatpacking operations continue to be big business in Northern Kentucky, with both small, family-run businesses such as Glier's, Heringer Meats, and Bessler's Meats, in Covington; Brooks Meats, in Walton; and Bill Finke and Sons, in Fort Wright, as well as larger national brands, including Blue Grass Quality Meats, in Fort Mitchell; and the Tyson Corporation, along US 27 just south of Alexandria.

While hundreds of workers chose meatpacking careers, an even

Wiedemann Brewery, Newport, Kentucky, 1913. Courtesy www.nkyviews.com.

larger number of men were called to the beer-brewing industry, which was booming in Covington and Newport by the 1850s. Covington's Duhme and Company Brewery in the Lewisburg neighborhood became a major producer, and soon the Lewisburg Brewery, Phoenix Brewery, and Covington Brewery were supplying the much-desired beverage throughout Northern Kentucky and elsewhere. Covington's other major producers included the Heidelburg Brewery at Fourth and Bakewell streets and the Bavarian Brewing Company, housed in a massive, castle-like structure on Twelfth Street near Willow Run Creek. Newport was home to several similar operations as well, but the Wiedemann Brewing Company was easily the most successful in the entire region. Located at Sixth and Columbia streets, it opened in 1870 under the John Butcher name.[26] By the 1860s, Greater Cincinnati and Northern Kentucky were a center for beer production and consumption: by the mid-1890s the average yearly beer consumption here was an incredible forty gallons per person, 250 percent higher than the national average.[27] During Prohibition, many smaller plants went out of business while the larger companies turned to alternative products; Bavarian to soft drinks and Wiedemann to rubbing alcohol, for example. After Prohibition, Wiedemann reopened in 1933 and employed hundreds of local residents for years, becoming the largest industry in Newport. Bavarian hosted a grand reopening in 1935 with 3,000 in attendance. Unable to compete with the national breweries, Bavarian eventually closed in 1959. Wiedemann was purchased by the G. Heilman Brewing Company of La Crosse, Wisconsin, makers of Old Style among other labels; the Newport facility was closed in 1983 and was razed a few years later.[28] The Bavarian building in Covington remained dormant for years before being remodeled into Jillian's, an entertainment facility with a microbrewery and bowling alley, but that was short-lived. After another twenty-year vacancy, the building was purchased by the Kenton County Fiscal Court in 2016. As of 2019, plans were underway to relocate many of the county offices there.

17

German and Irish Immigration, and Another War

Along with the industrial explosion in Northern Kentucky, another major shift took place between the 1830s and the 1850s, when Covington and Newport were inundated with German and Irish immigrants. In 1850, Louisville remained the most populous city, with 43,194 residents; but Covington had jumped to second place, with 9,408. Lexington was third, with 8,159; Newport was fourth, with 5,895; and Maysville was fifth, with 3,804.[1]

Maybe more than any other ethnic group, the newly arrived Germans proved incredibly important to the successful development of Northern Kentucky. By the 1850s Greater Cincinnati, including Northern Kentucky, was one of three major transplant regions for German immigrants, along with St. Louis, Missouri, and Milwaukee, Wisconsin.[2] The German population in Covington and Newport formed a congregation in 1841, with the assistance of Reverend Ferdinand Kühr, who is considered the German patriarch of Covington. Their church, Mother of God Catholic Church at Sixth and Washington streets, still stands as one of the most majestic church buildings in the entire region. The Germans soon opened additional churches, as well as their own schools, and established other organizations, such as the Turner Society. German immigrants also became owner-operators of bakeries, groceries, saloons, tobacco warehouses, hotels, and restaurants in the area.

Like the Germans, the Irish were one of the largest groups to settle in Northern Kentucky and arrived around the same time. Thomas Kennedy, in fact, who founded Kennedy's Ferry at what is now Covington, was of Irish descent. Unlike the Germans, the Irish came in two distinct waves, the first being Scots-Irish people, who were principally Protestant; and the second, who were Irish Catholics.[3] Covington, Newport, Maysville, and other locations provided ample employment opportunities for the Irish. By the 1840s, many Irishmen were among the workers on the Covington and Lexington Turnpike and later on the Covington and Lexington Railroad. In 1833, Covington's St. Mary's Church, later renamed the Cathedral Basilica of the Assumption, was founded and served the needs of the Irish, as did Newport's Immaculate Conception Catholic Church, St. Patrick in Covington, St. Anthony in Bellevue, and St. James in Ludlow. The La Salette Academy in Covington and Immaculata Academy in Newport were established as well.[4]

The influx of both German and Irish immigrants transformed the entire region socially, culturally, religiously, and politically; but, while the added population and revenue were good for the region overall, the change was far from well received by many, as ethnic discrimination became rampant. Many of the Irish despised the German immigrants, and vice versa. And many of the so-called natives—those born in the United States and already living in Greater Cincinnati—seemed to care for neither the Germans nor the Irish. Things got even worse in the 1850s when immigrants met with nativist opposition in the form of the Know Nothing (American Party) movement.[5] While the Know Nothing party was relatively short lived, secret societies were formed in Covington, Newport, and later Maysville to promote their basic agenda: the placement in government positions of only those who were native born. Nativist hostilities subsided for the most part with the coming of the American Civil War.

In 1845, the state of Kentucky requested that the remains of Daniel and Rebecca Boone be reinterred in Kentucky. Their goal, of course, was to officially recognize his importance in the state. The Boones had moved to Missouri around 1799, and Rebecca died there in 1813; Daniel died on September 26, 1820.[6] Some folklore exists suggesting that in response to Kentucky's request Missourians purposely turned over another person's remains in place of the famous pioneer in order to keep Daniel's for themselves. The facts to the contrary, however, are overwhelming. As a delegation began disinterment, it was realized that the wooden coffins had completely deteriorated and many of the smaller bones had turned to dust. The delegation from Kentucky carefully removed the larger bones and placed them in boxes, leaving the soil, which contained a good portion of the pioneer's remains. Jefferson Callaway, a former slave of Flanders Callaway who was asked to assist in the dig, found both of Daniel's silver sleeve buttons, with his initials, and gave them to a descendant, as noted by historian Lyman Copeland Draper and others. Several witnesses were on hand for this ceremony, and Missouri's own newspapers recorded the facts of the disinterment. Daniel and Rebecca Boone—at least most of them—are currently interred at Frankfort Cemetery. Ellison Williams Sr., one of Northern Kentucky's earliest residents and a longtime friend of Daniel Boone, traveled to Frankfort to take part in the official ceremony and served as one of the pallbearers. Afterward, he expressed to his closest friends the desire that his body be interred there as well. Williams died at his residence south of Covington on August 11, 1850, and was buried there.[7] However, ten years later his body was exhumed, taken to Frankfort, and reinterred not far from Boone, in grounds set aside for early pioneers.[8]

Stephen Foster

Stephen Collins Foster (1826–1864) wrote hundreds of songs during his lifetime, including "Camptown Races," "Oh! Susanna," "Jeanie with the Light Brown Hair," "Old Folks at Home," and, of course, "My Old Kentucky Home." Born in Pittsburgh, he was the tenth of eleven children of William and Eliza Tomlinson Foster. With some formal music training, by age eighteen he was writing both words and melodies; and by 1860, his was a household name throughout the country. While Bardstown, Kentucky, honors Foster, claiming that his inspiration for "My Old Kentucky Home" and other songs came from that location, Foster actually had a much stronger relationship with Covington and Augusta, Kentucky. Stephen's mother was the half-sister of both Dr. Joseph S. Tomlinson, president of Augusta College in Bracken County, and Dr. John Tomlinson, an Augusta physician. Stephen and his mother visited their relatives at Augusta often, as early as 1833. A historical marker there suggests that Foster actually got his inspiration for many songs from the beautiful Negro spirituals he heard that emanated from a small church located on a hill overlooking the town. Foster also worked for his older brother for several years on the Ohio River bank at Cincinnati, with a magnificent view of the stately mansions in Covington. There he witnessed river life firsthand and noted the mingling currents in American culture.[9] From wherever his inspiration came, Stephen Foster became the first true American composer, as the style of his music was unique, far different than what was being imported from Europe.

Meanwhile, out west, Texas had won its independence from Mexico after first suffering a devastating defeat at the Alamo, just outside San Antonio. Jim Bowie, born in Logan County (present-day Franklin County), Kentucky, as well as the famous Tennessee frontiersman Davy Crockett, were among the dead. The United States annexed Texas in 1845, making it the twenty-eighth state of the Union.[10] Immediately, America considered the Rio Grande as the border with Mexico, while Mexico considered the border to be the Nueces River, 150 miles to the north. When James Polk (1795–1849) was elected president in 1845, his main platform was to expand America's western borders even further, causing additional animosity with Mexico, which at that time controlled what is now California, Nevada, Arizona, New Mexico, Utah, and most of Colorado and Wyoming. By August 1845, President Polk had sent 4,000 troops to protect the new state of Texas. He also sent an offer to the Mexican government: $30 million for all Mexican-controlled land north of the Rio Grande. His offer was rejected.

President Polk then ordered General Zachary Taylor and his troops all the way to the Rio Grande, deep into the disputed territory. By late March 1846 they had reached the edge of the river and built an earthen fortress they named Fort Texas. Taylor's forces set up cannon artillery and took aim at the Mexican town of Matamoros. Polk, hoping the Mexican army would take the first shot, got just what he wanted. On April 24, 1846, Mexican troops fired upon a small group of American soldiers; in minutes, 11 Americans lay dead and another 52 were taken prisoner. Polk demanded that Congress declare war on Mexico, telling the public that the Mexican army had crossed into United States territory and ambushed defenseless American soldiers.

In Kentucky, Governor William Owsley (1782–1862) called for volunteer companies, hoping to muster as many as 2,400 men. In the end, nearly 13,000 answered the call. In Covington alone, three companies of infantry organized, as did companies from Newport, Gallatin County, and Boone County.[11] In a later request for troops, men mustered from Boone, Fleming, Campbell, and Mason counties. Several regiments formed at the Newport Barracks, including one commanded by John W. Tibbatts, a local Democratic congressman.

General Taylor sent 2,300 troops to Palo Alto, Mexico, but they were met by 3,200 Mexicans. Though greatly outnumbered, the Americans won a hard-fought victory. Taylor soon moved his men, including the newly arriving Kentucky volunteers, against the larger town of Monterrey. The first day proved disastrous for the Americans, but they were quickly able to regroup and won another victory. Meanwhile, troops under the command of General Stephen W. Kearney (1794–1848) made their way through the northern theater, with plans to secure present-day New Mexico and California. Since that territory was only sparsely populated, Kearney experienced little resistance. General Winfield Scott (1786–1866) then took command of the majority of Taylor's troops, planning an unprecedented water landing at Veracruz. The remainder of Taylor's men headed toward Buena Vista. Learning that Taylor's army had been split, Antonio Lopez de Santa Anna, leader of the Mexican Army, marched a force of 20,000 men north, engaging the US troops on February 23, 1847. Taylor's army experienced many casualties in the Battle of Buena Vista, as the Mexicans had total control of the situation. The Americans were in the middle of a full retreat when, incredibly, Santa Anna received word that a revolution was taking place in Mexico City and that his entire force was to go there immediately. In what became another US victory, 266 Americans were killed as well as an estimated 1,500 Mexicans.

On March 9, 1847, General Scott arrived at Veracruz with a force of 12,000 troops and eighty warships. Before firing one shot, he sent word that all civilians should evacuate. His warning was ignored. Scott then ordered a full bombardment. The largest cannon aboard the American ships at sea also fired upon the city. The barrage continued for three days and nights before officials within the fort surrendered. After American citizens received news of the great victory, however, they were far from joyous, learning that, of the 250 killed within the city, more than half were civilians, including many women and children.

Scott soon marched his men toward Mexico City, but Santa Anna met the invading army at Cerro Gordo. At that spot was a deep ravine surrounded by several rugged hills. Santa Anna placed eighty cannon atop the hills overlooking the ravine, but left the tallest hill unprotected, thinking it would be impossible for any troops to scale such a steep incline. Under the cover of darkness, however, Scott summoned his engineers to determine if there was any way to circumvent Santa Anna's plans. In this scouting party was forty-year-old Captain Robert E. Lee. The night before the battle Lee, who commanded the "Mississippi Rifles," supervised 1,500 troops as they dragged cannon to the top of the hill. At sunrise, the Mexican soldiers awoke to more than a dozen cannon aiming down on their camps. On April 14, 1847, the 12,000 Mexicans, mostly untrained volunteers, were no match for the expert Americans, who were only 1,500. The battle lasted just a few hours. Afterward, Scott and his army found only minor resistance as they continued their march to overtake Mexico City. The battle there began on September 12, 1847, and at the end of the day the Mexicans stood firm. On the second day, however, the Americans had far more success, and soon an American flag flew above Mexico's National Palace. While the United States won the war, the capitulation details were yet to be decided. Some in Washington wanted to annex the entire country of Mexico. Eventually a treaty was reached, and on February 2, 1848, the United States paid $15 million dollars, half of the original offer, for more than 500,000 square miles of territory.

Kentucky's service in the Mexican War was not forgotten. Monuments in Frankfort, Paris, Lawrenceburg, Midway, and Cynthiana were raised to honor those Kentuckians who had fought and died in the service of their country.[12] The city of Monterey in Owen County was named for the Battle of Monterrey, Mexico, and small neighborhoods in both Newport and Covington were named for the Battle of Buena Vista. John P. Gaines (1795–1857), a prominent Boone County landowner and politician, ran for Kentucky's Tenth congressional seat while a prisoner of war in a Mexican jail—and won the election. He later used his experiences to help him gain appointment as the governor of the Oregon Territory.[13] Likewise, Carroll County's Major General William Orlando Butler used his experiences to gain the nomination for US vice president in 1848.

18

Northern Kentucky in the Mid-1800s

By 1850 Newport was producing 900 tons of iron through two rolling mills, one owned by Daniel Wolff, the other being the Swift and Evans Company.[1] The same year also brought the Licking Iron Works Company, owned by Phillip Bush and his son John, to Covington. Ignatius Droege worked there a short time and later partnered with Charles Bogenschutz, who owned a hardware store along Pike Street, between Madison and Washington streets. The two men established another iron processing plant at Sixteenth Street along the Licking.

Richard Stewart Sr. opened the Stewart Iron Fence Company in Covington in 1856, and by 1886 the company had grown to over 150 employees. By the turn of the twentieth century, Stewart was known as the largest ornamental iron furniture manufacturer in the United States and the largest ornamental fence company in the world, employing over 700.[2] Stewart Iron Works created all the benches and amenities for New York's Central Park, the fences and gates around the Panama Canal, and the jail cells for such places as Alcatraz, Sing Sing, and Leavenworth.[3] Stewart's "golden age" was during World War I, as the company supplied motor trucks to the army, and immediately after the war, when they cornered the market for cemetery fencing across the nation. Stewart remained busy during World War II by supplying tank armor and portable Bailey bridges. In the 1950s and 1960s, Stewart manufactured chain link fences and won the contract to line the new superhighway system from coast to coast.[4] In 2019, Stewart Iron Works remains an important industry in the region.

Another major industrial operation opened in Covington in 1852, when the Hemingray Glass Company relocated there from Cincinnati. While the general offices remained in Covington for decades, the manufacturing operations moved to Muncie, Indiana, a few years later. Hemingray became one of the nation's largest producers of domestic and industrial glassware and was the world's largest producer of glass insulators for telegraph, telephone, and electric power distribution.[5]

Back in Campbell County, James McArthur, Henry Walker, and Washington Berry petitioned Governor William Owsley in 1848 to charter a town to the east of Newport, to be named Jamestown after the early pioneer and founder of Newport, James Taylor Jr. One year later, Governor John J. Crittenden was petitioned by two riverboat builders, Burton and Lewis Hazen, for a town adjacent to be named Brooklyn. These two towns merged in 1867 and became the present-day city of Dayton, Campbell County.[6]

In the early 1850s, Godfrey Frankenstein (1820–1873) was enjoying great success as an artist, painting mainly in oils. His works included various scenes around Cincinnati, especially the Mill Creek area, as well as at Yellow Springs, Ohio; Madison, Indiana; and even Niagara Falls. In 1851 Frankenstein stayed for several months at the home of R. F. Sanford, who resided along the Banklick Turnpike (3-L Highway) in present-day Fort Wright.[7] There he painted two works extremely important to Northern Kentucky history. The paintings are two views of what is now Madison Pike, one looking south from present-day Howard Litzler Drive, and the other looking north from in front of the Sanford home, just north of today's TANK bus garage. While Madison Pike exists today as a four-lane divided highway filled with commuters, it is truly remarkable to see how it looked in 1851.

On December 23, 1853, travel between Covington and Newport became much easier, but only temporarily. A suspension bridge was erected over the Licking River, but it collapsed less than a month later under the weight of too many cattle. An upgraded structure reopened in May 1854. A far more serious disaster was experienced at Maysville in August 1854 when the city's powder magazine exploded in the middle of the night. It was a "diabolical outrage," according to the *New York Times* the following day, when a "person or persons unknown fired off the magazine."[8] The facility, located at the bottom of the long hill leading into town from the south, housed 80 kegs, or about 35,000 pounds of black powder. Not a house in the city of Maysville, or Aberdeen,

A Country Road, by Godfrey Frankenstein, depicts the area that is now Madison Pike in Fort Wright. Godfrey Frankenstein (1820–1873), *A Country Road,* Kenton County, Kentucky, 1851, oil on canvas, 31 x 40 1/8 in. (78.7 x 101.9 cm), Cincinnati Art Museum: The Edwin and Virginia Irwin Memorial, 1997.

Ohio, across the river, escaped damage. A hole in the Court Street side of the First Presbyterian Church was never repaired and remains as a scar from the incident.

Discussion on the building of a railroad from either Covington or Newport to Central Kentucky began as early as the 1830s, but it took another two decades to raise the necessary funds. A Licking and Lexington Railroad Company was established in 1847, but little progress was made by 1849, when it was rechartered as the Covington and Lexington Railroad (C&L).[9] Surveys were conducted to determine the most desirable route, and eventually rails were laid along the western side of the Licking River and run from Covington to Paris. Construction began on the 78-mile run in July 1851, and a short run for the public was made from Covington on August 24, 1853, with stops at DeMossville and Grassy Creek. The span from Covington to Falmouth was completed in October of 1853. Earlier that year, Mortimer M. Benton (1807–1885), Covington's first mayor, became president of the company, taking over for Alexander Greer, who had worked hard to secure the success of the venture. Greer later established the Covington Locomotive Works at Third and Philadelphia streets; that complex, at its peak, included more than a dozen buildings, one of which stood three stories high. Initial orders of ten locomotives were placed with Greer's company by Ohio's Little Miami Railroad, as well as the C&L.[10] The entire stretch from Covington to Paris was completed in May 1854, and the company immediately began operating regularly scheduled trains. The express train left Covington at 8:00 a.m. and arrived at Cynthiana at 11:50 a.m., with stops at Benton, DeMossville, Butler, Falmouth, Collinsville, Boyd's Station, Berry, Robinson's Station, and Garnett's Station. Although passengers began traveling to and from both ends of the line, a major source of revenue was the shipping of livestock, principally hogs and cattle, from Central Kentucky to the stockyards at Covington.[11]

The Maysville and Lexington Railroad laid rails between Lexington and Paris, and in December 1853 the first train completed that eighteen-mile run. Because of the Civil War, however, completion of the entire route was delayed until 1872. Daniel Wolff of the Licking Rolling Mill acquired the Covington Locomotive Works in 1856, renaming the facility the Kentucky Locomotive and Machine Works; he expanded the business to include the manufacturing of boilers and engines for steamboats. In 1859, the C&L, Maysville and Lexington, and Lexington and Danville railroads became known as the Kentucky Central Railroad, run by John Talbot Levis, who had been associated with the Covington Cotton Factory, Licking Rolling Mill, and Northern Bank of Kentucky, among other endeavors. Almost immediately after the railroad arrived, several individuals began omnibus service in the region. At Covington, for instance, the Clayton and Grant firm offered rides from the depot "to any location in that city, Cincinnati, or Newport."[12]

By the beginning of the twentieth century, several companies were running trains throughout Northern Kentucky. These included the

Louisville and Nashville (L&N), which ran from Newport to Wilder's Station and into Milldale (Latonia), then to Maurice Station (present-day KY 17 at Pioneer Park), Independence, Banklick, Walton, Verona, Zion, Glencoe, Sparta, Sanders, Eagle, Worthville, English, and eventually Louisville and beyond; the Chesapeake and Ohio (C&O), which ran along the Ohio River from Newport to Melbourne, New Richmond Station, California, Foster, Bradford, Augusta, Dover, Maysville, and beyond; the Kentucky Central (KCRR), with stops at Covington, Milldale (Latonia), Decoursey, Culbertson, Grants Bend, Visalia, Benton, Morning View, Butler, Boston, Falmouth, Morgan, Boyd's Station, Berry, Robinson, Cynthiana, Paris, Lexington, and beyond; and the Cincinnati Southern Railroad (CSRR), which ran from Cincinnati to Ludlow, Erlanger, Dixon (present-day Industrial Road at the Boone-Kenton line), Richwood, Bracht, Crittenden, Sherman, Dry Ridge, Williamstown, Georgetown, Lexington, and beyond.

While Covington's public square remained the hub for the courthouse crowd, the railroad brought with it a major change. The depot was located at present-day Pike and Russell streets, and the entire stretch along Pike Street between Russell and Madison quickly became the city's primary commercial center for the rest of the nineteenth century and well into the twentieth century. Packinghouses, groceries, meat markets, printers, jewelers, saloons, lumberyards, machine shops, hardware stores, and more than twenty hotels cropped up in this area of the city.[13] One of the new business establishments was M. C. Motch, Jewelers, established in 1857. As of 2019, the store enjoys the extremely rare distinction of remaining open and under the ownership of the same family, over 160 years later.[14] At Newport, the main passenger and freight depot was established near Fifth (then Madison) and Saratoga streets; like Covington, hotels and various business establishments flourished within a several-block radius of the station.

In smaller cities throughout the region, fine business centers soon developed around the railroad and its depots, complete with hotels, banks, mercantile shops, and more. The railroad depot was the place to see who was arriving and who was departing. Friends were welcomed and loved ones were kissed good-bye. And because the Western Union telegraph office was at the depot, it was also the place to hear the latest news.[15] In Carroll County the towns of Carrollton, Worthville, Eagle

Railroad depot at Williamstown, Kentucky. Courtesy www.nkyviews.com.

Station, and Sanders each grew as a result of the railroad. Glencoe and Sparta in Gallatin County; Butler and Falmouth in Pendleton County; and Augusta, Brooksville, Foster, and Wellsburg in Bracken County all had depots. In Grant County, the towns of Blanchett, Corinth, Crittenden, Dry Ridge, Elliston, Mason, Sherman, Williamstown, and Zion each had railroad stations.[16] Erlanger's original depot has been saved and restored and is open as a museum. Covington's depot at Pike and Russell was later renovated into office space.

A bridge over the Ohio River had been discussed as early as 1815, but that major waterway was a quarter-mile wide at Covington, and such an engineering feat had never been accomplished anywhere in the world. A company was organized in 1828 for the purpose of building such a bridge, but dissolved just a year later. While many citizens on both sides of the Ohio showed great interest, an equal number of others, especially Cincinnati-based officials, wanted nothing to do with such a project, citing the possibility of losing both business and population to their southern neighbor. Eventually a study was done to determine the usefulness and profitability of a bridge. The first week of April 1856, ferry traffic from Covington's Scott Street included 1,480 crossings, with 29,311 passengers, 369 horses, 382 cattle, 1,566 drays (flat wagons), 627 buggies, and 450 other one-horse vehicles.[17] Officials on the Ohio side eventually agreed to a bridge, but placed several restrictive clauses within the working agreement: no piers were to be placed in the water; Cincinnati would dictate the span's height and length; and the bridge would have to be placed between Walnut and Central avenues and could not exit directly onto Vine, Race, Elm, or Plum streets.[18] The bridge's designer, German immigrant John A. Roebling (1806–1869; born Johann August Röbling), had planned to create the illusion of one continuous thoroughfare, connecting Covington's Scott Street to Cincinnati's Vine Street, and soon remarked that the new restrictions would deprive the area of the "finest and most significant avenue on this entire continent."[19] Several more years of delays followed, mostly owing to financial issues; but thanks to Covington businessmen Amos Shinkle (1818–1892) and Henry Bruce Jr. (1817–1891), on August 18, 1856, excavation began for the placement of the massive piers. Work had just begun when Irish workers went on strike, asking for an additional 50 cents per day in pay.[20] They were immediately discharged and replaced with German workers. The entire project, however, would soon be halted due to the outbreak of the American Civil War.

19

Slavery and the Underground Railroad

Slavery was nothing new to Kentuckians, having been an institution well before that state was ever settled. Many families throughout Virginia, Maryland, and elsewhere owned slaves prior to their migration to the West. However, by the time Kentucky became a state in 1792, Vermont, Rhode Island, Pennsylvania, Connecticut, New York, New Jersey, and Massachusetts had all abolished slavery at least to some degree, and both Ohio and Indiana were free states when they joined the Union in 1803 and 1816, respectively.[1] At the Kentucky Constitutional Convention in Danville in 1792, Article 9, which would legalize slavery in the state, passed easily, though sixteen men voted against it, including three from Northern Kentucky: Miles Withers Conway of Maysville; George Lewis, for whom Lewis County is named; and John Wilson, who later settled in Cincinnati. After the 1799 Constitution, when slaves were officially defined as perpetual chattel, the influx of slaves into Kentucky increased dramatically. Slave markets soon opened at Maysville and Washington, and by 1860 there were nearly 226,000 slaves in Kentucky, 11,000 in the northernmost counties.[2] Boone and Mason counties were the most saturated in the region, where slaves comprised as much as 40 percent of the total population.[3]

Unlike most slave states, however, Kentucky was not a land of large plantations, and most slaveholders owned four or fewer slaves.[4] These slaves built houses and fences, cleared fields, planted, harvested, took produce to market, and worked on the steamboats and river craft, all as forced labor. While many Northern Kentucky slaves worked in the fields and took care of their owners' homes, many others were able to obtain more skilled positions, such as iron workers, coachmen, masons,

imprudence, or the baneful habit of self-abuse. At the same time pointing out the *certain means of self-cure.*

By one who has suffered from the above cause, and from misplaced confidence in medical humbug and quackery. Single copies sent (post-free) on the receipt of a stamped envelope, bearing the address of the applicant.

Address, NATHAN MAYFAIR, Esq., Bedford, Kings County, N. Y.

dec 9-23-3m S.M.P., N.Y.

A LARGE NUMBER OF NEGROES WANTED!

The undersigned wishes to purchase throughout the year, a large number of

SOUND AND HEALTH Negroes OF BOTH SEXES.

FOR which the HIGHEST PRICE IN CASH will be paid at his Jail, opposite the County Jail, Short Street, Lexington, Ky., where either himself or his Agents L. C. & A. O. Robards, at all times may be found.

Any letters addressed to me concerning negroes, shall have prompt attention.

Dec. 15-25 6mo. R. W. LUCAS.

PIANO FORTES.

A. H. GALE & CO.

TAKE pleasure in inviting the attention of Artists, Amateurs, and the public generally to their NEW SCALE PIANO FORTE, just introduced. The growing desire for a Square Piano Forte that shall approach the Grand in volume of sound, and, at the same time, avoid the ungainly appearance of that three-cornered instrument, directed our energies to the production of

Typical newspaper advertisement for slaves wanted, this one from a Lexington, Kentucky, paper. Courtesy www.nkyviews.com.

blacksmiths, boot and shoemakers, and more.[5] At public sales, it was not uncommon for strong male slaves to fetch from $500 to $1,000, especially at the Lexington market. Higher prices were paid for mulatto (mixed-race) slaves. Of course, these mulatto men, women, and children were typically the sons and daughters of white slave owners.[6] The domestic slave trading at Washington later became the inspiration for Harriet Beecher Stowe's *Uncle Tom's Cabin,* as she observed the selling of human beings while visiting the Marshall Key House. Locally, slave owners often bought and sold slaves without a formal market, and frequently "hired out" slaves—an illegal but accepted practice.

Most supporters of slavery in Kentucky resided in the southernmost and westernmost counties, where slave-harvested crops such as tobacco and hemp were grown. Just as in the Deep South with cotton, slaves made up the majority of the workforce. In the north and east, however, Kentuckians were moving away from the idea of slavery. That region was far more diversified than the rest of the state, with the cultivation of grains and cereals, the breeding of horses and livestock, and, especially in the far north, the manufacturing of goods. A third group existed—those who were still wavering over the whole idea of slavery.

While many of these families were not financially tied to the practice of slavery, they justified it for several reasons; some saying it was "a necessary evil" for life in an agricultural state.[7]

Runaway slaves became a major problem, and several counties in Kentucky had enacted certain court orders providing patrollers to catch and return runaways, even as early as 1799. Even so, a slave's desire for freedom was never ending. Prior to 1830, runaway slaves generally acted on their own, usually fording the Ohio River at some point and escaping into Ohio or Indiana, where they hoped to find a group of free blacks, a peaceful Indian village, or an empathetic white family willing to take them in. By the 1840s, however, various groups opposed to slavery had formed in the North, and the number of successful runaways greatly increased. In fact, Boone County was losing 50 slaves a month by 1853.[8] A complex network was soon established, known as the Underground Railroad, whose members worked diligently to free as many slaves as possible, often sneaking them into their homes at night and later providing transportation to the northern states. The system was called a "railroad" because many of these volunteers would personally transport the runaway to the next safe haven, or "station," along the line. Northern Kentucky was home to many such stations, especially in Carroll, Boone, Bracken, and Mason counties, as well as at Covington. Runaway slaves were frequently caught, returned to their owners, and were severely punished, however; and those who had aided in their escape were generally prosecuted. The sheer number of known Underground Railroad workers and crossing sites in Northern Kentucky prohibits them from being listed in this brief summary. However, a few of the more well-known "conductors" and celebrated escapees include the following.[9]

Eliza Harris was the name informally given to a slave sheltered by Levi Coffin after she and her infant baby succeeded in making a treacherous escape over a frozen Ohio River. The harrowing event was later retold to Harriet Beecher Stowe, who used the woman as a character in *Uncle Tom's Cabin.* The woman had escaped from her owner in Mason County and made her way to the Ohio, but found it to be frozen over. She jumped onto a large chunk of ice, hopping from piece to piece as the ice sunk beneath her. Several times she pushed her child onto the next piece of ice and then pulled herself out of the freezing

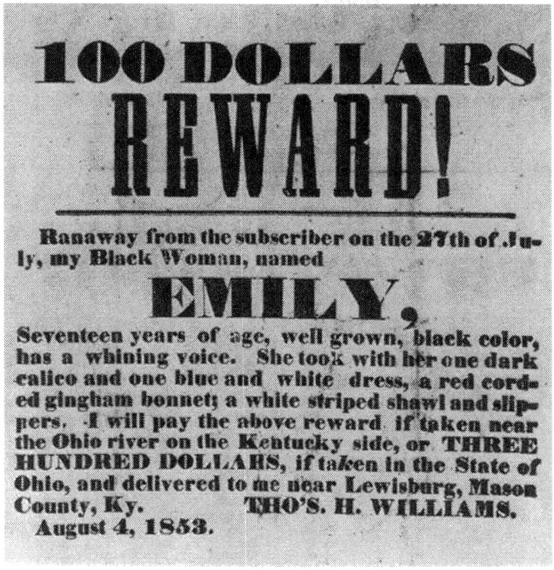

100 DOLLARS

REWARD!

Ranaway from the subscriber on the 27th of July, my Black Woman, named

EMILY,

Seventeen years of age, well grown, black color, has a whining voice. She took with her one dark calico and one blue and white dress, a red corded gingham bonnet; a white striped shawl and slippers. I will pay the above reward if taken near the Ohio river on the Kentucky side, or THREE HUNDRED DOLLARS, if taken in the State of Ohio, and delivered to me near Lewisburg, Mason County, Ky. THO'S. H. WILLIAMS.

August 4, 1853.

Newspaper notice for a runaway slave from Lewisburg, Mason County. Courtesy www.nkyviews.com.

water. A man on the other side of the bank scrambled to help her when she neared the shore and then directed her to a place of safety nearby, where she received dry clothing before being taken to a station along the Underground Railroad.

Henry Bibb (1815–1854) was born to Mildred Jackson, a slave working on a Trimble County plantation. As a youth, he was told that his father was James Bibb, a Kentucky state senator. Bibb saw each of his six younger siblings, all boys, sold away to other slaveholders. In 1842 he managed to escape to Detroit, from where he hoped to gain the freedom of his wife and daughter. Unsuccessful in this attempt, Bibb focused on his career as an abolitionist, traveling and lecturing throughout the United States. In 1849, he published his autobiography, *Narrative of the Life and Adventures of Henry Bibb, an American Slave,* which became one of the best-known slave narratives of the antebellum years. Bibb later migrated to Canada, where in 1851 he established the first black newspaper in that country, *The Voice of the Fugitive.*

Delia Webster (1817–1876) started the Lexington Female Academy after moving there from Vermont. In 1844, she was arrested and convicted of assisting several slaves in their escape to Ohio. Pardoned a year later, she returned to the northeast to teach, but in 1854 returned to

Kentucky and purchased a 600-acre farm in Trimble County, where she operated an important Underground Railroad station. She later taught school in Jeffersonville, Indiana.

Adam Crosswhite, Richard Daly, and others were "conductors" at several crossing points in Carroll County, including Hunter's Bottom. Daly assisted with the escape of at least thirty slaves before taking his own family of five to Canada in 1856. Crosswhite was a fair-skinned mulatto slave who, along with his wife and children, relocated from a farm in Bourbon County. When he learned that their owner planned to sell some members of his family, he enlisted the help of the Underground Railroad in nearby Madison, Indiana. The entire Crosswhite family escaped to Marshall, Michigan; but, wanting their valuable slaves returned, a posse of owners hired a spy to locate the Crosswhites and other fugitive slaves. Citizens of Marshall, however, helped hide the runaways, and a bronze marker at that site honors the Crosswhite family and those who risked their lives to harbor them.

John Pavy and others ran slaves from Ghent to Vevay, Indiana; and Elijah Anderson did the same from Carrollton. Pavy, a Baptist preacher, operated the first documented safe house in Switzerland County, Indiana. Anderson was referred to as the "General Superintendent" by northwestern Ohio abolitionists and was responsible for the safe travel of dozens of Northern Kentucky slaves. Brothers Alexander and Duncan Fuller were associated with the New Liberty Baptist Church near Quercus Grove, Indiana, a known station on the Underground Railroad, and those two men assisted fugitives from the Gallatin County region who arrived at Vevay, Patriot, Markland, and elsewhere along the river. Alexander Sebastian, the founding father of the church, ran slaves from the Warsaw area. One of the leading abolitionists in Bracken County was James Armstrong Thome. A graduate of Augusta College, Thome was a participant in the famed Lane Seminary Debates held on slavery in Cincinnati in 1834.

Addison White was born around 1821 and lived in Fleming County, Kentucky, with his owner, Daniel White. In 1856 he ran away, eventually arriving in Mechanicsburg, Ohio, where he sought refuge in the home of Udney Hyde. White's owner and some federal marshals eventually located the fugitive slave, but the Mechanicsburg townspeople surrounded the cabin and, armed with pitchforks and other weapons, refused to let the marshals take the slave. The marshals then attacked the defenders of the cabin, but eventually a mob of Ohioans detained the marshals and jailed them on the charge of assault with intent to kill. Eventually, Ohio governor Salmon P. Chase (1808–1873) negotiated the release of all prisoners, with all charges being dropped against both groups. Fearful that the court might return Addison White to his owner, Mechanicsburg residents raised $950 to purchase the slave's freedom. Addison spent the remainder of his life as a free man in Mechanicsburg and served two years in the Union Army during the American Civil War.[10]

Arnold Gragston, a black man, also assisted runaways to Ripley, Ohio; and John G. Fee was a famous abolitionist and educator in the region. Fee later founded Berea College at Berea, Kentucky. Maysville's Paxton Inn was rumored to be a station, and John P. Parker, a freed slave living in Ripley, Ohio, was likely the most active conductor in that region. Along with Reverend John Rankin of Ripley, Ohio, Parker was said to have been responsible for freeing dozens of Kentucky slaves. Reverend Elisha Green is also well known in the Maysville area. Green was a slave who became a minister, started the Bethel Church, and wrote an autobiography of his life. Other famous black people in the area include "Aunt" Polly Jackson, Rhonda Jones, and "Uncle" Billy Marshall, all of whom assisted in running slaves from Mason County. In addition, carriage makers Frederick and Jonathan Bierbower were known to hide slaves in their home at 38 West Fourth Street, in Maysville.[11] That property now houses the National Underground Railroad Museum of Maysville.

In Kenton County, many of the more elaborate homes along the riverbanks of the Ohio and Licking rivers had tunnels leading from hidden basement rooms to the water's edge. The rooms' initial use was simply to transport products from the arriving steamboats, but some became stations of the Underground Railroad. Henry Hathaway Jr. used his home on Highway Avenue in this fashion. Jacob Price, a free slave who became a preacher and successful business owner, also ran slaves at Covington. Slaves often accompanied their owners into Covington and Newport on business, and many runaways may have been aided in their escape plans by certain contacts they had met there. Newport's York Street Congregational Church was rumored to be another safe haven.

However, when the Kentucky Heritage Council funded a detailed study to verify such traditions in Northern Kentucky, it could not identify any reliable evidence of persons assisting the Underground Railroad within the city limits of Newport. Likewise, previous articles mention slave tunnels under the Covington castle estate of Daniel Henry Holmes, at what is now Holmes High School. However, since that building was not constructed until after the Civil War, there would have been no fugitive slaves to smuggle out.[12]

Of all the slave escape stories in Kentucky, however, none is more profound than that of Margaret Garner. Incredibly, it was later learned that her story, as remarkable as it may be, was far from unique among the tens of thousands of slaves who longed for their family's freedom.

Margaret Garner was born enslaved on June 4, 1834, at Maplewood Farm, a 300-acre plantation owned by John Pollard Gaines (1795–1857) on the north side of present-day Richwood Road, about two and a half miles west of Interstate 71/75. Gaines had purchased the property in 1825 from his father, Abner Gaines, who had brought the family to Kentucky from Virginia in 1797. When Abner came to Kentucky, he brought with him four slaves, and Margaret Garner descended from one of those unknown persons through a grandmother.[13] By 1820, Abner Gaines owned twelve slaves and had accumulated a sizable fortune raising hogs for the Covington and Cincinnati markets. At his death in 1832, his slaves, including Margaret's mother, Priscilla, became the property of his son, John Pollard Gaines, a successful lawyer with political aspirations. John had married Elizabeth Kinkead in 1819.[14] Priscilla became the family's maid and also cared for her owner's growing family. When Priscilla gave birth to Margaret, it was clear that the baby was mulatto (mixed race), and as such was believed to be the daughter of her owner, John Gaines.[15] As a child and early teen, Margaret also worked in the Gaines home. In 1848, John Gaines served in the Mexican War and afterward returned to Maplewood for a brief time. Having been elected to Congress, he resided in Washington in 1848 and 1849.[16] John then became territorial governor of Oregon, and in December 1849 he sold Maplewood Farm to a younger brother, Archibald K. Gaines.[17]

At age fifteen, Margaret married a fellow slave, Robert Garner, and in early 1850 she gave birth to a son, Thomas, who was most certainly

Robert's biological son. The paternity of her second son, however, is questionable. Born in 1852, Samuel was described as "a bright or light-skinned mulatto" and was born after Robert had been hired out to other families and was away from Maplewood. Two girls born to Margaret between 1853 and 1855 were described as "almost white."[18]

By late 1855 Archibald Gaines had been overheard talking about selling some or all of his slaves. Fearing the family might be split apart, Robert began making plans for an escape. By December the region was experiencing one of the coldest winters on record, with temperatures diving into the minus twenties. Rumors circulated that the Ohio River at Cincinnati had frozen over completely and that one could walk across the river on foot.[19] On Sunday night, January 27, 1856, Robert hitched two of his master's choice horses to a sleigh, stole a pistol, and bundled up his parents, Margaret, and the children for a journey through a steady but light snowfall.[20] The group traveled along the backroads and then north on the Covington and Lexington Turnpike toward Covington, risking slave patrols the whole way. They reached Covington around five in the morning, abandoned the sleigh, and crossed the iced-over river. At Cincinnati, Margaret had a free-black uncle, Joseph Kite, who lived along Mill Creek just west of the city. Robert had met Kite several years earlier when he drove hogs to Cincinnati. The runaways arrived at the Kite home before sunrise; and, while they rested and warmed themselves, Kite traveled to a known Underground Railroad station with plans to secure passage for the Garner family. Unfortunately, Archibald Gaines and US marshals were already on their trail.

It is impossible for anyone other than Margaret to know the pressures of her life. What she had endured at Maplewood can only be imagined. Margaret knew that if they were caught the family would most certainly be split up and, worse, was nearly certain that her two young daughters would soon suffer the same future as her past. Margaret decided that if they were discovered, she and her family would not return to slavery—no matter what.

While Kite was away, US marshals burst into the cabin. Robert took aim at the officers and fired off several rounds, wounding one, while Margaret barricaded herself with the children in a back room. Robert was quickly taken into custody, and another officer forced himself into the locked room. There he found that Margaret had secured a butcher knife and had slashed the throat of her youngest daughter, Mary, nearly decapitating her. She had also wounded the other children, but they were still alive. Margaret and Robert were arrested, and the surviving children were taken to safety.

In a two-week trial at Cincinnati, National Guard troops were summoned to suppress demonstrations in the streets. Abolitionist and lawyer John Jolliffe attempted to convince the judge that the Garner family should be considered free, since both Robert and Margaret had been permitted to make trips into the free territory on various errands. He was not successful. In the end, the Garners were returned to Gaines. Public outbursts continued for weeks. Immediately after the trial, Jolliffe suggested that Margaret be arrested for murder, hoping that she would be acquitted in Ohio and therefore have another chance for freedom. Gaines, however, realizing Jolliffe's plan, immediately separated the slaves and sent them to different plantations, preventing marshals from being able to serve any arrest warrant. Margaret ended up on a Mississippi plantation, where she died in 1858.[21]

Unknowingly, Margaret Garner contributed greatly to the antislavery movement. The trial, as well as the horrific details of the incident, made national headlines. It caught the attention of renowned abolitionists, as well as President James Buchanan (1791–1868) and the governors of both Ohio and Kentucky; and it polarized even more the feelings of the North and the South.[22] Margaret's story became the basis of the novel *Beloved* by Toni Morrison (1983) as well as the Richard Danielpour opera *Margaret Garner* (2005). Both are works of fiction, however; for a nonfictional account, see *Who Speaks for Margaret Garner?* by Mark Reinhardt (2010).[23]

20

The American Civil War in Northern Kentucky

Nationally, when the two drastically opposing philosophies regarding slavery eventually collided in 1860, the impact shook Kentucky to its core.[1] Probably more than any other state, families in Kentucky were often extremely divided on their views of slavery and the war in general. Kentucky, therefore, became the perfect example of what many have termed the "brother against brother" war.

Governor Beriah Magoffin (1815–1885) issued a formal proclamation of neutrality and advised Kentuckians to stay home and away from the fight.[2] While neutrality seemed a good idea, it would soon become impossible to achieve. Recruiters for both armies began enlisting men throughout the state, and rival factions organized militias. In elections held shortly after Magoffin's proclamation, the Unionists won overwhelming victories in both the state's congressional seats as well as the legislature. In a strong response, Southern sympathizers organized a rival government in Bowling Green, and in December 1861 Kentucky was admitted into the Confederacy as the thirteenth state, with George W. Johnson (1811–1862) governor. Magoffin eventually resigned and joined the Confederacy, as did John C. Breckinridge (1821–1875), former vice president of the United States and then Kentucky senator.

Kentucky's dual governments and military forces caused many divisions, even in the state's most elite families. In Northern Kentucky, John J. Crittenden's son, George, became a general in the Confederate army while another son, Thomas, was a general for the Union. Robert Breckinridge, John C. Breckinridge's uncle, had two sons fighting for the north and two for the south. Three grandsons of Henry Clay fought in Union blue while four were in Confederate gray.[3] While the great majority of men in Kenton and Campbell counties joined the Union, households in the other Northern Kentucky counties were often split in half. About 100,000 Kentuckians served in the Union, and after April 1864, when the Union army began recruiting African American soldiers in Kentucky, 24,000 joined to fight for their freedom. For the Confederacy, nearly 40,000 Kentuckians answered the call. President Abraham Lincoln (1809–1865) was quick to recognize the importance of the Commonwealth in the war when he said, "I hope to have God on my side, but I must have Kentucky."[4] He also stated that to lose Kentucky would be to "lose the whole game. We would as well consent to separation at once, including the surrender of this capitol [Washington, DC]."[5]

For the first few months of the war, both Union and Confederate units obeyed the governor's request and stayed away from Kentucky soil. Soon, however, Confederates took over Columbus, along the Mississippi River in the far western part of the state. Union soldiers under Brigadier General Ulysses S. Grant (1822–1885) made sure that the Confederates would advance no further north by establishing Federal camps at both Paducah and Smithland.[6] Grant, of course, was a major player in the war and lived for some time at the home of his parents, Jesse Root Grant and Hannah Simpson Grant, at 520 Greenup Street in Covington.[7] In January 1862, Confederate forces laid claim to parts of southeastern Kentucky including the Cumberland Gap, but Union forces secured the Cumberland River and later defeated the Confederates in that region.[8] In fact, Union forces had made all of Kentucky secure by the summer of 1862, before Confederate General Braxton Bragg (1817–1876) and Major General Kirby Smith (1824–1893) began a major offensive into the state.

Northern Kentucky became a major point of interest in the Civil War, as Union officials knew a Confederate victory over Cincinnati would be devastating. The Union could not allow rebel forces to take control of the major manufacturing plants there, or to take control of the Ohio River. Adding to Union frustrations, the *Cincinnati Daily Enquirer* on February 23, 1862, reported: "At two places between Carrollton and Madison, the Confederate flag is proudly displayed to every passing steamer, particularly those descending the Ohio loaded with troops." Action was needed immediately in the tri-cities of Covington,

Newport, and Cincinnati, and Major General Horatio Wright (1820–1899), the commander of the newly created Army of the Ohio, ordered thirty-five-year-old Major General Lew Wallace (1827–1905), then in Paris, Kentucky, with a small federal force, to fall back to the local area and take charge of its defenses.[9] A city in Kenton County, as well as the fort that was there, was named for Major General Horatio Wright. Lew Wallace may be best remembered for penning the epic novel *Ben-Hur* in 1880.

Free black males were not permitted to join the army at this time, but on September 2, 1862, Cincinnati mayor George Hatch gave an order that all able-bodied black males work "fatigue" duty for the Union army. As a result, hundreds of blacks in Cincinnati's poorest neighborhoods were rounded up by police and impressed into service in Northern Kentucky. Immediate public outcry, however, stopped this abusive action within days.[10] General Wallace, disgusted with how the men had been treated, placed Judge William Martin Dickson as commander of the "Black Brigade of Cincinnati." A promise of "fair treatment and the same pay as the white man" was quickly made. More than 700 blacks returned the following day; and in a few weeks these men and other volunteers built fortifications, cleared hundreds of acres of land for a clear field of fire, and constructed numerous rifle pits for the Union soldiers.[11] In all, a series of 28 hilltop fortifications were constructed under the orders of Generals Wright and Wallace—17 in Kenton County and 11 in Campbell County. Also, Ohio's Mt. Adams and Price's Hill, which featured a commanding sweep of the river and Kentucky's shoreline, were supplied with two batteries of artillery.[12] When the work was finally completed, many of those in the Black Brigade were inspired—and, more importantly, permitted—to join the Union army.

What became known as the "Defense of Cincinnati" began in early September of 1862, when Confederate forces had moved into Central Kentucky with plans to continue north through Covington.[13] Along eight miles of hilltops, from Ludlow to present-day Fort Thomas, volunteers and soldiers constructed rifle pits, earthworks, and fortifications later manned by 25,000 Union soldiers and as many as 60,000 local militiamen. When Major General Lew Wallace moved his headquarters from Cincinnati to Kentucky, he selected the main house at the Thompson Winery, at what is now Monte Lane and Vivian Place, Covington. The spot was designated Fort Henry, although no earthworks were ever constructed there. This was the approximate center of the Northern Kentucky fortifications; soon, telegraph lines connected the other sites with his headquarters. (A list of Northern Kentucky Civil War fortifications is given in Appendix A.)

Before long, parts of the Greater Cincinnati area were placed under martial law, including Covington. The fear of treason and traitors was great enough to make it a distinct possibility that the most innocent of remarks might be twisted into something disloyal. Many locals turned to the German language to carry on conversations when within hearing distance of strangers.[14]

A twenty-five-foot-wide pontoon bridge, made by connecting several coal barges together, was built to connect Cincinnati with Covington. As many as 85,000 Union soldiers and volunteers crossed the bridge into Kentucky, depicted in a mural on the floodwall in Covington.[15] Another pontoon bridge linked Kenton County with Campbell County and was located at present-day Eastern Avenue just south of Holmes High School. Local steamboat operator Captain John A. Duble organized a "navy" of steamboats to patrol the river. Each one of the sixteen vessels in the fleet was barricaded with hay bales to protect volunteers from small gunfire, and each was equipped with two six-pound cannon. The gunboats patrolled the Ohio River from Augusta to Lawrenceburg.[16]

Meanwhile, Confederate forces under Generals Smith and Bragg were advancing into Central Kentucky. After city leaders in Lexington heard that the rebels had planned to move on their town, an appeal was made to Northern Kentuckians for volunteers; and home guardsmen, such as Captain Gustavus Artsman and Amos Shinkle, were alerted to assemble their companies. At 4:00 a.m. on July 12, 1862, three trains with 700 troops and volunteers left Covington for the Central Bluegrass.[17]

Meanwhile, on July 4, 1862, then Colonel John Hunt Morgan (1824–1864), with nearly 900 men, marched from Tennessee to Glasgow, Kentucky, and captured Lebanon on their way to Harrodsburg and Georgetown.[18] Seeing that Lexington was too heavily fortified, the Confederates turned their attention to Cynthiana. Morgan was victorious there; but, with Union reinforcements closing in on him, he paroled all captured soldiers and escaped through Paris before leaving the state. In Morgan's First Kentucky Raid, he captured 1,200 Federal soldiers, acquired several hundred horses, and destroyed thousands of dollars in property. He unnerved Kentucky's Union military government, and President Abraham Lincoln received so many frantic appeals for help that he complained that "they are having a stampede in Kentucky."[19]

While no major battles were fought in the region, several minor skirmishes took place in the northernmost counties of Kentucky during the Civil War.[20] (Of course, the families of those killed or wounded in this region would not consider these altercations "minor.") By late August 1862, a Confederate force moved north with plans to overtake Cincinnati. They met with little resistance as they passed through Crittenden on the Covington and Lexington Turnpike. The Confederates, under the command of Kentucky colonel Basil Duke (1838–1916), were using the 2nd Kentucky Calvary—Morgan's men—as support.[21] By early September 1862, several small groups of rebel forces were within ten miles of the Covington city limits and had formed a line stretching from a point just south of the Ohio on the west and curving southeastwardly to a point just east of Banklick Pike.[22]

By September 9, a Confederate army under the direct command of General Henry Heth and a Colonel Hutchinson camped at Snow's Pond, situated along the Covington and Lexington Turnpike between present-day Richwood Road and KY 16, just north of Walton. On September 17 General Heth and Colonel Hutchinson sent a sizable scouting party toward Florence. The detachment of 101 Confederates moved north along the turnpike, where they were spotted by a smaller scouting party of Union soldiers just north of the town's main intersection. Shots rang out; and within minutes the Confederates were retreating down the pike, shooting back at the Union men the whole way. In the skirmish, one Union soldier and five Confederates were killed, with one Union soldier and seven rebels wounded.[23] One civilian, local farmer Larkin Vaughn, was shot and killed as he stood on the corner of Main and Girard streets.[24] Those injured were taken to nearby Florence Christian Church. The small party of Confederates rejoined their larger force at Snow's Pond; and on September 25, a force of Union troops from the 18th Michigan Volunteers, 10th Kentucky Calvary, and 4th Indiana Calvary from Fort Mitchel engaged what they believed to be a small contingency. Overwhelmed by a far superior force, the Federals surrendered without firing a shot. As many as sixty men were taken prisoner and later paroled.[25] A week earlier, around September 15, another rebel force of about forty men and a slightly larger number of home guards fought about two miles north of Independence. Amos Shinkle and Mortimer Benton's men captured five Confederate soldiers before the rebels headed south and escaped through the streets of Independence.[26]

Though they realized some minor success, the Confederates quickly found that Union troops had secured well the hills below Covington and Newport and that taking Cincinnati from a southern approach would be impossible. Colonel Basil Duke changed his tactics and moved toward Augusta, with plans to take that small village, cross the Ohio River, and attack Cincinnati from the east. On September 27, Duke, with 750 of Morgan's men and two small artillery pieces, was in position on the hilltops around Augusta and opened fire on a group of patrol boats on the river. The gunboats briefly returned fire, doing heavy damage to the Confederate encampments, but then withdrew upstream. The town had no heavy guns, and when Duke's forces rode into the small Bracken County city they expected a quick surrender. Instead, residents mounted a stiff defense and met the Confederates with a hail of gunfire. Ultimately, hand-to-hand fighting erupted when the rebels forced their way into homes and businesses.[27] Eventually, the Confederates forced the town's militia to surrender, but the townspeople had inflicted so many casualties upon the rebels they were forced to retreat and cancel their plans to attack Cincinnati. More than 10 percent of the attacking force became casualties, including Captain Samuel Morgan, cousin of John Hunt Morgan.[28] The rebels enjoyed a spree of looting, plundering, and burning many of the town's buildings before making their way back through Brooksville, Falmouth, and into Cynthiana.[29] The same month, 800 of John Hunt Morgan's Raiders took Maysville without a shot.[30]

Meanwhile, Bragg's main army had advanced into Central Kentucky where, on October 8, 1862, they met a force of Union soldiers under the command of Major General Don Carlos Buell (1818–1898) at Perryville, about ten miles southwest of Harrodsburg. In what was the only "major" battle of the Civil War fought in Kentucky, Bragg and his Confederate rebels had the early success. However, the Union forces were able to rally and win a decisive victory, forcing Bragg and his men to leave the state. The result of the battle was the worst loss of life ever on Kentucky soil, as 7,407 people were killed: 4,211 Union soldiers and 3,196 Confederates.[31] After the Perryville victory, Kentucky remained under Union control for the remainder of the Civil War. Various groups of Confederate raiders continued to wreak havoc in the state; but after Perryville, most of these men were nothing more than outlaws, draft dodgers, deserters, and those looking for personal gain—looters and such.[32] They scoured the countryside, raiding private homes, destroying railroad tracks, and burning bridges. Owen, Carroll, Gallatin, and Grant counties were often saturated by these so-called guerrilla gangs, while a few rebels made it into the streets of Covington and Newport.[33]

In late June and early July of 1863, John Hunt Morgan and nearly 2,500 hand-picked cavalrymen, along with two artillery pieces, crossed from Kentucky to Indiana west of Louisville in what became known as Morgan's Second Raid. From Indiana, the men marched through Ohio, traveling to just south of Youngstown. For forty-six days, they fought various groups of Union soldiers and home guardsmen, plundering homes and businesses the entire way. Morgan was eventually captured on July 26, 1863, and was taken to a penitentiary in Columbus, Ohio. After digging for several weeks through the concrete floors of the penitentiary, however, he and Captain Thomas Hines escaped on November 27, 1863. The two men boarded a train bound for Cincinnati; but, fearing they would be captured at the depot, they jumped from the train on the outskirts of town. The duo then walked to the Ohio River and caught the Fifth Street Ferry to Ludlow, Kentucky.[34] There they visited the home of a Southern sympathizer, Helen Ludlow, who provided them with horses and $60 in gold. The men headed west along the Ohio River before meeting with Benjamin F. McGlasson at the home of Francis Tupman, near Anderson's Ferry. There they received fresh horses and were taken down Zig Zag Road and along Gunpowder Creek to Dr. John Dulaney's home on Pleasant Valley Road. Dulaney led the men along the Florence Turnpike to the Piatt-Fowler home at present-day Union, and then along Clarkson Lane and Hathaway Road to the home of Henry Corbin, where they rested for the night. By morning, news of the pair had spread, and members of the Big Bone Baptist Church arrived to meet the rebel escapees. The men then continued past Big Bone Lick, led by Henry Corbin's son, Perry. After a short visit at the Richardson cabin on South Fork Church Road, the duo entered Gallatin County before heading south into Owen County.[35] There Hunt stopped at the home of J. J. Alexander, where a historical marker now stands near that spot, about twelve miles north of Monterey, near the intersection of KY 325 and KY 355. It is unfortunate no Unionists discovered Morgan during his escape, as within months he would take command of another huge force of Confederate rebels and inflict still more devastation and death upon the citizens of Kentucky.

Henry Bruce Jr.

Henry Bruce Jr. was born in Fleming County in 1817 and moved to Covington sometime before 1853. That year he purchased the Orr Academy–Rugby School at 630 Sanford Street, where he lived with his wife, Mary, who was also his first cousin. The couple raised four daughters, one being Pauline Duke, who married a cousin of Colonel Basil Duke of Morgan's Raiders; and another being Henrietta Green, mother of acclaimed primitive artist Mary Bruce Sharon. Henry Bruce Jr. fled his Covington home in December 1863, ahead of a contingent of Yankee troops who came to arrest him for allegedly financing the escape of General John Hunt Morgan from the Ohio Penitentiary at Columbus. Bruce escaped to Canada; after the Civil War he relocated to New York City, where he found great success operating hotels such as the Southern hotel on Broadway.[36]

Morgan and his men once again marched into Central Kentucky, reaching the outskirts of Cynthiana at dawn on June 11, 1864. Morgan divided his men into three columns, nearly surrounding the town with a force of more than 1,200 cavalrymen. A small group of volunteers and home guardsmen under the command of Colonel Conrad Garis, about 300 men total, constituted the entire Union force there. The civilian volunteers at Cynthiana even included a group of Cincinnati firemen.[37] Morgan's initial attack was launched at Keller's Bridge over the Licking River. The rebels were easily able to drive the Union forces back toward the depot and north along the railroad. Another Union force arrived by train shortly after, about 750 men of the 171st Ohio National Guard under the command of Brigadier General Edward Hobson

(1825–1901), but Morgan trapped this force in a meander of the Licking River. After intense fighting, Morgan forced Hobson to surrender, taking about 1,300 Union soldiers prisoner, thus ending day one of the battle with an easy victory for the Confederates. Morgan decided to take a chance the following day with another contest against superior Union mounted forces that were known to be approaching. Brigadier General Stephen Gano Burbridge (1831–1894), with 2,400 well-trained Union soldiers, arrived and attacked Morgan's army just after dawn on June 12. The result was a complete disaster for the Confederates, resulting in the destruction of Morgan's force as a viable unit. The rebels retreated through the streets of town, where many were captured or killed. A few were able to escape, however, including Morgan.[38] While this proved to be an important win for Union forces, 1,092 soldiers and volunteers were killed within their ranks, with another 1,000 lost on the Southern side. While Confederate forces left Kentucky for the most part, small pockets of guerrilla activity continued in the region. In October 1864, for example, the towns of Tilton and Hillsboro in Fleming County were terrorized and plundered, and the rebels killed the townspeople at will.[39]

Nationally, the Union army experienced a string of decisive victories beginning in late 1864 and stretching into April 1865. On April 9, after a major win at the Battle of Appomattox Courthouse, Robert E. Lee surrendered the entire Confederate army. The American Civil War was finally over. The war had led to the greatest loss of American life in conflict to date, with recent research indicating a casualty count as high as 850,000—more than the combined loss of every other war the United States has fought in for the last two centuries. It also saw an unprecedented level of destruction to private property, businesses, and government buildings. Two Civil War memorials can be found in Northern Kentucky, both located within Covington's Linden Grove Cemetery. The Veteran's Monument, also called the War Between the States Veteran's Memorial, is one of only two shrines in the state that celebrate soldiers on both sides of the conflict (the other being at Morgantown, Butler County). The Grand Army of the Republic Monument is the only Civil War monument in the state shaped like a sarcophagus.

21

Northern Kentucky after the Civil War

The Union's victory in the Civil War, the passage of the Thirteenth, Fourteenth, and Fifteenth amendments to the United States Constitution (abolishing slavery, granting African Americans citizenship, and giving former slaves the right to vote), and gains made during Reconstruction were all seen by black people in Kentucky as steps toward the fulfillment of the promises of freedom and human dignity. Unfortunately, all of these promises were broken a few years after emancipation, when new laws were passed that reinforced the continuation of a fully segregated society.[1] Among the new laws were those that forbade any person who was more than 12 percent African American from marrying a white person, and those that made it unlawful for blacks to attend schools with whites. In fact, schools for blacks were not permitted to be within one mile of a school for whites (600 feet in urban areas).[2]

Unlike most other areas of the state, some employment opportunities were available for blacks in Northern Kentucky, mostly as a result of river trade. Hundreds worked as steamboat loaders, cooks, polemen, maids, and stewards.[3] By 1870, Jacob Price (1839–1923) was listed in the local census as a laborer and minister of the Gospel.[4] Price, a black man who was freed before the end of slavery, had formed the First Baptist Church of Covington (African American) and, in that church, started the first school for black children in the city. He later operated a successful lumberyard at Fourth and Madison and was very active in civil, political, and educational rights for blacks. In 1939, the Covington Municipal Housing Commission named the new housing complex for low-income black people for Price.[5] In the mid-1870s, William Grant, a former Covington city councilman, ran for the Democratic seat in the

Kentucky legislature. One of his campaign promises was to the local black community. He met with several prominent African American leaders, including Price and Isaac Black, and promised that, if elected, he would revise the city's charter to establish a public school for blacks.

As with the South in general, however, in much of Northern Kentucky blacks were denied access to such places as parks, movie theaters, restaurant lunch counters, public bathrooms, and recreational facilities such as the YMCA.[6] Later, laws required special railway passenger cars for "colored people." In 1874, the Kentucky legislature passed laws creating a comprehensive public school system that solidified segregation in schools even more.[7] The William Grant School and Our Savior School in Covington, the Southgate Street School in Newport, the Paul Laurence Dunbar School in Elsmere, and the John G. Fee Industrial High School in Maysville were among the first schools built exclusively for black students in Northern Kentucky.[8] Others included one just north of present-day Turfway Park, at Idlewild, and at Burlington, in Boone County. In Kenton County, schools for blacks existed at Independence, Kenton, Key West, Milldale, Morning View, and Scott.[9] While it would be several decades before blacks would experience even the slightest sense of equal treatment, the Covington Library, which opened in 1900, gave blacks full access to its books and services from day one.

By this time, work had resumed on John A. Roebling's suspension bridge connecting Covington and Cincinnati. The piers were completed midway through the Civil War, and on Saturday, December 1, 1866, the span was opened to pedestrian traffic. Newspaper reports state that 166,000 people crossed that first weekend. The bridge was an engineering marvel; 1,057 feet between the midpoints of the towers made it the world's longest span at the time.[10] The bridge opened for vehicles on New Year's Day 1867 and has been reinforced and upgraded several times over the years. The John A. Roebling Bridge remains open today and is one of the most recognized landmarks in the entire region. In addition, each June Roeblingfest takes place on the Covington side of the bridge, with food and drink, tours, arts and crafts, and displays of local history.

The Beard family relocated to Covington from Cincinnati in the 1860s. Daniel Carter Beard (1850–1941) was one of six children born to James Henry and Mary Caroline Carter Beard. Daniel Beard became an acclaimed artist whose works were featured in several of Mark Twain's books. His true passion, however, was his love of the outdoors and nature, and his desire to teach boys the ways of the land. An early organization he founded, the Sons of Daniel Boone, became the Boy Scouts of America.[11]

In 1863, George W. Hill opened a general grocery store at Cherry Grove, just south of Williamstown. This became the forerunner to his 1865 enterprise at Covington, which became one of the largest feed and seed stores in the entire United States.[12] The same year, John Glauber opened a shoe store in Carrollton, located at 326 Main Street. When he died twenty-one years later, his son took over the business. Over the years, the merchandise sold in the store has changed, to include hardware, guns, and sporting goods, for example, but the store remains open in 2019.[13]

In 1866, work began on the fourteen-painting Stations of the Cross at St. Joseph Church in Covington. The young painter was Frank Duveneck (1848–1919), who was born in Covington and was residing with his parents at 1232 Greenup Street. At age twenty-one, Frank sailed to Germany and studied art at the Royal Academy in Munich. His talent was quickly recognized, and he received many awards. In 1872, while still in Germany, he painted what many believe to be his finest work, *Whistling Boy,* which now hangs in the Cincinnati Art Museum. Duveneck moved back to Covington, opened a studio at his home on Greenup Street, and taught in Cincinnati for several years; but, missing the culture of Europe, he moved back there in 1875. He married the following year, but his wife died of pneumonia in 1888. Devastated, Duveneck came back to Covington to teach and paint. Several of his students gained national acclaim, including Henry Farny, Dixie Selden, and Henry Twachtman. Long after his death, funds were raised to purchase some of his works, and descendants donated several others. Ten Duveneck originals are on display at the Kenton County Public Library at Fifth and Scott streets in Covington, while many others can be seen at the Cincinnati Art Academy and other museums around the world.[14]

Horse-drawn and, later, electrified streetcars were the first means of true mass transportation in American cities. In 1867, the Covington Street Railway began operating its first horsecars along the Madison Avenue route, and by 1868 more than 2,600 passengers per day crossed the Roebling Suspension Bridge on streetcars.[15] The Newport Street Railway also began in 1867, and soon streetcars ran between Dayton and Newport; Newport and Covington; and Covington and Cincinnati. Electric streetcars were the dominant form of urban transportation from 1890 through the 1930s. Streetcars ran on two rails and were powered by overhead wires. The streetcars' right-of-way was generally shared by horse and buggy and later by automobile traffic.[16]

Robertson County was formed from Bracken, Harrison, Mason, and Nicholas Counties in 1867, and was named for George Robertson (1790–1874), a well-respected judge and legislator. The son of Alexander and Margaret Robertson, this family moved to Kentucky in 1799, first settling at Harrodsburg. When Robertson County was formed, Mount Olivet became the county seat due to its central location, even though many locals had hoped nearby Kentontown would receive that honor.

With the advent of steamboats came steamboat accidents, and there have been several collisions and capsizes in the region. On December 4, 1868, two steamboats, the *America* and the *United States,* collided along the Ohio River just east of Warsaw, Gallatin County, and erupted into flames. While reports differ, the death toll was between 75 and 100. In 2019, a historical marker commemorates the event and stands along US 42 about a quarter-mile east of Warsaw.

March of 1872 marked a new era for the city of Newport, with opening ceremonies of the Louisville, Cincinnati, and Lexington (LC&L) Railroad Bridge across the Ohio. Located at the foot of Saratoga Street, the span included lanes for pedestrian and vehicle traffic. The town's population exploded once again, and by 1880 more than 5,000 new residents had arrived, a growth of 35 percent and an increase never again realized in the city.

West of the Licking, several families purchased property south of what were the Covington city limits just before and immediately after the Civil War. French-born Eugene Levassor (1789–1881), an acclaimed pianist, had moved to Cincinnati around 1820 and started what became a successful grocery and dry goods store. He purchased fifty acres between Madison Avenue and the Licking River and built an impressive mansion there. The Levassor family home remains along present-day Levassor Place. After working for Levassor for some time, Daniel Henry Holmes Sr. (1816–1898) opened his own store in New

Orleans. During the Civil War, Holmes purchased property just north of Levassor's mansion and moved his family to Covington. He continued running his business from there. When the war ended, he built a massive High Victorian Gothic house on the property. The estate went to his son after his death in 1898; eventually, the northern half was sold and became a subdivision. The remainder of the estate, including the house, was donated to the city to be used as a high school. From 1919, classes were held in the Holmes mansion until it was razed in 1936. New buildings were erected over time, and in 2019 Covington's Holmes High School campus has the appearance of a community college.

After working for the H. S. Pogue Company in Cincinnati, twenty-four-year-old John Roberts Coppin opened his own department store in Covington.[17] "General" stores had opened much earlier in the region, servicing customers with a wide variety of items, but the concept of a store with various "departments" within one building was fairly new, as most businesses in the urban centers specialized in just one line. In 1873, Coppin rented space on Covington's Madison Avenue and expanded several times before 1906. At that time, he purchased an empty lot on the northeast corner of Seventh and Madison and erected the first reinforced concrete skyscraper in all of Kentucky.[18] Known simply as Coppin's, the business thrived well into the 1970s. The opening of the Florence Mall in 1976, however, became an immediate threat to businesses in Covington and Newport. Coppin's Department Store closed permanently a year after the mall's dedication. The City of Covington used the structure for offices for a few years, and in 2016 the building was completely remodeled and reopened as the Hotel Covington.

In 1873, the Louis Fritz and Company opened in Covington on Pike Street near Craig. The firm produced soft drinks and other beverages over an incredible eighty-one years. At its peak, Fritz bottled 1,000 cases daily; popular flavors included cream soda, ginger ale, grape, lemon-lime, orange, root beer, sarsaparilla, and club soda. After several ownership changes, the company closed in 1957.[19] East of the Licking, the Newport Mineral Water Company was founded in 1886, producing soda water, seltzer water, and mineral water. The firm later expanded with a full line of soft drinks, but eventually closed in 1955.[20]

22

Northern Kentucky in the Late 1800s

With the American Civil War behind them, many Northern Kentuckians in the urban centers could engage in more leisure-time pursuits. Theaters were established in each of the region's cities, providing patrons with live-entertainment shows in the form of song and dance, dramas, light operas, and the very popular vaudeville performances. Some offered an even wider variety of options, including everything from amateur nights of music and comedy routines to exciting bouts of professional boxing.[1] Newport's Stadt Theater and Music Hall were open well before 1900, as was the Covington Theater, located in the Odd Fellows Hall at Fifth and Madison. While Covington and Newport were booming, however, neither holds the honor of hosting the state's first theatrical performance. That distinction occurred in tiny Washington, Kentucky, in 1797. Held inside the courthouse, the successful show included three plays by famous British playwrights, including Charles Macklin and Reverend John Home.[2] Junius Brutus Booth, father of actors Edwin Booth and John Wilkes Booth—President Lincoln's assassin—performed at Maysville on many occasions. By the late 1800s, Maysville had become a favorite stopover for traveling troupes of actors.

Although some Italian immigrants had entered the Northern Kentucky region decades earlier, the largest concentration arrived in the region from the mid-1880s through the late 1920s.[3] The majority of these immigrants arrived through Ellis Island, New York, which opened in 1892, and a good number of them were actually recruited by employment brokers working for the United States.[4] Dozens of these Italians started their own businesses, mainly in Covington and

Newport, and resided in homes or apartments above their mercantile shops. The small town of Clifton, later annexed by the city of Newport, became home to many Italian immigrants, and the area was nicknamed "Spaghetti Knob."[5] The Newport Rolling Mill provided unskilled jobs to many Italian immigrants, while dozens of tailors, seamstresses, and shoemakers plied their specialized trades elsewhere. By 1908, Newport's Hyde Park Clothes employed many Italians, who performed a variety of jobs, including everything from designing to pressing.[6] Several authentic Italian restaurants opened in the area as well, the most popular being Pompilio's, owned for more than fifty years by John Michael and Johanna Coletta Pompilio, and located at Sixth and Washington streets in Newport. The restaurant remains open and is well remembered by many locals as the shooting location for the "toothpick scene" in the film *Rain Man*.

Industry continued to grow throughout the region. In Carroll County, John Howe and his four sons were producing 6,500 yards of cloth per week at their woolen mills by 1878.[7] By 1882, the Jett brothers had established a distillery at Carrollton, producing Old Richland Whiskey. In 1898, they built a power plant in town and ran that for twelve years before turning it over to the city. It remained in service until after World War II. The Jetts also helped in the construction of a bridge over the Kentucky River and built the Carrollton Opera House at Fourth and Main streets. They also bought the Houghton House, which became the Richland Hotel and later, the Carrollton Inn.[8] The Carrollton Furniture Company was established in 1884 by H. M. Winslow, L. H. Henry, and W. F. Schuerman, and by 1900 the plant was operating from two five-story buildings.[9] Nearby, the Warsaw Furniture Factory, established by Owen Arthur Bogardus Sr., was the pride of Warsaw, employing almost 200 persons at its peak of production.[10]

In 1882, J. T. Hatfield started one of the first and most successful coal companies in all of Northern Kentucky.[11] Large supplies of coal arrived from the hills of Appalachia, first by barge and later by rail. Started as a small yard on Fifteenth Street in Covington, where he delivered kindling wood and coal to the neighborhood with a hand-pulled wagon, Hatfield turned his business into a major operation lasting many decades. Another large producer was the Montgomery Coal Company, located at Nineteenth Street adjacent to the railroad. Other suppliers in Kenton County included Economy Coal and the Latonia Ice and Fuel Company, both in Latonia. In Campbell County, Grimm Coal and Lumber opened at Brent; Breitsestein & Son located at Dayton; Bellevue was home to Peters Coal; and Newport had the Newport Coal Company at Twelfth and Columbia streets, as well as the Bell Coal Company at Sixth and Saratoga streets. In more recent years, Maysville has become a major supplier to the region.[12]

In 1883, a magnificent new courthouse was constructed at Newport, Kentucky.[13] The city's first courthouse had been a log structure, which was replaced in 1815 with a brick building. Remarkably, the 1883 structure still stands, with appropriate expansion, and today is still in use, located near the northwest corner of Fourth and York streets. Most Northern Kentucky counties established their first courthouses within log structures and replaced them many years later with finer stone or brick buildings. Some magnificent buildings were razed in the process, unfortunately, including two in Covington. Several new courthouses and other government buildings, far too many to be included in this brief summary, have been erected in recent years throughout Northern Kentucky, including those in Pendleton, Owen, Grant, Kenton, Mason, Fleming, and Boone counties.

The Latonia Racecourse opened on June 9, 1883, located at Thirty-Eighth Street and Winston Avenue, in what was Milldale. That town became the city of Latonia, but is now a part of Covington.[14] More than 10,000 spectators were on hand on opening day in what became one of the most successful tracks in the country. Black jockeys were prevalent at the Southern and Midwestern tracks, and Isaac Murphy dominated Latonia's top races. Many national racing stables were represented, and the horses that competed at Latonia were among the finest anywhere. Between 1883 and 1927, a total of twenty-seven Kentucky Derby winners raced at Latonia. The track changed owners several times; in 1919 it was purchased by the Kentucky Jockey Club, headed by Matt Winn, the man who made the Kentucky Derby famous.[15] The track's heyday was in the 1920s, when several legendary horses won the famed Latonia Derby, including Upset, the only horse ever to beat the great Man o' War. The Great Depression brought an immediate decline in attendance and purse sizes, however, and the track closed after the 1939 meet. The property was sold to the Standard Oil Company; and now

Aerial view of the Latonia Racecourse. Turfway Park.

the Latonia Shopping Plaza, including a Big Lots and other retailers, stands on the site.

Locals are familiar with what is known as the LLL (3-L) Highway. The name was derived from the location of the state's three popular horse-racing tracks, Louisville, Lexington, and Latonia. Signs proclaiming "LLL" were placed along the route, extending from Latonia (Old Madison Pike to Independence), then to Falmouth, Cynthiana, Paris, Lexington, Versailles, and eventually Louisville. While many previous articles cite an official 3-L horse-racing "circuit" or "association" run by the owners of those three tracks, there was no such organization. The road was simply named for the three cities that housed the three popular racetracks.[16] While the 3-L signage was only officially used from about 1924 to 1936, people throughout Kenton County still affectionately refer to present-day Madison Pike as the 3-L Highway.

The years 1883 and 1884 brought major flooding to the Northern Kentucky region. In 1883 the Ohio River crested at 66.3 feet, and it was quickly proclaimed by "experts" that the river would never reach that level again. Just one year later, the Ohio reached 71.1 feet at Cincinnati, and several river cities were devastated. In Mason County, eastern Maysville and the town of Chester were completely under water;

Augusta was also totally covered, and the Four Mile Bridge at California, Campbell County, was completely washed away. Residents at Boston in Pendleton County saw the river rise 12 feet in one day, and Warsaw and Carrollton residents met with a similar fate. Schools in Newport and Covington were used as temporary shelters for dozens of families. Although Covington experienced high water in many of its lower-lying areas, Newport was much harder hit, with nearly one-third of the town being submerged. The most long-term consequence of the 1884 flood by far was the US Army's decision to close the Newport Barracks. The installation had endured many floods over its eighty-one-year history, but in 1890 dedication ceremonies took place on a 111-acre site in the District of the Highlands. First named Fort Crook, the new post, as well as the town that quickly developed surrounding the fort, was named for General George H. Thomas (1816–1870), a Union Army commander known as the Rock of Chickamauga.[17]

Some of the first residents living in the "Highlands"—what is now Fort Thomas—were William Richard Taliaferro and his wife Alice Berry, whose father, Washington Berry, had given them 150 acres there. Taliaferro built a log home in 1830 and, although completely remodeled, the structure still stands at 1810 N. Fort Thomas Avenue.[18] Other early residents included Elli Kinney, whose massive estate later became Carmel Manor, and Samuel Shaw, whose home still stands on what is now Audubon Place. Long before Europeans were in the area, a bloody battle is believed to have taken place at what is now Fort Thomas between two groups of Indians, a Shawnee tribe who had sided with the British and possibly a group of Cherokee who were allied with the French. While little is known as to the reason for the 1749 conflict, between 500 and 600 graves were discovered once development began in the area, most found just east of present-day Highland and Grand avenues.[19]

The 1880s also witnessed the start of several distillery operations in Northern Kentucky. The Maddox-Hobart, Thorne, and Hazel Gap distilleries were successful in Campbell County, at a site that later became Tacoma Park. Just south of Newport, along Licking Pike, was home to the Old 76 Distillery, in operation until 1946. Not long after it was sold it was destroyed by fire. The Pogue family distilled spirits at Maysville; and in Boone County the Petersburg Distillery, largest in the entire state of Kentucky during the 1860s, operated from roughly 1836 to

1910. Between 1888 and 1913, Covington had at least thirty-five distilleries, the most successful including Crigler and Crigler, at Fifth and Scott; New England Distillery, on Pike Street near Washington; Sheldon Distillery, Licking Valley Distillery, and Sunnyside Distillery, all on Pike Street; Walsh Distillery, on Front Street; Old Kentucky Distillery, at Fourth and Court streets; Latonia Distillery; and Millbrook Distillery, Front and Scott streets.[20]

In 1886, Herman Eilerman (1830–1913) opened a men's clothing store on Monmouth Street in Newport. The business quickly expanded into another Monmouth Street location, and in 1892 he opened a small Covington store as well. In 1896, a new, four-story "flagship" location was built on the northeast corner of Covington's Pike and Madison, featuring a large bay window facing the corner and the first electric sign in all of Covington. Additional stores were later opened in Xenia and Lima, Ohio, Milwaukee, and Minneapolis.[21] Eilerman's enjoyed great success well into the 1970s. In 1887, Louis Marx and Brothers established furniture stores in both Covington and Newport. Like Eilerman's, their business remained successful well into the 1970s. In 1887, Dan Cohen established a general merchandise store on Pike Street in Covington, but in 1893 he began specializing only in shoes. He soon opened a second store, on Monmouth Street in Newport, and a third store in Cincinnati. Cohen transferred the business to his three sons before his death in 1903, and the business flourished—with thirty-eight stores throughout the Midwest at its peak. In 1910, the Covington store expanded and was the largest shoe store in Kentucky. The business finally closed in 1957.[22]

By 1890, Ralph M. Barker had opened a huge redryer plant for tobacco at Eleventh and Clay streets in Carrollton. More importantly, he went on to organize the Burley Growers Cooperative in order to assist farmers in getting better prices on their products and equipment. His 800-acre Richland Farm, located on US 42, included his exquisite mansion, a 203-foot brick cattle barn, and much more.[23] Massive tobacco warehouses were established throughout the state, but those in Carrollton and Maysville were among the largest and most successful.

From 1890 to 1892, all the horsecar transportation wagons were converted to the new electric streetcars. The Green Line Company installed lines from Covington to what were then the independent cit-

Green Line streetcar. Courtesy www.nkyviews.com.

ies of Latonia, Peaselburg, and Rosedale, and by 1895 routes extended to Southgate and Ludlow.[24] The following year, the business was purchased by a group of local investors including Richard P. Ernst, and a 90-by-370-foot streetcar storage facility was erected between Newport's Eleventh, Brighton, and Lowell streets. Nearby, a large electric power plant was built to supply power to the growing fleet of streetcars, and surplus power was sold to local merchants. Over time, the business of supplying power overshadowed the company's main interest, and a subsidiary company was formed: the Union Light, Heat, and Power Company. ULH&P soon became the main supplier of electricity to residents in the region. It was eventually sold to Columbia Gas and Electric (CG&E) and later to Duke Energy.[25]

23

Lagoon Amusement Park and the Start of the Twentieth Century

The Ludlow Lagoon opened on May 18, 1895, and featured a wide variety of attractions that were enjoyed by residents from the entire region. The Lagoon was created when Pleasant Run Creek was dammed to create a large lake, providing fishing, swimming, and boating. A bathing beach was constructed on the north side of the lake, and a large clubhouse featured sweeping views of the lake and park. A large dance pavilion, which drew thousands of dancers and bands, was termed the largest dance floor in the United States west of New York City.[1] Early rides included a toboggan sled, pony track, miniature gold mine, and scenic railroad. The most popular ride was possibly the roller coaster, which took riders over the lake and up and down several times before entering a circular building, where it spiraled in the dark before exiting. Over the years, a merry-go-round and 100-foot Ferris wheel were added, as well as a wooden "motordrome," or motorcycle racetrack. The park experienced four major setbacks after 1910, however, causing its eventual closing in 1918. A flood in early 1913 caused considerable damage. Repairs were made, but at enormous costs. A horrific accident on the motorcycle racetrack occurred in July of 1913, when a driver lost control and veered off the track into the grandstands. The cycle hit a gas lamp, causing burning fuel to spread over the crowd of more than 5,000. Seven people were killed and more than a hundred were treated for burns that night; several more died from their injuries over the following days. In July 1915 a tornado ripped through much of the park, causing more than $20,000 in damages. Finally, World War I and Prohibition saw the elimination of beer sales at the park.[2]

Roller coaster at Ludlow Lagoon Amusement Park taking riders over the lake. Courtesy Kenton County Public Library, KY.

In August 1891 Samuel Bigstaff, a major Newport residential developer, attempted to raise $200,000 to erect a toll bridge over the Licking River at Eleventh Street. Shortly after the venture got off the ground, however, construction stopped for lack of funding. Months later, in an effort to make up for lost time, King Bridge and Ironworks Company of Cleveland failed to properly set the bridge's piles, and on June 15, 1892, while 60 workers clung precariously to the bridge, it collapsed.[3] Men fell into the river only to be rained on by falling sections and debris from the broken span. More than half the workers were killed.

The same year, Joseph and Albert Andrews purchased the Newport Rolling Mill, and iron production in Newport grew to over 40,000 tons per year. Over time, Andrews Steel Mill was sold to Interlake Steel; and in 2019 the factory, now known as the Newport Steel Corporation, remains an important part of the region's industrial commerce. Other large, long-lasting manufacturers opened in the area as well, including Wadsworth and Company, fine watchmakers.

While Saint Elizabeth Hospital opened on East Seventh Street in Covington in 1861, by the mid-1890s two other hospitals also existed in Campbell County. Dr. J. L. Pythian had bedrooms in his office at 810 Washington Street in Newport, and Dr. J. Oliver had a similar operation in his home at Seventh and Isabella streets, though it seems the latter was in operation only from 1895 to 1897.[4] Dayton's Speers Hospital opened in 1897 and became a long-lasting and important facility to the region, eventually closing in 1973. In 1908, the Hayswood Hospital opened in Maysville, Kentucky, and remained until 1983, when it was replaced by Meadowview Regional Medical Center. That 101-bed facility remains the largest hospital in the region, outside of Boone, Kenton, and Campbell counties. Covington's Booth Hospital opened in 1914 in the former Shinkle Castle along East Second Street. The facility started as a Salvation Army home for girls and evolved into a general hospital for that group. Booth eventually moved to Florence and became part of the Saint Luke Hospital chain and, later, the Saint Elizabeth Medical Center group. Covington's Saint Elizabeth Hospital eventually moved from its original location to a larger facility at Twentieth and Eastern streets. By the 1950s, Carroll County Memorial Hospital had opened at Carrollton, and New Horizons Medical Center was established at Owenton. Later, the Saint Elizabeth group built a new complex in Crestview Hills and vacated the Eastern Avenue location. Afterward, Saint Elizabeth opened a regional facility in Grant County as well as a satellite center with an emergency room and doctor's offices in Covington, just south of Twelfth Street near Interstate 75.[5]

In early 1896, Northern Kentucky was home to a horrific and sensational crime, one that riveted much of the nation for several months. Early in the morning on a cold January 30, Jack Hewling, a fourteen-year-old farmhand on John Locke's property near what is now the YMCA on US 27 in Fort Thomas, discovered the partially dressed and headless body of a young woman later identified as twenty-two-year-old Pearl Bryan of Greencastle, Indiana. Two men were arrested within days, including Scott Jackson, her former suitor. The men were tried, convicted, and later hanged—the last public hanging in Campbell County. The whereabouts of the victim's head were never determined, however, and decades of rumor and speculation followed the event. Numerous sites in the area became referred to as haunted, including Bobby Mackey's, a local country music venue.[6] At least six separate folk songs, one published as early as 1913 and one as late as 2012, were written about the notorious event.[7]

That same year, Owen County native George Lee Wainscott (1867–1944) moved to Winchester, Kentucky, and operated the Rees House, a hotel. In 1902, he opened a bottling plant there and began producing fruit-flavored drinks and soda water. In 1926, after visiting northern Europe and tasting many ginger-based drinks, he returned to Winchester and produced what became Ale-8-One soft drink.[8] The unique, nearly indescribable taste became an instant success, and the drink is as popular as Coke or Pepsi within a fifty-mile radius of the bottling company. Vending machines offering the product exclusively can be found as far north as Fleming, Mason, Lewis, and Harrison counties. It has only recently become available in Kentucky's northernmost counties.

In 1897, William Remke opened a small meat market at Thirteenth and Holman streets in Covington. In its early years, home delivery by wagon accounted for as much as 75 percent of sales, and in 1922 the store moved to the northwest corner of Nineteenth and Holman. The store passed down to the three Remke sons, who in 1935 opened one of the region's first self-service grocery stores, located at Orphanage Road and Dixie Highway in Fort Mitchell. The business expanded again in the 1970s with the opening of several other locations, including Deer Park, Ohio; and Florence, Hebron, Independence, Newport, Crescent Springs, and Taylor Mill.[9]

Jackson Florist opened along the Banklick Turnpike, now Madison Pike, just south of Latonia in the 1890s. It immediately became a popular spot for those taking flowers to the nearby Mother of God Cemetery. The business remains family owned and operated and is still at the same location, offering a variety of products including lawn ornaments, trees, shrubs, and floral arrangements.

By 1900, Northern Kentucky had grown in similar fashion to many other metropolitan areas, especially those to the east. The first telephones, phonographs, and automobiles had arrived, though these luxury items were limited somewhat to the more well-to-do in the urban centers of Covington, Newport, and Maysville. Ready-made clothing, public utilities, brick-paved streets and sidewalks, public schools, and libraries had also entered much of the region. Covington remained the second largest city in Kentucky, after Louisville. Newport followed, and Lexington was fourth. Newport's final stage of expansion occurred between 1900 and 1936, when the city roughly doubled in size.[10] Steel remained the dominant industry there, due in part to the constant expansion of the Andrews firms. Joseph Andrews owned the Newport Rolling Mill, which made the sheet metal for the Globe Iron Roofing and Corrugating Company, which Andrews directed.[11] Also at Newport, the Evans Toy Company operated one of the biggest toy plants in the United States; and George Wiedemann produced more beer than any other brewery south of the Ohio River.[12]

In February 1900, thousands of local citizens visited the Odd Fellows Hall at Fifth and Madison in Covington to pay their respects to William Goebel (1856–1900). Those who had voted for him and those who had voted against him all joined in the sad occasion. Goebel had been the Democratic candidate for governor of Kentucky and in 1900 became the only United States governor to die in office at the hands of an assassin.[13] He had lived in Covington with his parents; after their deaths, he raised his younger siblings. He worked odd jobs while pursuing his education, eventually graduating from the University of Cincinnati Law School. Goebel became quite successful as a Covington attorney and excelled in politics as well. The governor's race in 1900 was so close that although his opponent, William S. Taylor, seemed to have won the race, a recount was requested. As the recount was being conducted, Goebel was walking near the capitol in Frankfort on January 30 when a shot rang out. As he battled for his life, the legislative committee determined *he* was the winner, and he was sworn into office. Goebel died on February 3, 1900. Several men were arrested in the ensuing investigation, including Henry Youtsey of Cold Spring, the probable assassin. Controversy continues to surround the event, however; and in the end those who had been convicted were pardoned.[14]

By the beginning of the twentieth century, Newport's Donaldson Lithographic Company had become known internationally for its high-quality, colorful circus posters.[15] Located in a four-story building at Sixth and Washington streets, across from Pompilio's Restaurant, it employed as many as 300 at its peak. The company was founded by William M. Donaldson (1840–1931), who lived most of his life in

Campbell County. He started a lithographic firm in Cincinnati in 1863, and as that business grew he relocated to Newport. While the company engaged in various printing services, its main focus by 1910 was creating circus posters for such names as Ringling Brothers, Buffalo Bill Cody, and Annie Oakley. Other commercial clients included Plymouth automobiles and Florsheim Shoes. In 1914, Donaldson started a second firm, located along what became Donaldson Avenue in Covington, between Madison and the railroad and between Twenty-First and Twenty-Fourth streets. There the focus was mainly on metal signs and tinwork for such things as powder cans. The Newport plant closed within five years of Donaldson's death, and Hyde Park Clothes moved into that location. The Covington operations ceased in 1988; that building was razed in 2002.

A group of Benedictine monks came to Covington from Pennsylvania in the late 1800s. They purchased property overlooking that city and Milldale (Latonia) and reestablished the old Thompson Winery. Soon they began producing altar wine and eventually supplied churches throughout the entire Midwest. In 1901, a few of the monks built a tiny chapel on the site to be used for private prayers. With Prohibition, the winery closed, and eventually so did the monks' compound. The property was eventually sold, and a subdivision was erected in the 1950s and 1960s. The chapel, however, was not razed and remained in the backyard of one of the new homes. It was eventually moved to the campus of Thomas More University and remains there, overlooking the lake near Turkeyfoot Road.

J. Robert Kelley and Albert B. Koett started what became the Kelley-Koett Manufacturing Company in Covington. They donated $1,000 worth of equipment to the new Saint Elizabeth Hospital and later developed a mobile X-ray table to treat military casualties. The company grew quickly and became one of the nation's top producers of X-ray equipment and accessories, employing more than 600 and reaping over $50 million in sales by the 1940s.[16]

One seemingly unimportant event took place in Covington in November 1905 that literally changed the entertainment world. A man had purchased a moving picture machine and was charging five cents' admission for folks to watch the silent film *The Great Train Robbery*. This was the first time anyone in the area had seen a "movie." A man from

Monte Casino Chapel at its original location in Covington, circa 1960. Courtesy www.nkyviews.com.

New York City happened to be in Cincinnati on business and had heard about this new form of entertainment. He attended a showing of the film, and one week later he had a theater of his own at Fountain Square. Within a year, he had opened dozens of theaters all along the east coast, and soon, discouraged by the few number of "new releases" available, he purchased and/or merged three different studios, which eventually became Metro-Goldwyn-Mayer (MGM) Studios. The man who saw his first motion picture in Covington, Kentucky, was Marcus Loew.[17]

Ice production was another major industry in the region at this time. In the early 1900s, ice was farmed from frozen lakes in the region and transported by horse-drawn wagon. In winter months, large blocks were cut and then stored until needed in large warehouses with thick walls insulated with sawdust.[18] Blocks weighing 50–75 pounds were placed into the top compartments of wooden "iceboxes," similar to today's refrigerators. The ice would keep the contents of the icebox

Ice delivery wagon driven by Jess Sanders at Third and Garrard, Covington, 1914. Courtesy Kenton County Public Library, KY.

cold. As the ice melted, water would collect in pans at the bottom of the box, and the pans would need to be emptied to prevent overflow. As electricity became available, ice was produced in large factories, but home delivery by horse-drawn wagon continued. One major operation in the region was the Latonia Ice and Fuel Company, started in 1902 by brothers Joe and Phil Mueller. Originally, ice was taken from a spring-fed lake at what is now the Transit Authority of Northern Kentucky bus barn along Madison Pike in Fort Wright. Later, a manufacturing plant was built on Latonia's Eugenia Avenue along the railroad tracks, where both ice and coal were sold. At its peak, the company could produce 100 blocks of ice, weighing 300 pounds each, per day. The Penn family ran a similar business on Newport's east side until 1959.[19] The longest-lasting operation, however, was Dusing Brothers Ice, located along Dixie Highway in Elsmere. This company, started by brothers Ben and Frank Dusing in 1928, eventually closed in July of 2017.

A huge demonstration in Maysville helped bring attention to a major problem affecting the region's tobacco farmers. In 1908, more than 5,000 men marched through the streets of town in support of the American Society of Equity. James B. Duke, later of Duke University and Duke Energy fame, had developed the American Tobacco Company, which cornered the market in cigarette production and sales. In fact, it became one of the biggest monopolies in US history.[20] Soon tobacco farmers were being paid less and less for their raw tobacco and had no one else to sell it to. Many families lost their farms or found themselves on the brink of bankruptcy. Farmers formed their own organizations, such as the American Society of Equity (ASE) in various Northern Kentucky counties. These organized farmers urged each other to stop raising tobacco altogether, or to at least hold out and not sell to Duke's trust. Some farmers chose to go against the ASE and continued growing tobacco. A radical group known as the "Night Riders" organized to pressure those farmers. In hundreds of instances, plant beds were scraped, salted, or sewn with clover. Empty graves were dug as threats. While the worst attacks occurred in Western Kentucky, barns and tobacco warehouses were burned in at least Augusta, Brooksville, Carrollton, Covington, Germantown, Maysville, Owenton, Sanders, and Walton.[21] With help from the National Guard, the Night Riders eventually disbanded by 1920.

24

The Basilica, World War I, and Prohibition

On June 29, 1910, the new Cathedral Basilica of the Assumption officially opened on Covington's Madison Avenue, just north of Twelfth Street. Ground was broken in 1894 and the first congregation met there in 1901, but after more funds were raised, a new façade was built, covering the plain brick front, and beautiful stained-glass windows replaced traditional glass. Once completed, the front elevation mimicked the Notre Dame Cathedral in Paris, and a total of 82 stained-glass windows were installed, including one of the world's largest, 67 by 24 feet, on the north-facing wall. The structure contains works by noted artists Frank

Cathedral Basilica of the Assumption, Covington.

Duveneck and Clement Barnhorn, and today the cathedral remains one of the most magnificent buildings in the entire region.

Also in 1910, brothers William and Charles Devou donated 500 acres of land to the city of Covington for use as a park, in honor of their parents.[1] The property was situated to the west of town and included the hilltops overlooking Cincinnati and the riverfront. Roads were laid out and the park opened in 1912, quickly becoming a favorite spot for Covington residents, as well as those from the entire region. A short-lived quarry was established within the park, and prisoners from the city jail worked to crush stone to be used on the city's streets. Around 1929, the quarry was closed and a lake was formed, known ever since as Prisoner's Lake. A nine-hole golf course was developed in the late 1920s and was redesigned in 1936. The former home of Thomas Montague was transformed into a clubhouse for both the golf course and a tennis club, and after being destroyed by fire in 1933, it was replaced by a new facility.[2] With help from the Works Progress Administration, three improvements were constructed in 1939: a shelter house, a swimming pool, and the Devou Park Band Shell. Forty thousand people attended the first concert that year. In 1950, a museum was established within the old Devou homestead and placed under the direction of area archeologist Ellis Cummins Crawford. Early exhibits at what became the Behringer-Crawford Museum included many items from Crawford's own collections, as well as unusual oddities from West Covington's William Behringer, including a two-headed calf.[3] The museum expanded greatly in the early 2000s and has become one of the main destinations for those interested in local history. The 1950s also saw the addition of the Memorial Building, which has hosted hundreds of wedding receptions, family reunions, and picnics over the years. Showing signs of wear, that building was replaced in 2003 by the Drees Pavilion, a large reception venue with sweeping views of the Ohio River Valley and Cincinnati. A second nine holes were added to the golf course in 1995, and in 2017 a new clubhouse was completed. Devou Park remains one of the nicest amenities offered in the city of Covington.

In 1913 the R. A. Jones Company relocated to Covington and built a factory on East Fifteenth Street east of Garrard. Lexington-based dentist Dr. Ruel Anderson Jones (1874–1941) started a soap company in 1905, each bar produced, labeled, and packaged by hand. Over time,

An enormous crowd attends a concert at the Devou Park band shell, 1939. Courtesy Kenton County Public Library, KY.

Jones realized the company's future was in high-quantity packaging and sold the soap business. In 1919 he introduced the first of many automatic cartoning machines, and in 1921 Cincinnati's Proctor and Gamble, the world's largest manufacturer of soap products, purchased a Jones cartoner to package soap bars.[4] By 1933, most of the world's mass-produced consumer products, such as razor blades and toothpaste, were packaged by Jones-made machines.[5] The company moved in 1966 to a 235,000-square-foot facility in Crescent Springs, and the firm remains one of the largest exporters of goods in the region, with annual sales topping $50 million.[6]

Covington experienced another important addition in 1913 when, under the guidance of attorney Richard P. Ernst, a new YMCA (Young Men's Christian Association) building opened on the southeast corner of Pike Street and Madison Avenue. Ernst had been named president of the Covington YMCA in 1892, a position he held until his death in 1934, and had quickly expanded programs to a point where a new, larger facility was necessary.[7] A YMCA had been established in Covington in

1857 and occupied a variety of small sites over the years, but the new facility had an indoor swimming pool, gymnasium, locker rooms, and a dormitory for short-term housing. A women's division was added in 1929. William Wade (1902–1983) served as director for fifty years, and the Covington YMCA later became known as the Wade Branch. A railroad YMCA opened in Silver Grove in 1914 to service the overnight needs of railroad workers, and a second opened in Covington in 1919, eventually locating at Seventeenth and Madison.[8] A YMCA existed on the military grounds of Fort Thomas and remained there until the army post closed. A new Campbell County YMCA opened in 1967 and still exists on South Fort Thomas Avenue near US 27. Another location opened the same year to serve residents of Florence, Erlanger, and Elsmere and was designated the Tri-City Branch, located on Main Street near Turfway Road. That branch closed when a new center opened in the 1990s near Burlington, named after benefactor R. C. Durr. During the 1920s, the Covington branch operated a camp in Rosedale called the Ernst Lodge, and Ernst later purchased the 80-acre Underhill Farm near Burlington. Before his death, Ernst gave the farm to the YMCA for summer outdoor recreation, such as swimming, boating, fishing, and hiking.[9] The intent was to bring urban children out to the fresh air of the country for a couple of weeks each summer. The site now consists of 350 acres and successfully operates as Camp Ernst. Besides the Durr Branch, which enjoyed a $2.7 million expansion in 2017, and the Campbell County YMCA, several satellite centers exist in the region, including a teen center at Dayton; pool and soccer fields at Independence; swimming pools at Union and Cherry Hill; and a YMCA at Maysville.[10]

J. B. Sanders purchased property in 1909 that included the Farmer's Bank, Huffman Blacksmithy, and Dry Ridge Creamery near present-day Grant County Farm Supply on Broadway in Dry Ridge. The property included a deep well that had struck mineral water instead of fresh water. The discovery of the spring prompted Sanders to build a hotel at the site. After 1915, the operation was known under a variety of different names, such as the Lake View Sanitarium and Hotel Company, although Carlsbad Springs Hotel remained the name on the sign. The term "spring" is really a misnomer in this case, however, as there actually is no spring. The water lies in deep wells and was pumped from the ground. The hotel was destroyed by fire in 1927, and eventually a new hotel was constructed. The popularity of mineral-water spas diminished over time, however, and pumping water from the wells became no longer profitable. While nearly all the mineral water springs in Kentucky eventually dried up, the deep wells at Dry Ridge remain, though hidden underground.[11]

While sawmills and lumberyards had existed in the region for decades, two men started a new business in 1915 that became the oldest lumber company still remaining in 2019. John Edgett and Blain Fulton opened a business called Edgett and Fulton Lumber on Crescent Avenue in Erlanger that year. In 1924, R. C. McNay purchased the business and changed the name to Boone-Kenton Lumber. In 1960, Warren Kelly took over and formed the Boone-Kenton Lumber and Building Supply Company. He also owned the Wildwood Motor Inn and was part owner of Ramada Inn, both in Florence. Two of his brothers started Kelly Brothers Lumber. Boone-Kenton Lumber survived three disastrous fires (1931, 1966, and 1972) and changed hands a few more times over the years, but as of 2019 is still a thriving business at the same location.[12]

By 1915, several bathing beaches existed along the Ohio River. These included the Queen City Beach in Bellevue and the Princess, Manhattan, Berlin, and Tacoma beaches in Dayton.[13] With frequent flooding, water pollution, and the later construction of dams upriver, these public beaches were relatively short-lived. Tacoma Park, however, outlasted the rest. Owner Tony Gesser constructed a 130-by-150-foot in-ground swimming pool filled with clean water from an artesian well, a 100-locker bathhouse, a roller coaster, a penny arcade, a combination dance floor and skating rink, and other amenities. Unable to fully recover from the Flood of 1937, however, the park closed in 1941.[14] While not located along the Ohio, Pleasure Isle was equally successful, especially after World War II. The state-of-the-art swimming pool was located along 3-L Highway just south of Hands Pike, and included a large beach along the adjacent Banklick Creek. After the success of larger facilities and amusement parks in the region in later years, attendance at the Pleasure Isle pool suffered and, after the widening of the 3-L, the facility closed in 1997.[15]

In 1917 the United States entered World War I. Suddenly, North-

Manhattan Bathing Beach, Dayton, Kentucky, circa 1910. Courtesy Kenton County Public Library, KY.

ern Kentuckians with German heritage found themselves in a precarious position.[16] The overwhelming majority of them were loyal Americans, of course, and many of these families had lived in the United States for generations. Some of their non-German counterparts, however, viewed them with distrust. A Citizens Patriotic League was formed in 1917 and was, unfortunately, successful in eliminating many aspects of German culture and language in the area.[17] Schools stopped teaching the German language, the Covington Public Library removed its sizable German-language collection, and the circulation of German newspapers all but ceased. The German National Bank in Covington was renamed People's Liberty Bank, and Newport's German Bank became American National Bank. German-sounding street names were also changed, and many citizens began spelling their names differently: Braun to Brown and Baumann to Bowman, for example.[18] The Citizens Patriotic League often used violence to achieve their goals, and several instances of such activities are worth noting. On June 5, 1918, Reverend Anton Goebel, pastor of St. John Catholic Church on Pike Street in Covington, was attacked on the porch of the rectory. A farmer in rural Kenton County who was accused of supporting the German war aims was tied to a tree and whipped.[19] The League hired a private detective agency, which placed listening devices inside a Latonia shoe store owned by Charles Schoberg. As a result, three local men, all upstanding citizens of the area, were convicted of espionage and sentenced to prison; in 1921, after a successful petition drive by their friends, they were released and pardoned.[20] This Anti-German hysteria, as it was called, changed much of the region forever.

As early as the late 1800s, farmers across Kentucky often struggled due to seasonal crop failures and the rising costs of feed and equipment. At a meeting in Louisville in November of 1919, the Kentucky Farm Bureau was established to be the "voice of Kentucky agriculture." Farm Bureau organizations in other states joined together and worked diligently for the local farmer, and when farm foreclosures became rampant after 1932 they worked with President Roosevelt on what became the Agriculture Adjustment Act of 1933. In Kentucky, separate organizations were formed in each county, and today the Kentucky Farm Bureau has grown to over 500,000 members. They continue to work for the local farmer, with specialized insurance services and with such programs as Agriculture in the Classroom and Certified Roadside Markets. They are also a strong supporter of the Future Farmers of America program in the schools. Their television program *Bluegrass & Backroads,* which began in 2003, is enjoyed by both farmers and city folk and can be seen on various KET stations.

Another nationwide development took place in 1919 that literally changed the course of Northern Kentucky, especially the city of Newport; the impact of this change lasted nearly five decades. Prohibition began with the ratification of the Eighteenth Amendment to the Constitution, which prohibited the importing, exporting, transporting, selling, and manufacturing of intoxicating liquor, and enforcement of the Volstead Act began on October 10, 1919.[21] While many states were already "dry," many citizens within those states continued to drink alcohol, which was supplied by bootleggers or produced in their own backyard or basement stills. Like other metropolitan areas, Northern Kentucky had many groups rallying for passage of what was termed the

Volstead Act, but a far greater number of citizens were opposed to it. Individuals and small organized groups began stockpiling liquor almost immediately, for their own personal consumption as well as to sell for profit. It did not take long, however, for the Mafia to jump in with a plan to manufacture and supply alcohol to all who wanted it. Prohibition, in fact, was the sole reason for the mob's long-lasting success in this country; but in the end, Prohibition also proved with little doubt the government's inability to regulate its citizens' behavior.

Locally, George Remus was by far the king of the bootleggers. He and his associates ran railroad boxcars full of illegal whiskey and made millions. Almost immediately, Covington and Newport became home to dozens of "speakeasies," places that secretly served alcohol to the public. These places appeared to be nothing more than small restaurants, but owners could press a buzzer to allow access to a secret basement room, back room, or second floor, where the liquor was served. Gambling soon went hand in hand with these establishments, and in many locations telegraph and later telephone lines were installed to allow for horse-race betting all across the country. Prostitution also expanded significantly in Newport, and it was said that it was easier to find a prostitute than a corner newspaper stand. Most importantly, corruption within the ranks of government officials and law enforcement became commonplace, a trend that would last well into the 1970s. Raids were often made into suspected clubs, but owners were usually tipped off in advance of such raids, so that when inspectors arrived no alcohol or gambling paraphernalia would be found. Many police officers and other public officials made more per month in bribes and kickbacks than some factory workers made in a year. On a more positive note, the downtown districts of Newport and Covington became bustling places of activity, due in part to the gambling halls and speakeasies, with many restaurants, department stores, and shops being open twenty-four hours a day.

25

Northern Kentucky in the 1920s and 1930s

By the 1920s, for the first time ever in United States history, more people lived in cities than on farms. In addition, the nation's total wealth more than doubled between 1920 and 1929.[1] In Northern Kentucky, the urban centers of Covington, Newport, and Maysville prospered greatly as a result of this new wealth and population distribution. While the automobile had been available much earlier, few could afford that luxury until the 1920s, and by the end of the decade gas stations, auto repair shops, motels, and restaurants sprang up all along the major highways, such as Dixie Highway (US 25), Alexandria Pike (US 27), and the 3-L Highway (KY 17).

The early twentieth century also saw a tremendous housing boom nationwide, and Northern Kentucky, especially the cities of Covington and Newport, benefited greatly. Neighborhoods that never existed before rose up almost overnight, including Peaselburg and Latonia, now parts of Covington; and Clifton and Cote Brilliante, now within Newport's city limits. Such a need existed for fine-quality homes that could be erected quickly that several companies offered them through mail-order catalogs—not just the floor plans, but all the materials needed to properly construct a home from the ground up. One of the largest companies was Sears, Roebuck and Company, which sold more than 100,000 kits from more than 400 different models between 1908 and 1940.[2] Hundreds of these homes can still be found in the region, especially in Fort Mitchell, Latonia, Ludlow, and Elsmere.[3]

Showing motion pictures became the rage by the early 1920s. Live entertainment theaters in Newport, Covington, and Maysville quickly altered their stages to accommodate movie screens. The Covington

Theater and Newport's Music Hall and Stadt theaters were among the earliest to make the change. Early films had no soundtrack, and piano players were hired to add a certain ambiance to each film. By the end of the 1920s, "talkies" were being produced, and patrons were amazed to be able to hear the actors' dialogue for the first time. From 1910 to the 1930s, more than fifty movie theaters opened in Northern Kentucky. A few of the more successful included Covington's Colonial, Kozy, Gayety, and Hippodrome; Latonia's Kentucky and Delbee; Newport's Myrtle, Music Hall, Clifton Gardens, Colonial, Hippodrome, Grand, and York; and Maysville's Nickelodeon, Pastime, and Russell.[4]

The early 1920s were not all peaceful and carefree, however. Things turned extremely violent in Newport in November 1921, when management at the Andrews-run steel plants decreased wages to its hundreds of employees, mainly because of heavier competition. The unionized workers went on strike and were given an ultimatum: go back to work at the reduced rate or be fired. Thousands returned to work, but more than 1,000 continued their strike. In a city whose labor force equaled 10,000, long-lasting friendships ended, neighbors split into factions, and some families broke apart.[5] Within days, the strikers became violent, harassing workers who remained on the job. Houses were burned, and windows of the factory buildings were shot out. A mob carrying torches marched up Waterworks Road to burn the homes of Joseph and Frank Andrews, but they backed off when armed residents confronted them.[6] Governor Edwin P. Morrow (1877–1935) was asked for assistance, and 200 guardsmen were sent to Newport on December 24, with another 130 arriving four days later. The violence continued, in fact escalated, into February, and more troops, along with a tank company, arrived on the scene. The strike, which ended with a union defeat, proved to be one of the darkest times for Newport.

As the population of Northern Kentucky grew, so did industry. Many companies opened to answer the demand for pasteurized, homogenized, and refrigerated dairy products.[7] By 1920, fifty-four dairies were operating in the region. Though they may not have been the first, Newport's Trauth Dairy, which was purchased by Mayfield Dairies in 2000, is the only one of these early companies remaining in operation. In 1920, Louis Trauth purchased the Fred Schuerman Dairy, situated where the Newport Shopping Center sits today; over the years,

Phillip Sauerbeck Dairy milk wagon. Courtesy www.nkyviews.com.

he expanded and relocated his business to Eleventh and Monmouth streets. Campbell County was home to several other successful operations, including Sealtest, Clover Leaf, George B. Moock's dairy farm, Hiland Dairy, Phillip Sauerbeck, and Feldman's Dairy. In Kenton County, Buttermilk Pike was said to have been so named because transporting milk over the bumpy dirt roads on a humid day would churn it into buttermilk.[8] List Dairy, Thirs Dairy, and Echo Dairy operated in along Buttermilk Pike and the adjoining hills as early as the 1880s; and in present-day Edgewood, successful dairies were run by the Requardt and Foltz families. Other Kenton County operations included the Rehkamp Dairy on 3-L Highway, Trenkamp and Hanneken dairies at Covington, and the Ratterman family's Latonia Springs Dairy. In 1928, the Carnation Company came to Maysville and canned milk for several decades, and in Owenton the Kraft Company ran a processed cheese factory for many years.[9] From the late 1800s through the 1950s, horse-drawn milk wagons and, later, mechanized trucks delivered milk and other dairy products door to door. The advent of grocery stores with refrigeration cases of course brought an end to that quaint service.[10]

The mid-1920s also saw the beginning of a long-lasting poultry business in the region. Years earlier, John Tewes Sr. and his family moved from Covington to Amsterdam Road and started raising chickens in their basement. By 1925, the family had moved to a sprawling farm at what is now Charter Oak Drive in Edgewood and began selling eggs to local stores and to individual families through home delivery. In fact, more than 100 customers were on their weekly route, with eggs selling for 10 cents a dozen. Tewes Poultry Products continues their family-run business, now specializing mostly in turkeys, along Crescent Springs Pike in Erlanger.[11]

The 1920s, unfortunately, brought several disastrous fires to Northern Kentucky. On June 7, 1921, an explosion was the cause of a fire at Burlington that destroyed two businesses, two apartments, and the post office.[12] In Dayton, on January 20, 1924, Dayton High School at Eighth and Walnut streets was completely destroyed, as frozen hydrants handicapped the efforts of the firefighters. In Grant County, flames ripped through the business district at Dry Ridge on February 25, 1927. Eleven businesses and several homes were destroyed, as was the historic Carlsbad Hotel. Later that year, three businesses and a home were destroyed in Williamstown.

On a happier note, several local individuals found great success in the 1920s. While still a student at the University of Cincinnati, Covington-born George S. Sperti (1900–1991) became somewhat of a local celebrity when he invented a utility meter and was paid $30,000 by General Electric. After his 1923 graduation from the College of Engineering, he held the first patent for fluorescent lights and developed the Sperti Sunlamp. Sperti later founded the Saint Thomas Institute, working mainly on products for the food and drug industry. There, he helped develop such products as Sperti Ointment and Burn Salve, and Preparation H hemorrhoid cream.[13]

In 1929, a Greek immigrant's dream came true when he opened what became a long-lasting regional restaurant chain. Nicholas D. Sarakatsannis (1900–1984) arrived in the United States in 1914 and worked in various restaurants, including Cincinnati's Empress Chili. In a small front room at 733 Monmouth Street in Newport, in 1929 he started Dixie Chili, Northern Kentucky's first chili parlor.[14] He sold 9 gallons of chili on his first day in business; today, an estimated 150 gallons are prepared daily for the company's three locations (Covington, Newport, and Erlanger),[15] with Dixie's canned products shipped worldwide. Dixie was soon followed by other chili parlor chains in the region, such as the extremely popular Skyline and Gold Star, as well as several "mom and pop" operations, such as Covington Chili. The 1930s also saw the first White Castle restaurant open in the region, at 825 Madison Avenue in Covington. In the 1990s, that company opened a distribution center along Madison Pike in South Covington.

In 1929, Covington's L. B. Wilson started WCKY, Northern Kentucky's first commercial radio station, one of the first in the United States.[16] While commercial stations were relatively new, amateur radio also had early roots in the Commonwealth. The world's first mass exhibition of radio transmission and receiving occurred on January 1, 1902, in Murray, Kentucky, when Nathan Stubblefield transmitted his son's voice about one mile to an audience of roughly 1,000 people.[17] Radio was possibly the greatest invention since the wheel, allowing mass communication for the first time in human history. By 1932, it was estimated that 64 percent of the population of the United States owned a radio; and in 1950, even after television had begun to gain in popularity, 40 million Americans, or about 94 percent of the population, listened to radio.[18] Northern Kentucky was later home to other important radio stations, such as Maysville's WFTM (still operating with both AM and FM stations); WCVG (which has changed hands and formats numerous times and is currently a gospel station); Newport's WNOP (for decades a jazz-oriented station, now a Catholic-based religious station); WNKU (based on the campus of Northern Kentucky University until 2017); WNKR (based in Williamstown–Dry Ridge and in 2019 a country station); and WZIP (no longer on the air, its tower still standing alongside Interstate 71/75 at Goebel Park in Covington).[19]

By the mid-1930s, several men who were successful in the local bootlegging game had opened new businesses, mainly in Newport, and each of these establishments included illegal gambling. Pete Schmidt, one of George Remus's original henchmen, opened the Glenn Hotel on Monmouth and would later open the Beverly Hills Country Club just south of Newport. Buck Brady ran the Primrose Club in present-day Wilder. Other successful clubs included the Flamingo, the Alibi, the

Bluegrass Inn, Grandview Gardens, Guys and Dolls, the Latin Club, the Merchant's Club, the Tropicana, and the Yorkshire in Newport; and the Kentucky Club, the Golden Horseshoe, the Lookout House, and the Press Club in Kenton County.[20] Mafia groups from both New York and Cleveland entered the region at this time and took over the more successful clubs. Generally, owners would be given an ultimatum: they could stay on as managers, but the Mafia would receive the profits from the business. Those who refused would often watch their clubs burn to the ground or, in very rare instances, they themselves would simply disappear. By the 1940s, more than forty-five illegal gambling casinos were operating in Kenton and Campbell counties, each controlled by the Mafia.[21] While most of the clubs were dark and dingy dives, one drew crowds from the entire Midwest, due mainly to the nationally known entertainers who performed there. The Beverly Hills Club (later known as the Beverly Hills Country Club) hosted such names as Frank Sinatra, Dean Martin, Jerry Lewis, and Marilyn Monroe, and unlike many of the illegal establishments, offered "fair," not "fixed," gambling. The Mafia did not stop with complete control of the gambling clubs; prostitution was taken over as well. While a portion of most of the women's income had always gone to their "managers," these men were now paying a good portion of their income to the mob. So brazen was the operation that two houses of ill repute once operated within a block of the Newport police station. There were even "day houses" and "night houses" to accommodate men working various shifts in the region; and at least fifteen brothels were operating in Newport by the mid-1930s. Prohibition ended in 1933, but by then the damage was done. Newport had been completely overtaken by the Cleveland Syndicate, and their strong-arm control over Northern Kentucky would continue well into the 1970s.

One friend of the Mafia, though there was likely no mutual respect, was John Thompson (1860–1940). Thompson was born in the historic Southgate House (present-day 24 East Third Street in Newport), and his ancestors are a true who's who of Newport history; they include General James Taylor, Nathaniel Southgate Shaler, and Dr. Louise Southgate. Thompson eventually reached the rank of brigadier general, but his claim to fame is due to his later accomplishments. After World War I, he started the Auto-Ordnance Company, and in 1919 he

Newport's Flamingo Casino. Courtesy Kenton County Public Library, KY.

developed the Thompson Machine Gun, or what became known as the tommy gun.[22] A historic marker stands outside the Southgate House to commemorate his achievements.

Meanwhile, Clara Rich opened a restaurant along Dixie Highway in Erlanger, mainly to feed the local tobacco and railroad workers.[23] From its earliest beginnings, the Colonial Cottage was known for its fried chicken, meatloaf, and wonderful cream pies. Rich later sold the business, and in 1987 a new, larger building was erected. The restaurant has changed hands since, but remains a favorite dining location. In recent years, Colonial Cottage has become one of the leading servers of goetta, a German-inspired breakfast food found only in the Greater Cincinnati–Northern Kentucky region. Made of pork, steel-cut oats, and spices, the product is typically manufactured in a loaf, which is cut into slices and fried in a similar fashion to sausage patties. Gliers Meats in Covington is by far the leader in production, with nearly one million pounds packaged annually, representing 99 percent of all goetta consumed in the United States.[24]

Covington-born Haven Gillespie (1888–1975) grew up on Third Street between Madison and Russell, and dropped out of school in the fourth grade. He eventually worked for the *Cincinnati Times-Star,* but also entertained local audiences as a singer-songwriter, mainly as the opening act for other performers. In his early twenties, he had some success with songs such as "You're Just the Girl I've Met in My Dreams" and "When I Am Gone," but in 1925 his "Drifting and Dreaming" was a national success. He eventually wrote songs performed by Frank Sinatra, Dean Martin, and Louis Armstrong. Gillespie's career peaked in 1934, when he teamed with friend and music composer John Coots. Gillespie wrote his memorable lyrics after overhearing a mother scold her unruly child that Christmas was fast approaching and he'd better behave. Gillespie and Coots's "Santa Claus Is Coming to Town" sold 100,000 copies of sheet music and 30,000 records in less than twenty-four hours and remains a holiday favorite.

With cities expanding and the population growing, so were traffic and pollution. In the 1930s, several summer resorts opened throughout the region. At Latonia Lakes, for example, 900 cottage sites were sold beginning in 1931 in the small community located just east of Taylor Mill Road near Hands Pike. With lakes for fishing, boating, and swimming, the resort was destined to become a long-lasting recreational spot for urban residents wanting to get away from the inner-city noise and dirt. Other similar resorts included the White Villa Country Club (Decoursey Pike in southern Kenton County); Bethel Grove (Visalia); Crystal Lake (Ryland); Ryland Lakes Country Club; and Martz's Grove (Ross, Kentucky). Many of these resorts, unfortunately, suffered financially after the onset of World War II.

While white families enjoyed the luxury of living wherever they wanted, black people and other minorities in the urban centers of Covington and Newport were being greatly discriminated against, unknowingly being funneled into specific neighborhoods within those cities through a practice known as "redlining." The term refers to various policies developed by the Home Owners Loan Association, created in 1933 by the Franklin Roosevelt administration to reduce home foreclosures during the Great Depression, and later institutionalized by the 1937 US Housing Act, which established the Federal Housing Association (FHA). These federal agencies determined whether areas were deemed unfit for investment by banks, insurance companies, savings and loan associations, and other financial service companies. Unfit areas were physically demarcated with red shading on maps; in contrast, zones that were to receive preferential lending status were marked with green shading. Over many decades, neighborhoods that local banks deemed unfit for investment were left underdeveloped or in disrepair. Loans for new business ventures in these areas, even those on a small scale, were commonly rejected outright. When existing businesses failed, new ones were not allowed to replace them, often leaving entire city blocks empty and crumbling. This discriminatory practice was almost universal across the country well into the 1950s.[25]

The Dixie Terminal opened in Cincinnati in 1921, and suddenly commuting across the Ohio River from Northern Kentucky became easier than ever. Green Line streetcars and, later, motorized buses carried thousands of commuters across the Roebling Suspension Bridge. On the Cincinnati side, a ramp (signed for bus traffic only) took these vehicles overtop Fort Washington Way and into the second floor of the large brick structure. Once inside the terminal, riders would disembark as other buses were being loaded with return passengers. Although working in Cincinnati was already a common practice for Kentuckians, the opening of the Dixie Terminal resulted in even more Kentucky residents taking jobs in Cincinnati (and to a far lesser degree, Cincinnatians moving to jobs in Kentucky).

26

The 1937 Flood and World War II

Northern Kentucky suffered through many floods, and will likely endure others, but none devastated the region more than the Great Flood of 1937. Over the course of ten days, the Ohio River swelled to 79.99 feet at Cincinnati, more than 27 feet above flood stage.[1] With a wetter than average January, the Ohio River stood at 70.4 feet on January 28, with predictions that it would crest at 72 feet. A day later it was at 72.8 and still rising. By then, as many as 15,000 Northern Kentucky residents had already been forced from their homes.[2] Floodwaters had closed Lunken Airport (Cincinnati Municipal Airport), and eventually only the top of the control tower remained visible. Many of the bridges connecting Kentucky to Ohio were closed, leaving only the Roebling Suspension Bridge open, but only for the transportation of vital supplies. By the first part of February, special permits were needed to cross. Raging floodwaters broke electrical cables, sparking a fire in the Camp Washington area of Cincinnati. Gasoline from breached fuel tanks at the Standard Oil storage plant nearby quickly fueled the flames. Thirty-five fire departments converged, including help from as far away as Columbus, Ohio. The fire itself caused an estimated $2 million in damages over three miles of Cincinnati.[3] Police lines were drawn on the perimeters of Covington and Newport to stop people who came from the outlying areas to stare at the incredible sight.[4]

As the flood disaster reached epic proportions, President Franklin Roosevelt declared a state of emergency and ordered government agencies to respond in "war-time" fashion.[5] National Guard troops supplemented local police forces, and the New Jersey Coast Guard arrived with small cutters to navigate the city streets. When the floodwaters finally

(*Above*) The Great Flood of 1937 and the Covington courthouse. Courtesy Kenton County Public Library, KY. (*Below*) Flood survivors in a canoe outside the Newport courthouse. Courtesy Kenton County Public Library, KY.

began to recede, many residents throughout the region had to continue with water rationing and without electricity for weeks. Truckloads of food and supplies were sent to Cincinnati and Northern Kentucky from the entire Midwest. In the end, Northern Kentucky communities suffered more than $1 million in damages, and 50,000 residents were left homeless, and more than 150 were killed.[6] In addition, 55 percent of Newport was under water, 60 percent of Dayton, 40 percent of Bellevue, 20 percent of Covington, and 37 percent of Ludlow. Bromley was an island completely surrounded by water, and the towns of Silver Grove, Melbourne, and Rabbit Hash were completely covered.[7]

Sadness turned to delight in 1939, especially for the region's children, when Bill Martin opened Johnny's Toys along Decoursey Pike in Latonia. The store quickly became the premier place to shop for toys, models, train sets, dolls, and board games. The store eventually relocated to the Latonia Shopping Plaza. Over the years, Johnny's became a small regional chain, with stores in Greenhills and Norwood, Ohio, while the main store moved to Howard Litzler Drive. Possibly its most popular feature was the "birthday castle." Children who were registered would receive a postcard on their birthday with a key they could use to enter a large castle within the store. Once inside, they could select from one of the hundreds of free gifts. In the early 2000s, and with the opening of mega chains like Toys "R" Us, the popular family-run business closed. Today the site is a children's play center called Totter's Otterville, operated by a relative of Johnny's. In earlier days, fine toys were often sold in some of the better hardware stores and five-and-dimes, such as Federle's general store and Hart's Hardware in Newport, the Klingenberg chain of hardware stores, and Landwehr's Hardware in Covington.

In 1941, area horse-racing fans applauded a local jockey who had achieved greatness. Edward "Eddie" Arcaro (1916–1997) was born in Cincinnati and was raised in both Newport and Covington. He dropped out of school at age thirteen and galloped horses at the original Latonia Racecourse, with hopes of becoming a jockey.[8] He went to Mexico, where there was no age restriction for jockeys, and lost forty-five races before his first win. He moved back to the United States when he turned sixteen and became one of the winningest jockeys of all time. He remains the only two-time winner of America's Triple Crown, with mounts on Whirlaway in 1941 and Citation in 1948.

World War II began in Europe when Adolf Hitler's German army invaded Poland. Most Americans wanted the United States to stay out of the war, but in 1940 a draft was instituted in order to build up America's armed forces. The Americans were suspicious of the Japanese but assumed that if they would strike, they would do so against US bases in the Philippines. As a result, reinforcements and supplies were sent there, including the 38th Tank Company from Covington, which became part of the 192nd Tank Battalion.[9] When the Japanese instead launched a surprise attack on Pearl Harbor in Hawaii on December 7, 1941, Kenton County's William Richardson was aboard the battleship *Arizona* when it was hit by a bomb that detonated its powder magazine and sank the ship. Richardson was among the 1,177 men killed.[10]

The United States needed to retaliate, and Bracken County's Captain Thomas Cline was placed in charge to test the idea of launching land-based bombers from aircraft carriers. His efforts, along with those of many others, were behind the successful raids on Tokyo in April of 1942.[11] The United States then began a series of island-hopping raids to cut off Japanese supply lines. Campbell County's Edward Ahrens was among the many Marines who went ashore at Guadalcanal, but was killed in action. Owen County's Willis Augustus Lee Jr. commanded the battleship division that engaged and beat the Japanese naval force sent to protect the islands. US forces soon began building airfields, naval facilities, and supply depots on those islands. On New Caledonia, Kenton County's John Herndon, an African American with the Navy Seabees, helped build a large air and supply base, while Campbell County's Charlie Tharp worked with the Seabees in the Marshall Islands.[12] Bracken County's John Capito earned a Silver Star and Purple Heart for driving a bulldozer across a creek under fire in order to clear a path for advancing tanks and infantry.[13] Kenton County's Lawrence Keller was a cryptologist decoding Japanese messages, and Leroy Waller was an engineer who helped build the Burma Road. Franklin Runyon Sousley (1925–1945) was born at Hill Top in Fleming County and was killed in action during the Battle of Iwo Jima. He is best known for being one of the six flag raisers atop Mount Suribachi on February 23, 1945, as shown in the iconic photograph *Raising the Flag on Iwo Jima.* And the USS *Kenton,* named for Kenton County, Kentucky, was part of the largest amphibious invasion of the Pacific war against the island

Iconic Iwo Jima photograph depicting (from left to right) Ira Hayes, Harold Schultz, Michael Strank, Rene Gagnon, Franklin Sousley, and Harlon Block. Associated Press/Joe Rosenthal.

of Okinawa. Alvin C. Poweleit (1908–1997) was a resident physician at Covington's Saint Elizabeth Hospital before joining the US Army Reserves as a captain in 1937. He became the medical officer of Kentucky's newly formed 192nd Tank Battalion and served in the war in the Philippines, where he saved many lives. After the war, he returned to Northern Kentucky, where he established a successful medical practice specializing in ear, nose, and throat treatment.[14]

In the European war, Germany was initially seen as a more important threat than Japan by President Franklin Roosevelt, and the first American troops landed in England in January 1942.[15] Among them was Piner's Jesse Auton, who evaluated sites for potential air bases for the newly formed 8th Air Force. Owen County's Gerald Johnson was an American ace, chalking up eighteen victories by the end of the war. By this time, German submarines had advanced to the eastern coast of the United States, and Owen County's Evan Yancy, later an admiral, commanded the destroyer USS *Clemson* and modified its equipment to better detect the enemy's submarine depth, enhancing the success of antisubmarine operations.[16] The first major action Americans were involved with in Europe was the invasion of North Africa in November 1942. Covington's 106th Coastal Artillery Battalion fought in the battle of Kasserine Pass and later participated in the invasion of Sicily, as did the 103rd Automatic Weapons Battalion, a National Guard unit from Covington. In June 1944, Allies launched the invasion at Normandy, and Northern Kentuckians fought there on land, at sea, and in the skies. By the war's end, 589 Northern Kentucky soldiers, sailors, and marines were listed as either killed or missing.[17]

On the home front, Northern Kentuckians experienced the rationing of such materials as gasoline, rubber, sugar, and meat.[18] As both men and women went off to war, many women left the home to work in war plants. Companies involved in war production in the region included Newport Steel and the Wadsworth Watchcase Company of Dayton, both of which began making shell casings and machine guns. Many Kentuckians also went across the river to work at the Curtiss-Wright aircraft plant, the Crosley Corporation, and other firms. As for the military, the Fort Thomas Military Reservation served as an induction center to process many of the soldiers as they joined.[19]

On a lighter note, a unique opportunity became available for young women as a direct result of World War II. With young servicemen away fighting, Chicago Cubs owner Philip Wrigley devised a plan to organize a professional baseball league for women, and the All-American Girls Professional Baseball League (AAGPBL) was born. While hundreds of girls tried out for the various teams, only a few were selected. Covington-born Patricia "Pat" Scott (1929–2016) traveled to Wrigley Field and not only made the league but enjoyed a successful, although short-lived, career. In 1952, Scott pitched for the Fort Wayne Daisies when they defeated the Rockford Peaches in the season championship. The 1992 hit movie *A League of Their Own,* starring Geena Davis, Madonna, and Tom Hanks, portrays that season. In 1988, the National Baseball Hall of Fame in Cooperstown, New York, honored the AAGPBL, unveiling a permanent exhibit called "Women in Baseball," which includes a photo of Scott pitching for the Daisies.[20]

The need for a new airport to serve the Greater Cincinnati area was made clear by the late 1930s, also as a result of the war. Lunken Airport on Cincinnati's east side was hindered by continuous fog issues, as well as constant flooding. In addition, leading up to World War II, the US Army Corps of Engineers was caught with virtually no paved runways except at civilian airfields.[21] A national airbase program was started, and soon more than 300 airports were built or improved using federal funds. The land, however, had to be provided by local governments. The search was on for a replacement for Lunken. Soon level farmland in rural Boone County was selected and approved by elected officials in Boone, Kenton, and Campbell counties. In May 1943 groundbreaking ceremonies commenced, and the official grand opening of what was to be known as the Greater Cincinnati Airport took place on October 29, 1943, with an estimated 50,000 people attending.[22] The airport has grown significantly from its early days, from a little over 300,000 passengers per year in 1947 to over 20 million in 2019. With the designation CVG, representing Covington (the largest city near the airport at the time), the Greater Cincinnati–Northern Kentucky International Airport is now a major hub for both Delta Airlines and DHL Worldwide Express, a package and freight overnight carrier.[23]

The opening of the airport was the second news event of the year that brought attention to rural Boone County, Kentucky. On August 17, 1943, Karl Kiger, vice-mayor of Covington, was killed along with his six-year-old son at the family's summer home outside Florence.[24] His wife was also shot but survived. Their sixteen-year-old daughter, Joan Kiger, was convicted of murder, but was later acquitted, being declared insane by the court. Rumors and conspiracy theories, however, surrounded the event for many decades.[25]

The year 1943 also brought the opening of an unusual but greatly successful business in Northern Kentucky. John Lawrence Griffin moved to Falmouth, purchased an old pickup truck, and began picking up dead farm animals and selling them to rendering plants in Ohio. His family later built its own processing plant in Pendleton County and began production of mainly fertilizer. Today, the multimillion-dollar Griffin Industries operates thirty locations in fourteen states, with a fleet of 1,100 trucks and trailers and over 900 employees.[26]

Marianne Theater, Dayton, Kentucky.

Movie theaters continued to thrive into the 1940s, with as many as fifty movie houses operating in Northern Kentucky at one time. Favorites included Dayton's Marianne and Dayvue; Fort Mitchell's Four Star Dixie; Newport's State and Hippodrome; Covington's Madison and Liberty; Maysville's Russell; and Falmouth's Pastime. Towns such as Carrollton and Williamstown also had their own theaters. In addition, the region's first drive-in theater opened in May of 1947. The Florence Drive-In was situated about a quarter-mile southeast of the intersection of Turfway Road, US 42 and US 25. It was followed by the Dixie Gardens Drive-In, located along Dixie Highway in what is now Fort Wright; the Pike-27 Drive In, situated along US 27 in Campbell County; and Dayton's Rivervue Drive-In, located along KY 8 just east of the city limits.[27] Other drive-in theaters existed at Carrollton and Maysville. With segregation still in full swing, many theaters had separate entrances for black patrons. On Covington's east side, two theaters later opened exclusively for blacks, while public parks, playgrounds, and public transportation remained segregated.

The Green Derby Restaurant opened in Newport in 1947 and

Green Line bus in Cincinnati, Ohio. Note the Dixie Terminal to the upper right. Courtesy Kenton County Public Library, KY.

quickly became a regional icon. Over the years, it has become well known for its cream pies, one-of-a-kind potato puffs, hot slaw, and one of the best fish sandwiches anywhere.[28] It remains open and is a frequent stop for Bengals and Reds players, local politicians, and celebrities.

Northern Kentucky's Green Line transit system reached its peak in 1946, with a record 41 million passengers.[29] That year the company also reached a deal with the board of the airport in Boone County to provide scheduled bus service from downtown Cincinnati. After World War II, the company converted all of its electric streetcars to motorbuses, and in 1947 the last streetcar in Campbell County, the Number 11–Fort Thomas route, became a motorbus operation. The final run of the last electric streetcar in all of Northern Kentucky, the Number 1, Fort Mitchell route, took place on July 2, 1950. Green Line buses continued to operate in Northern Kentucky until November 1972, when the Transit Authority of Northern Kentucky (TANK) was established. In 2019 TANK operates numerous bus routes throughout the region, including the Southbank Shuttle, which runs between the riverfronts of Bellevue, Newport, Covington, and Cincinnati.[30]

27

The Gourmet Strip, Civil Rights, and Urban Flight

By 1950, millions of travelers from Michigan to Florida utilized the Dixie Highway (US 25) through Northern Kentucky. As a result, dozens of restaurants opened along the stretch from Covington to just south of Williamstown. A similar trend occurred along KY 17, US 42, and US 27, but the eateries along Dixie Highway were far more successful, and that road became known as the "gourmet strip." Many of these establishments offered gambling during the heyday of that vice in the region. Some of the more popular restaurants (from Park Hills running south) were the White Horse Tavern, the Town and Country, the Old Mill Grill, Lookout House, Oelsner's Colonial Tavern, the Hearthstone, Robertson's, the Dixie Tea Room, Stevie's Clubhouse, Retschulte's Five Mile House, the Roundup Club, the Cabana, the Colonial Cottage, the Dixie Club, the Caintuckee Grill, and Williamstown's Halfway House.[1] The elimination of widespread illegal gambling in the 1960s, along with the opening of Interstate 75 in 1963, which routed drivers away from the state highways and onto the "superhighways," or "freeways," resulted in the eventual closing of most of these businesses. In 2019, only a few of the original "gourmet strip" establishments remain. The Town and Country is now the Garden of Park Hills reception hall, the Old Mill Grill building is now Chef Barone's catering, the Dixie Tea Room is now Greyhound Grill, and Retschulte's Five Mile House became Barleycorns. The Colonial Cottage and the Dixie Club remain much as they were decades earlier.

Although television sets were produced well before World War II, few American homes had that luxury until after the war. In Northern Kentucky, Cincinnati-based broadcasting stations have always provided the region's local programing. Cincinnati, in fact, topped the nation in the number of live, local programs being aired in the 1950s. Popular shows on WLWT included *Midwestern Hayride,* the *Ruth Lyons Show,* the *Bob Braun Show,* and the *Paul Dixon Show,* each with live audiences. WCPO's *Uncle Al* invited children into the studio for games and prizes, as did WKRC's *Skipper Ryle.* Bob Shreve played Lucky the Clown and Roger the Robot on *Uncle Al,* and later Shreve hosted the long-running *All Night Theater,* sponsored by the Schoenling Brewery. WXIX came on board in 1968 and featured *Larry Smith's Cartoon Club* in the afternoons. A puppeteer, Smith featured such characters as Hattie the Witch and Snarfie the Dog. Another popular program on WXIX was *Scream-In,* where the wildly dressed Cool Ghoul (Dick Von Hoene) hosted a late-night horror film every Saturday. Later, television shows were generally syndicated from New York and Los Angeles, and nearly all locally produced shows ended. For news, WCPO's Al Schottelkotte was by far the most trusted and most watched, anchoring the 6:00 p.m. and 11:00 p.m. newscasts for nearly thirty years.

Several major fires occurred in Northern Kentucky in the 1950s. On February 15, 1950, the Covington Paper and Woodenware Company at 212 Greenup Street was leveled. Flames spread to neighboring buildings as firefighters attacked the blaze for more than eleven hours. A month later, the 100-year-old Phoenix Hotel in Walton was destroyed. On February 7, 1952, flames erupted inside Lincoln Elementary School in Dayton while more than 300 students were in their classrooms. With previous training and drills, all students and school staff were able to evacuate safely, but the building was completely destroyed. On March 21, 1956, most of the tiny town of Milford, along KY 19 in Bracken County, was annihilated by flames. Fire departments from Cynthiana, Augusta, and Brooksville assisted, but the post office and six businesses were lost. And on September 2, 1957, flames hit the Perry and Derrick Company on Lindsey Street in Dayton. Fueled by exploding paint and thinner cans, the building burned in dramatic fashion.[2]

The early 1950s also brought the country's involvement in the Korean War (1950–1953), and Northern Kentuckians served in every branch of the armed forces during this conflict. Some volunteered, some were drafted, and some who had been in World War II were recalled to active duty. The highest-ranking officer from the region was Jesse

Auton, an Air Force brigadier general from the Piner area of Kenton County, who served as director of fighter operations for the Strategic Air Command. Of the 868 Kentuckians killed in action, 69 were from the northernmost counties.[3]

Back home, the 1950s saw the start of one of the most successful businesses in the region when S. David Shor started the Duro Bag Manufacturing Company in Ludlow. Other plants opened in Covington and Florence; but the company's major expansion took place in the 1970s, when operations began in Florida, Texas, Wisconsin, and New Mexico. The company remains the largest supplier of paper bags in North America, operating twelve plants with more than 2,500 employees.[4]

A. L. Heger had started a nursery and landscaping company in Lakeside Park back in 1929, and later added a farm on Spruce Drive in Florence to stock the nursery. Andy Biedenharn worked for Heger for several years, and in 1955 Biedenharn purchased the Florence business when Heger passed away. Andy's son, Jerry Biedenharn, began working there when he turned fourteen and bought the business in 1972. Jerry's children, Jeff and Jody Biedenharn, took over in 2007. As of 2019 Dixie View Nursery, now on Eads Road in Crittenden, remains one of the more successful operations of its kind in the region. Back in 1939, Heger began building a nativity scene each year for Western-Southern Life Insurance Company, which was put on display first at Lytle Park and then in Eden Park in Cincinnati. When the Biedenharns took over the business, they continued in Heger's footsteps. During the Christmas season of 2018 the seventy-ninth display was constructed, certainly one of the longest-running Christmas traditions in the entire region. Other favorite nurseries in Northern Kentucky include Ammon Nursery, opened in 1950 by Dick and Shirley Ammon and located along Camp Ernst Road in Boone County; and Maddox Garden Center and Landscaping, opened around 1983 along Dixie Highway just south of Weaver Road.

The Civil War officially abolished slavery, but it did not end discrimination against black people. They continued to endure the devastating effects of racism, and by the 1950s African Americans had had more than enough of prejudice and violence against them.[5] They, along with many white citizens, began an unprecedented fight for equality that spanned more than two decades. The civil rights movement is a broad term encompassing the strategies, groups, and social movements in the United States whose main goals were to end racial segregation and discrimination against African Americans. Locally, William Fouse, principal of Covington's William Grant High School, and William Humphrey, principal at Maysville's John G. Fee High School, both served as presidents with the Kentucky Negro Educational Fund. The National Association for the Advancement of Colored People (NAACP) had offices in Northern Kentucky for many years. In addition, a local branch of the Congress for Racial Equality (CORE), under the leadership of Reverend Joseph Garr, put pressure on local governments and businesses, especially in Covington, to hire more blacks and to pay those already employed a fair wage.[6] Between 1954 and 1970, protests nationwide often produced crises, but also brought about productive dialogue between activists and government authorities on the federal, state, and local levels. Boycotts, sit-ins, and marches took place across the country, especially in the South. As a direct result, several new laws were enacted. For example, the Civil Rights Act of 1964 expressly banned discrimination based on race, color, religion, sex, or national origin in employment practices; it ended unequal application of voter registration requirements; and it prohibited racial segregation in schools, at the workplace, and in public accommodations. Four years later, the Fair Housing Act of 1968 banned discrimination in the sale or rental of housing. While a wave of inner-city riots undercut some support from the white community, the movement was successful overall in bringing at least some sense of respect and equality to a long-discriminated-against race.

Certainly the most divided issue with the new civil rights laws had to do with schools. After the 1954 ruling that segregated schools were unconstitutional, local school districts were required to integrate black students with white. While heated discussions took place at various board meetings throughout the region, for the most part the process of integration was fairly smooth throughout Northern Kentucky, mainly because blacks made up such a small percentage of total students in area school districts.[7] In fact, many schools in the outlying areas of Boone, Kenton, and Campbell counties had no black students at all.[8]

In Covington, however, things were much different. The school board and most administration officials were openly hostile to the whole action. Surprisingly, so were the majority of both black and white parents. They resented the federal government's inserting itself and imposing its will at the local level when both races were quite content with the way things had been working.[9] Parents of students at the all-black Lincoln Grant School had typically attended the school themselves, knew the teachers well, and were quite satisfied with both the quality of the school and their children's education. In the end, the decision to close that school and integrate all-white Holmes High School was a federally enforced decision rather than one willingly made by the local school board. Once at Holmes, these black students—a lopsided minority of the student body—became lost in the shuffle. Few black teachers relocated there, few black students immediately involved themselves in sports and other activities, and the cafeteria became completely segregated. Nonviolent protests ceased, and racial tensions soared within the school and community. Fistfights between students were frequent. On February 19, 1970, Principal Richard Williams, along with several teachers and students, were assaulted in the halls of the senior high building by a gang of twenty-six black students who had obviously planned the attack.[10] The victims sustained only minor injuries, but the black students were immediately suspended from school. In the aftermath, the student gang delivered a list of nineteen requests to the Covington school board, which they demanded be met before they would consider returning to class. The organized students were upset with the low number of black teachers; the lack of black history or heritage being taught; and the fact that no blacks had been accepted on the cheerleading squad or basketball team. They also wanted a Black Student Union organized. Although the board saw most of their demands as frivolous, they did address the lack of black teachers, stating that many of the teachers at Lincoln Grant had chosen not to transfer or retired within the first year of integration, and that few black teachers were graduating from college with teaching degrees. Racial tensions continued at Holmes well into the late 1970s. Not surprisingly, white parents began looking into private schools for their children or moved to districts out of the city.[11] They fled the inner city to gated communities and sprawling subdivisions in the suburbs and never looked back. Far less documented is the fact that many black families, those with the leverage to get out of the inner city, often did the same.[12]

While it seemed like a great idea on paper, many now in Washington, including some earlier proponents of the idea, later admitted publicly that forced integration was not working and that the emphasis should actually be on improving neighborhood schools wherever people lived.[13] One aim of integration was to provide better-quality education to black students enrolled in what were often seen as academically inferior schools, the overall hope being that widespread neighborhood diversity would soon follow.[14] Unfortunately, the overall quality of classroom instruction fell off markedly in many districts. Often white students were required to repeat material learned in earlier grades because teachers found that the black students had not yet received it. While there was a slight improvement toward a healthier racial composition in schools into the early 1980s, a drastic reversal followed. In 2019, America's schools are still as racially divided as ever, income inequality is growing, and mass incarceration has hobbled an entire generation of young black men.[15] In retrospect, the lesson learned is that institutions do not integrate; people do.

One national trend that went hand in hand with the civil rights movement was urban flight, a social phenomenon that resulted in the mass exodus of families from the inner cities into the suburbs.[16] This trend began in Northern Kentucky in the late 1950s, but its true impact on Covington and Newport was not fully realized until the late 1970s and beyond. In Covington, especially, the process began as a direct response to growing racial tensions and the forced integration of the public school system. Two other factors, however, are often overlooked by historians. Many families, both white and black, simply wanted homes with larger yards, cleaner air, and safer streets with less traffic—leaving without any racial motivation whatsoever. Families who lived in what were once quiet neighborhoods, such as Peaselburg and Lewisburg, for example, fled not long after the opening of Interstate 75. The so-called baby boom was another common cause. Nationally, about 4 million babies were born each year during the 1950s and 1960s, and in many instances the older homes within Covington and Newport were simply no longer sufficient to accommodate these growing families.[17]

The majority of black families and other minorities had little means to leave the inner city and were forced to remain. Urban flight was soon followed by urban decay. Various neighborhoods in both Covington and Newport, and in lesser degrees at Ludlow and Dayton, experienced tremendous disrepair and neglect. Homes and businesses were abandoned. The depopulation brought about less tax revenue, which in turn brought about decaying infrastructure. Unemployment skyrocketed, as did crime. Real estate values dropped, and the future of the once-thriving inner cities was in serious jeopardy.

At the same time urban flight was taking hold, a major commercial development opened in Newport, which marked the beginning of a several-decade downward slide for the core business tract in that city. On a former orchard owned by the Schneider family, located at present-day Carothers Road and Monmouth Street, ten stores opened their doors on November 16, 1955, at what was Northern Kentucky's first "shopping center," including the first national chains: J. C. Penney's department store, Walgreens drug store, and F. W. Woolworth's "5&10" store. Two regionally successful grocers, Albers and Kroger, as well as two shoe stores and a restaurant also opened at the Newport Shopping Center.[18] While the shopping center was an overall asset to Newport and the region as a whole, businesses along Monmouth Street and elsewhere in the downtown center saw an immediate decrease in revenue, a loss of customers that was never really reversed.

On a more positive note, work began in 1956 on one man's dream for a serene site of refuge and meditation for followers of Christ. Eighteen years earlier, Reverend Morris Coers of Covington's Immanuel Baptist Church had visited the Holy Land and had a vision to replicate Jesus's tomb on local land for those who could not afford to travel abroad. A two-acre plot was located along Covington's Edgecliff Road, and construction began on the Garden of Hope. Over time, a huge Italian-marble statue of Jesus delivering the Sermon on the Mount, a stone Chapel of Dreams modeled after a sixteenth-century Mexican mission, and a carpenter's shop were added. After Coers's death in 1960, the site was cared for by volunteers from the church. With decreasing funds, however, it fell into disrepair during the late 1970s. New volunteers revamped the site, and in 2019 the Garden of Hope continues to greet hundreds of visitors from all across the country each year.[19]

In 1957, a group of Newport church members, fed up with Newport's image and lawlessness, formed the Social Action Committee (SAC). Their goal was to gather evidence of illegal activities in the various clubs and give the material to Commonwealth attorney William Wise.[20] The SAC hoped Wise would present the findings to a grand jury, but that never materialized. The committee could not go to the Kentucky state police, as that option was only available if Kentucky's governor ordered state intervention. Governor A. B. "Happy" Chandler (1878–1991) refused to become involved, however, explaining that Newport's people "had a right to have it dirty."[21] Crime and corruption continued in Newport, at least for the time being.

Two years later, a new business venture opened in Boone County, offering "legal" gambling to many Northern Kentuckians. After the old Latonia Racecourse closed in 1939, Northern Kentucky found itself without a horse-racing track for nearly twenty years. In 1959, however, a new track was built on the outskirts of Florence and was given the Latonia name. The track was quite successful over the next twenty-five years, and in 1986 it was sold to Jerry Carroll and James Thornton, who renamed it Turfway Park. Thornton owned several gas stations and convenience stores in Kentucky, and Carroll had been successful in real estate. Carroll, in fact, owned the property where the track stood as well as over 300 adjacent acres (along present-day Houston Road), and had plans to develop the entire area for commercial use.[22] Under Carroll's control, the track was extremely successful and innovative. In 1994, the Racebook opened, simulcasting races on monitors in the park, allowing patrons to wager on races as far away as Australia—a common practice at tracks worldwide today.[23] Facing stiff national competition, Carroll sold the track in 1999 to a partnership made up of the Keeneland Association and Harrah's Entertainment. The track changed owners again in later years, but remains a popular entertainment spot in the region in 2019.

Back in Newport, the so-called reformer groups never gave up. In 1961, a new group known as the Committee of 500, made up mostly of non-Newport residents, presented to newly elected Kentucky governor Bert T. Combs (1911–1991) a petition with 500 names, demanding the end of illegal gambling, crime, and corruption in their state. Combs considered the problem a local matter, but agreed to study the situation. Meanwhile, the group placed former Cleveland Browns football star and local celebrity George Ratterman on the ballot for sheriff of Campbell County. Ratterman pledged that he could not be bought by organized crime, and the Mafia realized they had a serious problem.

Thoroughbred racing at Turfway Park in 2009. Dwight Brown—Turfway Park.

Mob men Charles Lester and Tito Carinci soon devised a plan to disgrace Ratterman. He was invited to a meeting where he was drugged and then photographed in bed with one of the mob-controlled club's nearly naked showgirls, April Flowers. A simple drug test proved Ratterman's innocence, however, and the incident made national headlines. With clear evidence of corruption in the ranks of several local police officers and other high-ranking officials, Governor Bert Combs had little choice but to launch a full investigation, even sending the Kentucky State Police to take control of the city until the investigation was over. In the end, illegal gambling operations essentially ceased, and many of the mob's leaders left town for Las Vegas, which was just being established at the time. Unfortunately, a separate faction from New York's syndicate entered Newport, and soon the city was overrun with adult bookstores, an X-rated movie cinema, and nightclubs offering nude or seminude dancing.

28

Interstates and Higher Education

Interstate highways (also referred to as expressways or superhighways) completely changed the face of Northern Kentucky beginning in the early 1960s. These massive roadways not only altered the landscape of the region; they also greatly affected the area's population, housing development, employment, and shopping, and are responsible for the later growth of such cities as Dry Ridge and Crittenden in Grant County, Cold Spring and Alexandria in Campbell County, the sprawling subdivisions in Boone County, the industrial parks in Erlanger and Independence, and the overall success of the Greater Cincinnati Airport.[1]

Designated Interstate 75, the first expressway's initial stretch, that being from Covington to Florence, was completed in 1962, and travel all the way to Lexington was made available a short time later. Interstate 71 came a few years after, bringing traffic into the region from Louisville and Columbus. The Brent Spence Bridge, a unique double-deck structure built at what was the mouth of Willow Run Creek in Covington, takes both highways across the Ohio River. Brent Spence, for whom the bridge was named, had retired from the US Senate in 1962 after serving Kentucky for thirty-two years. Currently plans are being made to replace the bridge, which had been considered unsafe and obsolete a few years earlier. This would be the second major alteration since I-75's construction, the first being the relocation of a two-mile stretch from Covington to Fort Wright, eliminating what was once called "Death Hill." Interstate 275, a "bypass" completed around 1979, completely encircles the Greater Cincinnati area and has made travel to southeastern Indiana and the eastern suburbs of Cincinnati much easier. A "spur," designated Interstate 471 and completed around 1981, runs from Cincinnati to Highland Heights. Interstate 75 remains the main corridor through the entire region.[2]

Immediately after the completion of I-75, service stations, fast-food restaurants, and hotels opened at nearly every interchange along the route. Just as quickly, similar businesses along the old thoroughfares, such as Dixie Highway (US 25), the Alexandria Pike (US 27), and the 3-L Highway, began to close due to the sudden drop in business. At Fifth Street in Covington, Quality Inn built an eighteen-story hotel (owned by Radisson Hotels in 2019) with a unique feature. The entire top floor, housing a restaurant with glass exterior walls, rotates, making a full revolution each hour, thereby providing diners with a spectacular view of the Cincinnati skyline and much of Northern Kentucky. At Dixie Highway in Fort Mitchell, the first shopping plaza in Kenton County opened in the late 1950s, featuring a Kroger supermarket and several specialty stores as well as the extremely popular Robertson's Restaurant. Further south, the Drawbridge was a massive motel and convention center complex, serving patrons for many decades before being razed in the early 2000s. Motels and restaurants were also built at Donaldson Road, at US 42, and further points to the south.

Development at exits along I-71 and I-275 was slower in coming, due to the more rural location of those highways. Transformation of the landscape after the completion of I-471, however, was quite swift. In Southgate, acreage across from Evergreen Cemetery was completely developed, initially housing a Drug Emporium. A Jeff Wyler automobile dealership and several other retail establishments sit at that spot in 2019. Much of the hillside between East Tenth Street and Carothers Road was removed for the construction of the Newport Pavilion, a huge shopping center including a Kroger Superstore, Target, T. J. Maxx, Dick's Sporting Goods, and numerous other specialty stores and restaurants. Along the Ohio between Newport and Bellevue, a variety of hotels, condos, and restaurants have opened in recent years, completely transforming the riverfront.

By 1962, Glencoe-born Mary Frances Penick (1931–2004) was nationally known as the singing star "Skeeter" Davis. When she was a teen, her family moved to near Covington, and Skeeter began performing country music with fellow Dixie Heights High School student Betty Jack Davis. As the "Davis Sisters" (they were not related), the duo sang with Flatt and Scruggs on the television program *Kentucky Barn Dance* and seemed to be on the road to stardom when a car crash killed Betty Jack and seriously injured Skeeter. After recovering, Skeeter had a string of solo hits, including "Set Him Free" (1959), "I'm Falling Too" (1960), and "My Last Date with You" (1960). However, her 1962 hit "The End of the World" was by far her biggest, earning her a Gold Record and a lifetime of fame. She became a frequent guest on *The Grand Ole Opry, Hee Haw,* and *American Bandstand* and, years later, a section of KY 22 in Dry Ridge was named in her honor.[3] Kenny Price, nicknamed the "Round Mound of Sound" due to his robust size, enjoyed similar fame in the country music world. Born at 1311 Holman Street in Covington, Price spent most of his childhood on a farm outside Florence. He began singing in school talent shows and for small audiences in honky-tonks and roadhouses in the region, but by the mid-1950s was appearing on *Midwestern Hayride* and the *Arthur Godfrey Show* in New York. Price composed nearly 1,000 songs in his long career, 34 of which became chart singles. He was a regular on *Hee Haw,* displaying not only his musical talents but also his wonderful comedic antics.[4] Taylor Mill's Carly Pearce (b. 1990) was performing at Dollywood six times a day, five days a week, by age sixteen, and later celebrated her first Top 40 hit with "Wasn't That Drunk." In 2017, at the age of twenty-seven, she landed her first number-one single on the country music charts with "Every Little Thing."[5]

In the 1960s, ice skating, roller skating, and bowling were quite popular forms of recreation throughout Northern Kentucky. The Dixie Gardens Ice Bowl, adjacent to the Dixie Gardens Drive-In movie theater in present-day Fort Wright, was likely the most popular place for ice skating. The facility closed in the mid-1980s, not long after the drive-in was vacated. Of course, skating on frozen lakes in the region dates back to the late 1800s. Roller skating existed in the region as early as the 1890s at venues such as Newport's Masonic Hall and the Odd Fellows Hall in Covington. Popular roller-skating establishments in the 1960s and later included Jimmie's Rollerdrome in Elsmere, Lloyd's in Latonia, the Fundome at I-75 and Donaldson Road in Erlanger, Alexandria's Reca Roller Rink, and the Maysville Roller Rink.[6] Bowling had also been a popular sport for decades, but reached its peak popularity from the 1950s into the 1970s. Early alleys included the Highland Pike House in the Peaselburg neighborhood of Covington, where a ten-pin contest was held in May of 1877.[7] Popular lanes during the sport's heyday included Glenn Schmidt's and Walt's Center Lanes in Newport, Bellevue's B&J Lanes and the Bellewood Super Bowl, LaRu Lanes in Highland Heights, Southern Lanes just north of Alexandria, Latonia's Bowlounge and the American Legion Hall, Lookout Bowl in present-day Fort Wright, Florence Bowl, Kenton Lanes and Ten Pin Lanes in Erlanger, Cherokee Bowl in Independence, and Covington's Dixie Bowl. Super Bowl in Erlanger opened in 1999, and years later Star Lanes opened at Newport on the Levee. Bowling alleys also existed in Maysville, Walton, Dry Ridge, and elsewhere.[8] While the popularity of bowling declined after the 1980s, there now seems to be a resurgence taking place. Bellewood, LaRu, Southern, Florence, American Legion, Super Bowl, Double S Entertainment Center in Flemingsburg, and Star Lanes remain in 2019.

The most unusual museum in the region opened in Fort Mitchell in 1963, when William S. Berger founded the Vent Haven Museum, housing his forty-year collection of more than 500 ventriloquist's dummies and supporting memorabilia. Berger died in 1972, and the museum's president, John Brooking, constructed a building in Berger's honor that proudly displays the collection. More than 1,000 people visit the museum each year.[9]

The success of the Greater Cincinnati–Northern Kentucky International Airport unfortunately brought with it several airline disasters over the years. In November 1965, 58 of the 62 people on American Airlines flight 383 were killed when the plane crashed; and, almost exactly two years later, TWA flight 128 crashed, killing 70.[10] In both instances, planes arriving from the north over the Ohio River fell short of the runway, crashing into the steep hillside along KY 8 above the town of Constance. Many years later, in 1983, a fire started by a smoker in a rear restroom caused an Air Canada flight to be diverted to the Kentucky airport while flying to Toronto from Dallas–Fort Worth. Twenty-three people were killed by the toxic smoke filling the cabin before any rescue efforts could be made once the plane landed.[11]

Plane crashes were not the only disasters in Northern Kentucky during the 1960s. On the evening of January 6, 1962, flames struck Highlands Junior High School in Fort Thomas, causing more than

$500,000 in damage. Nearly a dozen of the 118 firefighters on the scene were injured, two seriously. The Avenue Nite Club in Bellevue was hit by fire on March 23, 1963, killing two. This blaze was believed to be started by a discarded cigarette thrown into a trash receptacle just before closing. On March 1, 1964, a tremendous fire swept through the Duro Paper Bag Company in Ludlow. Sixteen nearby homes were damaged, seven of which were total losses. Two hundred firefighters from ten cities fought what was Kenton County's biggest fire to date. And in April of 1968, a series of tornadoes moved across the region, generally from Falmouth to Maysville, causing nearly $4 million in damages. Five people were killed during the storms and more than 150 were injured. Over 200 people were left homeless.[12]

Nationally, 1965 also saw the first major battle between North Vietnamese and United States forces in the Vietnam War. Between 1966 and 1969, more than 543,000 US soldiers fought in the region. Of the 1,103 Kentuckians killed in the war, 109 were from the northern counties. In addition, two remain classified as missing in action: Captain Joseph Shaw Ross from Campbell County and Gary Lee Hall from Covington. The most decorated soldier from the region was Sargent Charles "Chalkie" Fleek of Boone County, who on May 27, 1969, threw himself on a live grenade, thereby saving many others. Due to his extreme heroism, Fleek was awarded the Medal of Honor.

In Carroll County, construction began in 1965 on the Dow Corning chemical plant. What began as a firm with sixty workers with offices inside an old drive-in theater grew to a factory with hundreds of employees. Now encompassing more than 1,600 acres, it is one of the largest silicone materials plants in the world.[13] Gallatin Steel, located just outside Warsaw, is another major corporation in the area. Purchased by Nucor Corporation in 2014 for roughly $770 million, the plant has a total work capacity in 2019 of about 27 million tons.[14]

September 1968 saw the opening of Thomas More College (now Thomas More University) in Crestview Hills, with President Lyndon B. Johnson as a surprise guest.[15] The institution had begun in 1921, when the Sisters of St. Benedict opened the Villa Madonna College on their property in Villa Hills. That school relocated to the St. Walburg Academy property on East Twelfth Street in Covington in 1928. In 1934, the all-male Covington Latin School began offering college-level courses at what they called Thomas More College, at their campus at Eleventh and Madison streets. That school became coeducational in 1945, and enrollment increased to a point that a new campus location was necessary. Although property was originally purchased in Campbell County, another site along Turkeyfoot Road in what is now Crestview Hills was chosen in 1954.[16] Enrollment in the Roman Catholic liberal arts college currently exceeds 2,000.

More groundbreaking ceremonies took place on March 31, 1971, this time in Highland Heights, for the construction of the first building on the new campus of Northern Kentucky University.[17] That school's roots were planted back in 1946, when the University of Kentucky offered extension classes in the region, first at the Trailways bus station and later at First District School, both in Covington. In 1961, classes moved to a new facility in Park Hills, on land once a part of Devou Park.[18] As enrollment increased, the need for a full-scale campus was realized. Today, school enrollment is over 15,000, with a faculty of more than 2,000.[19]

29

Inner-City Decay, Poverty, and the Region's Worst Disaster

By the 1970s, urban flight was rampant in the inner cities of Covington and Newport, and both towns were in the middle of a thirty-plus-year decline. Many residential homes, tenant dwellings, and businesses were left vacant as more and more families fled to the suburbs. As a direct result, the number of families living below the poverty line increased dramatically.

Poverty is certainly nothing new to Northern Kentucky. Throughout this region's history, past generations tried to tackle the problem. While the issue of homelessness is largely ignored in today's world, that was not the case when Covington and Newport were young, growing cities and nearly everyone knew one another. It was not possible to ignore the poor.[1] In the late 1800s, family and friends, as well as local church congregations, were called upon to help care for the indigent, the ill, and the aged. By the mid- to late nineteenth century, poorhouses were being established nationwide, but they quickly proved unsuccessful. Often they were poorly managed and dirty, and they mixed women with men, young with old, and healthy with sick.[2] Kenton County operated a poorhouse in Independence, and the city of Covington had a so-called pesthouse off of Kyle's Lane, which cared for the poor who were sick. By the early twentieth century, Kenton County officials realized that the poorhouse was failing, and in May 1907 they opened a state-of-the-art infirmary located on Glenn Avenue, which was later known as Rosedale Manor (in 2019 known as Rosedale Green, a senior living facility specializing in memory care, rehabilitation, and long-term care).[3] By the late nineteenth century, it was clear that other special services were needed, specifically to care for children: orphans, children who were neglected or abused, those with single parents who had to work, and more. The Saint John's Orphan Society of Kenton County was formed in 1848, and by 1868 had established an orphanage on the outskirts of Covington, what is now the Diocesan Catholic Children's Home on Orphanage Road in Fort Mitchell. Businessman and philanthropist Amos Shinkle (1818–1892) was concerned for poor Protestant children, and in 1880 he and others chartered the Covington Children's Home. First located at Fourteenth and Madison, it was relocated in the 1920s to Devou Park, where it remains today as the Children's Home of Northern Kentucky.[4] Although by the 1960s it appeared that local communities and city leaders had the issue of poverty in check, the problem actually worsened in the following decades.

The 1960s was the last time Covington's population reached over 60,000; it had peaked at 65,252 in the 1930s. Newport's population peaked in the 1950s, with just over 31,000 residents, and Maysville reached a high of 8,652 that same decade. (See Appendix B.) While Maysville experienced some urban flight, that city suffered far less change than Covington or Newport. Population and commercial activity in Covington continued to decline, even after the construction of the Internal Revenue Service (IRS) service center, which brought nearly 3,000 new jobs into the region. Covington's Coppin department store, both Eilerman's stores, and both Louis Marx & Brothers furniture stores closed in the early 1970s, and other stores such as JCPenney and Sears vacated Covington and Newport and relocated to the suburbs.[5] Enrollment in the Covington and Newport school districts decreased dramatically, and new schools such as Conner High School in Hebron (1970) and Scott High School in Taylor Mill (1978) were built to handle the rapid influx of students moving to the suburbs. By the mid-1970s much of the business districts of both Covington and Newport had nearly become ghost towns. Many storefronts remained empty for decades, while others were replaced with far less attractive commercial endeavors, such as tattoo parlors, pawn shops, and cash advance outlets.

In the mid-1970s, Covington officials began plans to revitalize the city, focusing on a small portion of its downtown, specifically the stretch of Pike Street between Madison and Washington. The project, known as Old Towne Plaza, failed miserably. However, with federal grant money and at a location nearer the interstate, the Main Strasse

Carroll bell tower at Goebel Park, Covington.

Village hosted its first Octoberfest a few years later with great success. The neighborhood stretching from the Ohio River to Pike Street and from Interstate 75 to roughly Johnson Street was turned into a German-inspired village with restaurants, taverns, and shops. The Goose Girl fountain (inspired by a Brothers Grimm fairy tale) was added at Sixth and Main Streets, and a tower featuring mechanical, musical fairy-tale figures that revolve in a forty-three-bell carillon was erected at Sixth and Philadelphia streets.[6] Over the years, other festivals have been added, including Mayfest, GoettaFest and Mardi Gras, and thousands visit the village each year. Today, however, Cincinnati's newly developed riverfront entertainment district as well as Newport on the Levee have taken some of the business away from the quaint village. Beginning in the 1970s, Covington also took steps to develop and better define its many unique neighborhoods; and later, with help from a community-driven Center for Great Neighborhoods, signs were installed to denote the city's many unique areas, such as Peaselburg, Austinburg, Kenton Hills, Botany Hills, and Latonia.

Newport's downtown core also went through a major change beginning in the 1970s; some termed it the city's "Second Cleanup." Even after illegal gambling and most Mafia-controlled businesses were chased away in the 1960s, Newport remained a center for vice and prostitution due to the more than twenty bars that offered various forms of nude dancing, bookstores offering explicit adult content, shops with coin-operated peep-show booths, and the Cinema X adult movie theater.[7] Over the years, various city commissioners and mayors ignored the problem, believing that adult entertainment was good for the city. However, others eventually entered the fight and finally made progress against such establishments. The Cinema X and a nearby bookstore were raided several times, and eventually both were permanently closed.[8] New ordinances were also enacted; and, over the years, nude dancing was banned and prostitution, which had been big business in Newport as far back as the early 1800s, was finally erased from Newport's streets. Afterward, Newport's leaders made strategic plans to develop its riverfront and core to focus primarily on "family-friendly" tourism instead of the "sin city" draw of the past.[9] It would take another twenty years, however, before those dreams were fulfilled.

While urban flight negatively affected Northern Kentucky's two largest cities, several other parts of the region experienced great financial gain and tremendous population explosions. In Kenton County, cities such as Erlanger and Independence grew significantly during the 1970s. In Boone County, the opening of a massive shopping mall in 1976 marked the beginning of one of the biggest housing booms in the entire nation. Florence Mall, still Northern Kentucky's largest shopping mall, contained three department stores and 130 specialty shops when it opened its doors. JCPenney and Sears relocated there from Covington, and within a few short years commercial activity along Mall Road and nearby Houston Road brought the opening of literally hundreds of other stores and restaurants. At the mall, a million-gallon water tower stands as a regional landmark. For a short time, the message painted on the tower read "Florence Mall," but the National Highway Beautification Act prohibited advertising a nonexistent entity, and the mall was still a couple of years away from opening. Florence mayor C. M. "Hop" Ewing came up with an idea to slightly alter the sign, and from that point on it has read "Florence Y'all." The Crestview Hills Mall opened

Water tower at Florence Mall, 2017.

many years later, but never had more than a 10 percent occupancy. It was eventually razed, and the open-air Crestview Towne Center has since flourished on the same site. In Erlanger, the massive Showcase Cinemas opened in December of 1974, drawing moviegoers of all ages to the first multiscreen facility in the region. It closed in 2008, however, and was eventually razed, making room for a business park.

As the population grew, and with the construction of new homes, shopping centers, and roadways, cities and counties throughout the region soon realized the need for green space. Boone County eventually became home to the Boone County Arboretum, Boone Cliff State Park, Big Bone State Historic Park, Boone Woods, and various smaller city parks and nature preserves. Many of these include walking/running trails, playgrounds, softball/baseball fields, and basketball courts. Pioneer Park, Middleton-Mills Road Park, Devou Park, Doe Run Lake, and other small-scale parks now serve the residents of Kenton County.

A. J. Jolly and Pendery Sports Park are among Campbell County's largest recreational areas, and other sizable parks have been established in the neighboring counties as well, including Grant County Park in Dry Ridge and Kincaid Lake in Pendleton County. By the 2000s, dog parks became the rage, and several specialty tracts for canines were established in the region, including at Burlington, Newport, and South Covington.

Several golf courses have been established throughout the region as well, and the more popular public courses now include Fairway (New Liberty), Perry Park (Owen County), Sugar Bay (Warsaw), Lassing Pointe (Union), A. J. Jolly (Campbell County), Northern Kentucky Golf Club (Butler), Twin Bridges and Hickory Sticks (California), Boone Links (Florence), Meadowood (Burlington), Devou Park (Covington), Twin Oaks Golf and Plantation Club (Latonia), Kenton Station and Laurel Oaks (Maysville), and the Golf Courses at Kenton County (Independence). Several private members-only clubs exist in the region as well, including Summit Hills, Fort Mitchell, Highland, Triple Crown, Maysville, and Eagle Creek.

One of the region's biggest fires occurred on August 14, 1973, when the Lookout House, a popular dinner theater along the "gourmet strip" and a longtime Northern Kentucky landmark, caught fire in midafternoon. Closed for remodeling at the time, the arson-suspected blaze completely destroyed the business, and flames and smoke could be seen for miles. The Lookout Corporate Center, a multistory office building, now stands at the site.[10] Although the Lookout House fire was spectacular, it paled in comparison to another event that would hit the region just four years later.

On May 28, 1977, the state of Kentucky experienced its worst tragedy since the Civil War, and Northern Kentucky, unfortunately, was home to this disastrous fire. The Beverly Hills Supper Club in Southgate, known as the "Showplace of the Nation," was packed over the Memorial Day weekend. More than 2,000 patrons hoped to have a special night they would always remember. They were not denied.

The club had its beginnings in the 1930s, when it opened as one of many illegal gambling casinos in the area. Run by a Mafia group known as the Cleveland Syndicate from the early 1930s into the 1960s, it gained national attention for its gourmet dining and top-notch entertainment. Celebrities who graced the stage during its heyday included

Frank Sinatra, Dean Martin, Louis Armstrong, and Mel Tormé. After a crackdown on illegal gambling, the club was sold, and new owners revamped the operation. From the early 1970s, the Schilling family ran an extremely successful dinner theater, and a new group of popular entertainers performed in an expanded main showroom.

At around 9:00 that Saturday night, smoke began seeping through the ceiling in one of the smaller party rooms, and waitresses immediately alerted club owners that there was a fire. A mass evacuation of the club followed, but it was hindered by heavy smoke near the front entrance. For many, escape routes followed narrow hallways and out through a kitchen service entrance. Still, nearly all the patrons and staff in the massive club were able to escape with little difficulty, except for those in the main showroom, known as the Cabaret Room. There, guests had just been seated for the first of two shows that night and were enjoying the comedy routine of Tetter and MacDonald, the warm-up act for headliner John Davidson. When a busboy took the stage and gave the warning that everyone should leave, only about one-third of the audience was paying attention; some even thought he was part of the act. Minutes later, flames and smoke entered the large room, cutting off the main means of escape and forcing everyone toward two emergency exits. Then the power went out, and total chaos ensued.

By 10:30 p.m., more than 100 firefighters were on the scene, and futile attempts were being made to rescue anyone still alive. By midnight, over 500 emergency personnel were working the tragedy from as far away as Harrison County, Kentucky, and Blue Ash and Colerain Township in Ohio, manning nearly sixty pieces of firefighting apparatus. By sunrise, more than 100 bodies had been pulled from the smoldering club, and dozens more would be retrieved in the following days. In all, 169 people were killed and nearly 100 were taken to several regional hospitals. The Fort Thomas Armory was used as a makeshift morgue, where for the next few days family members went body to body in search of their loved ones, who had been carefully laid side by side on the gymnasium floor.

Initial reports cited numerous code violations, locked emergency exits, and gross overcrowding as reasons for such a high death toll. Some newspapers erroneously reported that there were as many as 4,000 peo-

Beverly Hills Supper Club fire as seen from the club's driveway. Originally published in the *Kentucky Post*, May 29, 1977. Courtesy Kenton County Public Library, KY.

(*Above*) Bodies scattered on the lawn near the club's chapel. Originally published in the *Kentucky Post*. Courtesy Kenton County Public Library, KY. (*Below*) Fort Thomas Armory becomes makeshift morgue. Originally published in the *Kentucky Post*. Courtesy Kenton County Public Library, KY.

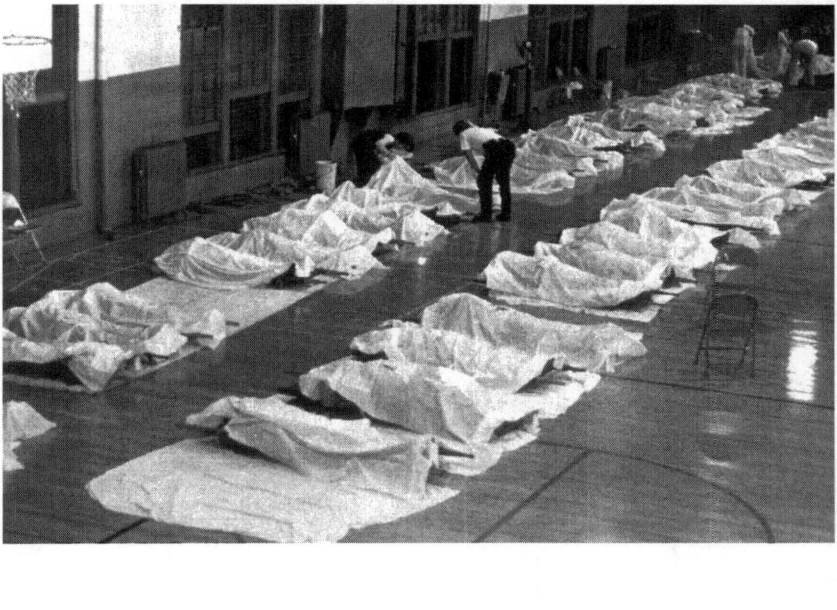

ple in the main showroom. However, a grand-jury investigation quickly proved many of these accusations false. Still, inaccurate facts about the fire circulated through the region for decades, including the "fact" that the fire was caused by faulty aluminum wiring. In reality, no one died as a result of minor code violations; the Cabaret Room was packed, but was not "grossly overcrowded," as there were 1,051 patrons in a room designed to hold 1,000; the only locked exit door was far away from the Cabaret Room and was blocked by fire early in the event; and aluminum wiring was never determined to be the cause in the initial investigation. In later civil suits, aluminum wiring was targeted by a group of attorneys, but no physical evidence was ever introduced to support such findings. Even the actual number of fatalities continues to be falsely reported by the media as 165. It was determined soon after the fire that unborn children would be included in the official death toll and, since four women were pregnant at the time of the fire, the true number of fatalities is, and always has been, 169.

A five-year study was conducted in the early 2000s by nationally recognized fire science experts and a former Kentucky state fire marshal. They concluded that the initial investigation by Governor Julian Carroll and the Kentucky state police had been drastically flawed and that there was a "rush to judgment," simply blaming faulty wiring.[11] During the reinvestigation, it was learned that parts of the club had been bulldozed just two days after the fire; the state police did not permit fire marshals into parts of the club after that Monday following the blaze; only certain pieces of information were made public; and many facts—including the discovery of timers in the rubble and witness statements about suspicious people being in the club the morning of the fire—had been purposely omitted from the official Kentucky state police report. Governor Steve Beshear formed a special task force to look into reopening the case, but that panel included no fire science experts or fire investigators, only lawyers. Forty years after the tragedy, rumors of a conspiracy and/or Mafia involvement remain as strong as they were immediately after the fire.[12]

A historical marker sits at the bottom of the club's original driveway along US 27, about an eighth of a mile south of Interstate 471, and a larger memorial, erected by a group of volunteers, overlooks the interstate from the tragic site. In 2017, during a memorial held in Southgate to commemorate the disaster's fortieth anniversary, plans were announced for the possible construction of a permanent memorial near the site of the tragedy, but as of 2019 no progress has been made toward that goal.

30

Local Sports Figures, and Hollywood Comes to the Midwest

Following the Beverly Hills Supper Club fire, better news arrived later in 1977, when *Sports Illustrated* named Covington-born Steve Cauthen Sportsman of the Year. Cauthen (b. 1960) grew up on his parents' farm at Walton and began galloping horses at age five. He won his first race as a jockey in 1976 at Cincinnati's River Downs, and went on to be that track's most winning rider that year, with a record-setting 120 wins. In 1977, Cauthen was the first jockey in the world to rack up $6 million in winnings with fewer than 300 wins; and, on Affirmed, he became the youngest to win the coveted Triple Crown.[1] He also enjoyed great success in Europe and was inducted into the Racing Hall of Fame during the first year of his eligibility.

Northern Kentucky was home to other prominent sports personalities over the years. Jim Bunning (1931–2017), who went on to serve Kentucky as a congressman, was born in Southgate and enjoyed a seventeen-year career in Major League Baseball. He once pitched a perfect game for the Philadelphia Phillies. Dave Cowens (b. 1948) was born in Covington and raised in Newport, where he attended Newport Catholic High School. He is a seven-time National Basketball Association (NBA) All-Star and, as a player and coach, spent more than forty years in professional basketball. David Justice (b. 1966) was born in Cincinnati, but attended Covington Latin School and Thomas More College. In 1985, he began a long career in professional baseball, playing for the Atlanta Braves, the Cleveland Indians, the New York Yankees, and the Oakland Athletics. Shaun Alexander (b. 1977) was born in Fort Thomas and later attended Boone County High School, where he set many school records. After excelling at the University of Alabama, he became one of the best running backs in the National Football League (NFL), playing most of his career for the Seattle Seahawks. As a head coach at UCLA, John Wooden (1910–2010) won ten National Collegiate Athletic Association (NCAA) national championships in a twelve-year period, including a record seven in a row, and his teams won an NCAA men's basketball record eighty-eight consecutive games. Wooden was named national coach of the year six times. Born in Indiana, Wooden started his coaching career at Dayton High School, Dayton, Kentucky. His first year at Dayton, the 1932–1933 season, marked the only time he had a losing record (6–11) as a coach. A native of Newport, Kentucky, Donna Murphy was one of the most prolific basketball players in Kentucky high school and college basketball. As a player at Newport High School, she earned Kentucky's first official Miss Basketball award in 1976, after averaging 35 points and 20 rebounds. At Morehead State University, she amassed 2,059 points and 1,442 rebounds and set thirteen individual records. Murphy also played professionally and enjoyed a long coaching career for both high school and college teams. Stephen J. Flesch (b. 1967) enjoyed a successful career as a professional golfer, competing on the PGA Tour. Born in Cincinnati, Ohio, Flesch attended Covington Catholic High School in Park Hills, Kentucky. After graduation, he played golf at the University of Kentucky and turned professional in 1990. He had eight professional wins and was featured in the top 50 of the Official World Golf Rankings, reaching a career high of 24th in 2004. Thomas Thacker (b. 1939) played basketball on three national championship teams: in the NCAA (at the University of Cincinnati 1960–1961 and 1961–1962), the NBA (for the Boston Celtics in 1967–1968), and the ABA (for the Indiana Pacers in 1970–1971). Grant County's Arnie Risen (b. 1924) enjoyed a successful career with Ohio State University, leading that team to the NCAA championships in 1944–1945. He also played for the Boston Celtics.

Film crews from Hollywood arrived in Augusta, Kentucky, in 1978 for the filming of a made-for-television miniseries titled *Centennial.* High production costs and other restrictions of shooting in Hollywood and New York had caused moviemakers to look for other alternatives, and the Greater Cincinnati–Northern Kentucky region soon became home to several major motion picture filming sites. *Eight*

Men Out (1987) used Latonia's Railway Museum of Greater Cincinnati as a backdrop. *Lost in Yonkers* (1992) utilized several area neighborhoods, especially in Ludlow. Other movies partially filmed in the region include *Fresh Horses* (1987), *A Rage in Harlem* (1990), *Airborne* (1993), *Milk Money* (1994), *Rabbit Hash: The Center of the Universe* (2004), *The Old Man and the Gun* (2018), *Reprisal* (2018), and *Extremely Wicked, Shockingly Evil and Vile,* a biopic about serial killer Ted Bundy (2019). The highest-grossing movie filmed in Northern Kentucky is *Rain Man* (1988), starring Dustin Hoffman and Tom Cruise. This Oscar-winning film featured scenes inside Pompilio's restaurant in Newport, the Roebling Suspension Bridge, Columbia Parkway in Cincinnati, Evergreen Cemetery in Southgate, Interstate 275 in Boone County, the Greater Cincinnati–Northern Kentucky International Airport, and St. Ann's Convent along KY 8 in Melborne.[2]

Several Northern Kentucky natives have "made it big" in Hollywood over the years. Academy Award winners include Robert Surtees, cinematography; George Clooney, acting; and Bub Asman, editing. Along with Una Merkel, George Clooney and Rosemary Clooney are the region's most well-known film stars. The world premiere of Rosemary's first feature film, *The Stars Are Singing* (1953), was held at the now-historic Russell Theater in Maysville.[3] Her most popular film was undoubtedly *White Christmas* (1954), where she costarred with Bing Crosby, Danny Kaye, and Vera-Ellen. Her brother, Nick Clooney, enjoyed a long career in the local news business, while Nick's son, George Clooney, remains a popular film star. Behind the camera, Anna Bell Ward was a producer of western films in the 1940s, and Covington-born photographer George Hurrell honed his craft shooting a unique style of glamour stills for the stars.[4] Boone County's John Arrasmith, historian and artist, crafted $10,000 worth of American Indian arrows for the Oscar-winning film *Dances with Wolves* (1990).[5] Arrasmith has either acted in or created costumes, weapons, or other Indian artifacts for movies such as *Last of the Mohicans* (1992), *Geronimo* (1993), and *Last of the Dogmen* (1995). Lee Roy Reams (b. 1942) has enjoyed an extremely successful career on Broadway, appearing in such hits as *42nd Street, Hello, Dolly!, Applause,* and *The Producers.* A 1960 graduate of Holmes High School, Reams's dancing and acting skills rewarded him with the honor of performing before several presidents and teamed him

Parade and street dedication in Maysville, early 1953, in honor of Rosemary Clooney. Courtesy www.nkyviews.com.

with such stars as Ann Miller, Ethel Merman, Anne Bancroft, Mitzi Gaynor, and Goldie Hawn.

Maysville, unfortunately, found itself in the national news on July 27, 1980. The strongest earthquake ever recorded to originate within the boundaries of Kentucky occurred that day and was centered near Sharpsburg, Bath County. Its effects were felt throughout the region and as far away as Canada.[6] Maysville was the hardest hit city in Northern Kentucky, where more than 300 buildings received some type of damage.

On October 9, 1980, just before lunchtime on a busy school day, an explosion rocked Simon Kenton High School as workers from UHL&P were working on a natural gas line servicing the school. In just minutes, and thanks to years of fire drills, students and staff were able to quickly evacuate the smoke-filled building. One student, however, was killed in the initial blast. A second explosion occurred just as firefighters from fourteen departments were arriving, injuring twenty first responders.[7] The school was heavily damaged; and, while repairs were being made, students attended nearby Scott High School. The Simon Kenton boys' basketball team, having to practice and play at makeshift locations, miraculously rallied from the tragedy and won the state championship that year.

At Newport, an illegal fireworks factory situated at 938 John Street exploded on April 2, 1981, devastating a six-block area of the city. Two persons were killed and twenty others were injured as debris rained down on the city, causing several small fires. More than 250 structures in Newport received some degree of damage. In Covington four years later, a 118-year-old landmark was lost on May 16, 1985, when lightning struck St. Aloysius Church in the Main Strasse area of town. More than 100 Covington and Fort Mitchell firefighters battled the blaze for hours, but the structure was a complete loss.[8] In September 1986, Covington's Mother of God Church was also hit by fire. As crews were making repairs to the roof and cupola overtop of the sanctuary, welding torches ignited the wooden substructure. Because the fire was discovered immediately, the church was saved.

In early 1981, one family in Independence mysteriously vanished without a trace, leaving neighbors puzzled. Just six months earlier, Martin and Karen Scott, along with their two children, Matthew and Gina, had made their new home in the Beechgrove area of town. Fifteen-year-old Matthew enrolled at Simon Kenton High School, while twelve-year-old Gina went to Twenhofel Middle School. Unbeknownst to their neighbors, Martin Scott had been placed in the US government's new witness protection program two years earlier, and Beechgrove was the family's third relocation. Martin Scott was in fact Henry Hill, one of the most famous mob "rats" in US history, whose life was later portrayed by Ray Liotta in the movie *Goodfellas.* Before the 1980–1981 school year was over, the children got off their bus one afternoon only to be greeted by federal agents. Henry's cover had been blown once again that day, and the family was gone before midnight.[9]

The year 1983 brought the birth of the Kentucky Wool Festival in Falmouth, after community leaders there had searched for a special summer theme that might entice tourism into the county. Kentucky was at one time a leading state in wool production, with Pendleton County among the top producers. The Woodhead family, English immigrants who had first settled in the textile regions of New England, came to

Falmouth in the early 1800s and, soon after the Civil War, opened the Pendleton Woolen Mills, one of many successful businesses during that period. The Kentucky Wool Festival pays homage to an aspect of early Pendleton County economy and heritage, and in 2019 the festival remains an extremely successful event, bringing thousands into Falmouth each year.[10]

The East Newport National Historic District was also established in 1983. Once home to some of Newport's wealthiest citizens, such as Cincinnati-based grocery store founder Barney Kroger and Newport brewery magnate George Wiedemann, the neighborhood consisted mainly of rental properties after families moved to the suburbs. By the late 1980s, however, new families moved into some of the magnificent two- and three-story mansions, and the entire region was rediscovered.

Maysville also saw significant changes beginning in the 1980s. The city limits were extended to include the "top of the hill," and several businesses moved to the outskirts of town, including the hospital, the consolidated school system, and many doctor's offices. The AA Highway, completed in the late 1980s, became home to many of the town's industries and restaurants and quickly became the main artery from the southeast into Newport and the Greater Cincinnati region.

In the late 1980s, the Werner Company of Chicago purchased the Kentucky Ladder Company, located in Carrollton. Originally opened as the Adkinson Brothers Lumber Yard in the 1890s, the company became quite successful, and in 1945 it was purchased and became known as the Rich Ladder Company, a major producer of wooden ladders. In 1966, the company became the Kentucky Ladder Company. After Werner took over, the business became the largest supplier of ladders and climbing products in the world.[11]

The decade of the 1980s would not end without another horrific tragedy. On May 14, 1988, a thirty-five-year-old factory worker, Larry Mahoney, drove his pickup truck the wrong way on Interstate 71 in Carroll County. Between Carrollton and the Trimble County line, near mile marker 40, an intoxicated Mahoney first hit a car and then collided head-on with a school bus filled with children and chaperones returning from an outing at Cincinnati's Kings Island amusement park. Upon impact, the front door of the bus was wedged shut and the gas tank exploded, spewing burning fuel throughout the passenger com-

Police photo after the school bus tragedy near Carrollton, Kentucky, May 15, 1988. Kenton County Historical Society.

partment. While some were able to escape through the rear emergency exit and side windows, most were burned alive. In what was the worst drunk-driving accident in United States history, 27 people were killed (mostly children) and another 34 were injured. Mahoney sustained only minor injuries and served nearly eleven years of his sixteen-year sentence on various charges.[12]

31

Revitalization Explodes in Covington and Newport

By 1990, city leaders in Covington had intensified their plans to change the image of their town from a city of decline to one of progress. As a result, several major developments enhanced the city, especially along the riverfront. Two separate condominium projects were completed on or near Riverside Drive, and later the $110 million, eighteen-story RiverCenter office tower and 230-room Embassy Suites Hotel were completed between Madison Avenue and Scott Boulevard. With tax incentives, Fidelity Investments opened a 2,000-employee campus in 1994, and a few years later the IRS completed the Gateway Center on Scott Boulevard, employing another 2,000. In 1997, RiverCenter II was completed, and a year after that the $30 million Northern Kentucky Convention Center was built across the street from a new Marriott Hotel at the foot of Madison Avenue. Meanwhile, nearly 600 new residential homes were built in subdivisions including Crystal Lake, Ridgeport, Clover Meadow, and Heathermoor. In 2008, Corporex completed a twenty-two-story luxury condominium project called the Ascent at Roebling's Bridge. The ultramodern, wedge-shaped structure designed by architect Daniel Libeskind won the 2008 CNBC property award for best high-rise in the Americas.[1]

Covington's riverfront also became home to a magnificent work of art when artist Robert Dafford was commissioned to create a unique and memorable landmark along an existing eyesore, the floodwall along the Ohio River from the Suspension Bridge west to Madison Avenue. Beginning in 2008 and taking over six years to complete, seventeen mural scenes (each 25 feet tall by either 20 or 40 feet wide) were created, depicting various scenes important to the region's history.[2] The

Ascent at Roebling's Bridge.

Roebling Murals on the floodwall at Covington have since been visited by tens of thousands. Earlier, in 1988, Dafford and his crew had completed a similar work on the floodwall in Maysville, depicting various historic scenes from the Maysville region. In 2017, many of those panels received much-needed restoration.

Newport's plans to redefine the city were emerging as well, starting with the opening of Newport on the Levee, a 350,000-square-foot regional entertainment facility. The complex grew to include a twenty-screen movie theater, live performance venues, and eateries featuring cuisine from nearly a dozen countries.[3] The area is home to numerous festivals throughout the year, including ItalianFest and GoettaFest. Along the riverfront, the Newport Aquarium opened in 1999, immediately followed by what became known as the World Peace Bell. At the southeast corner of Fourth and York streets, a tower was erected to hold a 66,000-pound bell with a 7,000-pound clapper. The bell measures twelve feet in diameter and has become a symbol of the desire for world peace. It remains as one of the largest free-swinging bells in the world and is visited by thousands each year.[4] In addition, the old Louisville and Nashville (L&N) Railroad bridge between Newport and Cincinnati, built in 1872 and replaced in 1896, underwent a major change in 2003. The railroad had ceased to use the bridge back in 1984, and vehicular traffic halted in 1992 when it was deemed unsafe for heavy loads. Rather than demolish the bridge, the city of Newport and the Commonwealth of Kentucky turned it into a pedestrian-only walkway.[5] In 2019, the Purple People Bridge, so named for its unusual color, carries thousands of citizens and regional visitors between the many points of interest on both sides of the Ohio River.

In more recent years, Covington and Newport officials began banking on a popular housing trend occurring across the nation: the migration of young professionals into the inner city, what some describe as "reverse urban flight." Former vacant structures and dozens of rundown houses have been purchased and renovated into beautiful single-family and multifamily homes, and in Covington three major upscale housing projects were also completed or started in recent years. Covington, in fact, witnessed a slight increase in population from 1900 to 2000. In November of 2015, groundbreaking commenced for a $3.3 million redevelopment of what is known as the Boone Block, situated on the eastern side of Scott Boulevard near Fourth Street. The large structure was molded into nine single-family townhomes, completed in 2017. The Mutual Building, on the southwest corner of Pike and Madison, was also redeveloped, renewing the historic building into fifteen one-bedroom apartments and several first-floor commercial spaces. Construction began in 2017 for Duveneck Square, where the entire area along Washington Street between Pike and Eighth streets will eventually include more than 150 apartments, commercial spaces, and greenspace. A planned enhancement along the Interstate 71/Interstate 75 corridor is the renovation of the old Bavarian Brewery at Twelfth Street into offices for the Kenton County Fiscal Court, and barely in the planning stages is the development of the old IRS facility, located north of Fourth Street between Madison and Johnson, which is scheduled to close in 2019.

At Newport, over $1 billion of investment money has been allo-

Plaza at Newport on the Levee.

Goettafest in Newport, with the Purple People Bridge in the background, 2017.

Newport Aquarium and riverfront, 2018.

cated or is planned for the city's riverfront. Construction is complete on the SouthShore riverfront condos, located at 400 Riverboat Row, and the Vue190 upscale apartment development is nearing completion nearby. The One Riverfront Place office building, situated at Dave Cowens Drive and Washington Avenue, remains at near capacity; and Ovation, a proposed $800 million redevelopment of Newport's riverfront at the confluence of the Ohio and Licking rivers, will soon offer a first-class mixed-use development in the urban core. The site is planned to include approximately 1,000 new housing units and one million square feet of office space, and is expected to provide additional lodging and entertainment amenities for the flourishing city and region.[6]

Much of the success in the recent growth and development of the entire Northern Kentucky region can be attributed not only to the work of various city administrators, but also to several outside organizations, such as Northern Kentucky Tri-Ed, Covington Renaissance, Vision 2015, and the Southbank Partners. These groups specialize in marketing the region both nationally and internationally as a prime location for new or expanding businesses and assist local companies in growing

Riverfront view of Covington, 2018.

View of Covington from Devou Park, with Cincinnati in the background, 2018.

their existing customer bases. Cities from Ludlow to Dayton have benefited from their efforts, and their project planning continues in 2019. One of the main projects of Vision 2015, later known as Skyward, was the Licking River Greenway and Trails. Covington was the first city to begin implementation of the trail, breaking ground in 2010, and to date it has grown to a more than five-mile multimodal structure connecting the neighborhoods of Latonia, Wallace Woods, Austinburg, Eastside, and Historic Licking Riverside. Trail access can be found behind Holmes High School at the corner of Levassor and Eastern Avenue, the dead end of East Sixteenth Street, in Clayton-Meyer Park, and behind Randolph Park. The city of Wilder began construction on the trails in 2013 and has since completed paths connecting the City Building to Frederick's Landing; and other cities have either broken ground or will be doing so in 2019.

While Covington and Newport, and to a lesser degree Ludlow, Bellevue, and Dayton, can boast about recent development, planned projects, and even slight increases in population, those cities continue to experience the effects of urban decay, poverty, and high unemployment rates. Like many urban centers across the nation, these towns are experiencing what many now define as "concentrated poverty." It is no surprise that problems such as crime, welfare dependency, nonmarital childbearing, and unfavorable health, educational, and work outcomes are concentrated in high-poverty areas. In the inner city, resources are often tied to a person's specific neighborhood. Public education, for example, is usually funded from local property taxes, and its quality varies dramatically across communities in the United States. Because people's social networks are also geographically rooted, those living in high-poverty neighborhoods have fewer social links to good jobs. Poor people living in disadvantaged neighborhoods not only have to cope with their own poverty, they also have to deal with the problems of so many of their neighbors.[7] Homelessness, of course, is just one result of poverty. While accurately counting homeless adults is often difficult, Northern Kentucky school districts counted 2,939 students as homeless during the 2016–2017 school year, a 26 percent increase from 2014–2015. The figure includes students in Boone, Campbell, Gallatin, Grant, Kenton, and Pendleton counties.

Newport has seven public housing communities with more than

475 units for families and senior or disabled households.[8] The city is home to hundreds of upscale condo units and million-dollar homes, but the average family income is only $32,000 a year, well below the state's median income per family of $45,000.[9] Furthermore, a staggering 20.7 percent of families in Newport live below the poverty line.[10] Things are slightly better in neighboring Covington, where the average family income is $38,000 a year and 15 percent live below the poverty line.[11] Covington, however, with far more residents than Newport, has a much wider variance in income levels. Families in South Covington and Wallace Woods, for instance, average from $55,000 to near $70,000 a year, while those in East Covington (from Madison Avenue to the Licking River and from Eighth Street to Twentieth Street) average only around $21,000 per year.[12] And, like many urban centers across the country, Northern Kentucky's two largest cities are home to numerous tattoo parlors, cash-checking and payday loan companies, bars, and pawn shops—businesses that often go hand in hand with lower-income neighborhoods and poverty in general. In 2019, a wide range of social service organizations are scattered about the city and the entire region, providing much-needed help to many lower-income families.

Various community support organizations exist in 2019 to help those in need throughout Northern Kentucky. United Ministries in Erlanger helps by offering emergency food supplies, a thrift store, discounts on prescription medication, and family support. The Northern Kentucky Community Action Commission helps to provide affordable housing options, such as apartment complexes in Boone County and the newly remodeled Lincoln-Grant Scholar House in Covington.

Other challenges continue to face administrators in the numerous cities and towns within Northern Kentucky. Many define progress as the destruction of older, dilapidated buildings followed by new construction. Others treasure the more historic structures and work to revive or repurpose them into viable dwellings and commercial opportunities. City leaders struggle with the decision to allow destruction in the name of progress, but at the same time want abandoned homes and businesses eliminated from their towns. In Covington, entire city blocks have fallen to the wrecking ball since 2015, but in most cases the buildings were unsalvageable. Covington has enjoyed wonderful success stories in recent years, but the overall progress seems to be much slower there than in Newport. Since most changes in Newport have been along the riverfront, citizens and frequent visitors can easily see the changes that city has made. Covington's challenge in rehabilitating and promoting new construction is far greater than that of Newport, of course, since the population of Covington is nearly triple in number and the city limits encompass over 350 percent more area (13.7 square miles versus Newport's 3 square miles). While Newport has the luxury of focusing their revitalization efforts mainly along the riverfront, Covington has several "business centers" or "entertainment districts" to deal with: the riverfront, downtown, Latonia, Main Strasse, the Pike Street corridor, the I-75 corridor, and others. When new money becomes available, such as federal grants, it is far more challenging to decide where the money should be spent.

In Cincinnati, the answer was getting city leaders out of the equation. In 2001, a private company was formed to address the Over-the-Rhine neighborhood, which was voted the most dangerous in the entire nation at the time. Freed from ordinary political constraints and focused on its task of reversing that neighborhood's downward slide, the Cincinnati Center City Development Corporation (3CDC) invested or leveraged more than half a billion dollars into Over-the-Rhine, buying and rescuing 131 historic buildings and constructing 48 new ones, while maintaining subsidized housing, rehabilitating parks, and driving out criminals with better lighting, cameras, liquor store closings, and the development of vacant lots.[13]

Possibly the biggest challenge for city leaders as of 2019 is dealing with a disturbing heroin and opioid epidemic that has strangled much of the region. While widespread drug use has existed for decades in many cities and suburbs across the nation, heroin took an unusually strong hold in Northern Kentucky after 2010. Nearly four out of ten adults surveyed in 2016 said they knew a friend or family member with heroin problems.[14] In a seventy-two-hour period in March 2017, fifty-one deaths were reported in Northern Kentucky, bringing that weekend's total in all of Greater Cincinnati to 121.[15] Deaths by drug overdoses in 2016 were nearly five times the number of people killed in car crashes.[16] In many jurisdictions emergency medical personnel carry ready-to-use syringes with special antidotes to revive victims while they lay on the streets or sit unconscious in their cars. In 2019, numerous clinics exist to help those with addiction, including the Northern Kentucky Medical Clinic, the Metro Treatment Center, and Square One Addiction Center, all in Covington; and Crossroads and Transitions, with locations in many counties.

32

Some River-Town Charm Remains

While the visual changes in Covington and Newport are obvious, many once-rural cities have experienced sensational changes as well, especially during the past twenty-five years or so. With the mass exodus from the inner cities, outlying towns in the region have witnessed tremendous growth. Independence, for example, has grown from around 1,700 residents in 1970 to more than 27,000, about a 1,500 percent increase, while Union experienced an incredible 3,000 percent rise, growing from just over 200 residents to nearly 6,000 in that same time frame. Grant County's population has risen from about 10,000 in 1970 to over 23,000 in 2019, due almost exclusively to the I-75 corridor. New subdivisions, industrial parks with colossal warehouses, and condominium and apartment complexes now reach far and wide in what was once rolling farmland. In Campbell County, the entire stretch of US 27 from Highland Heights to Grant's Lick is now a four-lane divided highway, home to several shopping plazas, specialty retail outlets, fast-food restaurants, and other business ventures. The 3-L Highway in Kenton County has changed in similar fashion over the past fifty years. The area between Highland Avenue and Orphanage Road has become a bustling retail center, with a Walmart Superstore and more than a dozen other businesses. In addition, a full-scale industrial park now stands along Banklick Creek just south of Interstate 275, where several pioneers had bravely built their first homesteads. And US 42 from Florence to Union is almost unrecognizable to residents and visitors who were there in the 1970s. The once winding, scenic country road has become six lanes of hard pavement, handling more than a million vehicles per week. Two new high schools, Ryle and Cooper, and several other schools opened

Flemingsburg, Kentucky, during Court Days, a two-day annual festival for the community with games, prizes, entertainment, and more. Courtesy Flemingsburg Rotary Club.

in recent years to accommodate the growth in Boone County. Erlanger, Highland Heights, and Wilder have also expanded tremendously over the past fifty years.

While many outlying cities grew significantly, several of the old business districts of those towns have remained unchanged. In many cases, new roads built to ease congestion with the increased population totally bypassed the old town squares, as was the case with Florence, Union, Alexandria, Flemingsburg, Maysville, Williamstown, Brooksville, and other communities. At Independence, there is little change visible within a half-mile of the courthouse, but with the addition of a massive elementary and middle school campus north of town and shopping centers and eateries south of town, the city's overall appearance has been drastically altered. Likewise, the intersection of Main and Shelby streets in Florence and the crossroads of Main and Washington streets in Alexandria look much like they did fifty years ago, while a view from less than a mile in any direction from those spots offers a totally different perspective.

For those appreciative of the slowed-down, country lifestyle of what were the old river towns of the region, several cities have been able to keep that wonderful charm. Augusta, for instance, remains much as it was a hundred years ago. While some industry has arrived, such as Berry Global, the central part of the city stands as a tribute to the families who settled there over a century ago. Historic structures such as the Rosemary Clooney home and the General John Payne home remain, though altered. The historic ferry connecting Augusta with Brown County, Ohio, continues daily operation, and the town hosts several festivals each year to celebrate its heritage.

Carrollton has experienced tremendous industrial growth along the Ohio River, with such companies as North American Stainless and Dow Corning. BPB Celotex opened a gypsum board manufacturing plant there in October 2000, with an annual production capacity of 700 million square feet of board. At a cost of about $72 million with about 100 employees, the company is one of the largest manufacturers of interior wall and ceiling products for residential and commercial use in the world.[1] In addition, KY 227 leading into town from Interstate 71 is now lined with hotels, restaurants, and other commercial endeavors. Yet the main section of town remains much as it was a century ago. The city is filled with structures built in the mid- to late 1800s, and the historic Masterson House (c. 1790), the oldest two-story brick structure between Cincinnati and Louisville, still stands proudly along the river.[2] The city's population has changed very little in the past fifty years, going from 3,226 residents to about 3,800. Recently, a walking-biking trail opened along the Ohio River, named for Charles William Webster, a former mayor, druggist, and well-loved community leader. At Point Park, the annual Fourth of July celebration is attended by thousands.

Much like Carrollton, nearby Warsaw continues to offer all the appeal of a small rural community. The Riverside Bed and Breakfast, located within the former home of James H. McDanell Sr., militia captain and state senator, is one of many historic structures in town. The tiny hamlet found itself in the national spotlight in 2000, however, when the Kentucky Speedway opened. NASCAR fans from the entire Midwest were ecstatic when owner Jerry Carroll chose a 1,000-acre tract near Sparta for the $152 million project. More than 300,000 spectators attended the first season, and the track remains a popular stop

Downtown Carrollton, Kentucky, 2018.

on the racing circuit.[3] Two other auto racing tracks predate the Kentucky Speedway. Thorn Hill Drag Strip, situated along Decoursey Pike in southern Kenton County, and the Florence Speedway, located along US 42 near Union, are still in operation, though with limited events.

Ludlow and neighboring Bromley have retained much of their historic beauty as well, though both cities have supplemented their rich architecture with new development. Moving forward, Ludlow officials broke ground in May of 2017 for the first phase of the Riverfront Commons walking and biking trail, and began construction of a community space and train-viewing platform adjacent to the city building. While Bellevue and Dayton have welcomed new high-rise condominiums, fine dining establishments, the New Riff Distilling company, and new boating marinas, the "Avenue," as it is called by locals—that being Bellevue's Fairfield Avenue and Dayton's Sixth Avenue—still offers a variety of small, mom-and-pop–style businesses, and that two-mile stretch bustles with busy shoppers every day. Bellevue has worked hard to carefully mix the new with the old; and two designated historical districts exist in 2019, put in place in part to help enhance the city's identity, both aesthetically and economically.[4]

Downtown Maysville, Kentucky, 2018.

Everything from historic row houses to modern subdivisions and golf course estates can be found today in and around the historic city of Maysville, while within two miles of town remains an impressive farming community. The AA Highway is home to many commercial endeavors, which have allowed the main downtown district to keep its historic appearance. Other cities in the more rural areas of the region, such as Owenton, Brooksville, Williamstown, and Falmouth, have also witnessed very little change over the past fifty years. Owenton, for example, has increased its population by only 300 over those five decades, while during that same time frame the population of Falmouth has fluctuated by a total of only 47 people.

The 1993 Nobel Prize brought world-wide attention to Pendleton County, when the award in Physiology or Science was shared by Richard Roberts and Cynthiana-born Phillip Allen Sharp. Sharp was raised in Pendleton County and graduated from Pendleton County High School in 1962. Afterward, he became a highly successful biochemical research scientist.[5] While working at MIT in 1977, Sharp discovered that a gene could be present in several well-separated DNA segments, a discovery significant to cancer research. In 1985, he became director of the MIT Center for Cancer Research and cofounded Biogen, Inc. (1978), one of the nation's first biotech companies, and Alnylam Pharmaceuticals (2002), both of Cambridge, Massachusetts.[6] Sharp Middle School, located along US 27 about six miles north of Falmouth, was later named in his honor. The city of Falmouth found itself in the news once again in 1997, when the town was inundated with floodwaters. The Licking River flood stage is 28 feet at Falmouth, but when the river eventually crested at 52 feet in March, 80 percent of the town was under water.[7] Structural damage reached more than $36 million, with more than 700 buildings flooded and 110 completely destroyed. Thirty-seven businesses never reopened, and more than 1,500 residents were displaced because of the flood. Five people were killed.[8]

An extremely popular television series put little Crittenden, Kentucky, on the map in 2000. The show *Survivor* takes a group of people from all walks of life and strands them, often on a deserted island. Through the help of a host, they are paired against each other in teams and are required to perform various tasks and physical challenges. At the conclusion of each episode, the castaways vote a fellow team member off until only one survivor is left, who walks away with a million dollars. Crittenden's Rodger Bingham (b. 1947), nicknamed "Kentucky Joe," did not win that season, but he quickly developed into one of the most popular contestants in the history of the long-running series and became a local celebrity.

In 2007, tiny Petersburg in Boone County received national attention when the Creation Museum opened nearby. The ministry Answers in Genesis opened the 75,000-square-foot museum, which presents an explanation of the creation of man and the universe based on the Genesis narrative in the Bible. Approximately 4,000 patrons visited the museum on opening day, and the site remains a popular attraction.

An offshoot of the Creation Museum, the Ark Encounter opened in July 2016 at Williamstown. The park's feature attraction is a full-scale replica of Noah's Ark, standing 510 feet long, 85 feet wide, and 81 feet high.[9] The ark contains 132 bays with models of animals that were purported to be on the ark, dioramas of Noah's workshop, and other displays. After feasibility studies projected that the park would provide

Ark Encounter grand opening in Williamstown, Kentucky, July 7, 2016. Courtesy Answers in Genesis/Ark Encounter.

a boom to the state's tourism industry, the Ark Encounter received tax incentives from the city, county, and state to induce its construction, drawing great criticism from some groups concerned with the separation of church and state.[10] A dispute over the park's hiring practices also arose when the US Federal Court ruled that the organization could require Ark Encounter employees to sign a statement of faith as a condition of their employment.[11] Nevertheless, in its first week of operation, more than 30,000 people visited the park, and it remains one of the top tourist attractions in all of Northern Kentucky.[12]

From the arrival of the first European settlers in the late 1700s to the building of the Ark at Williamstown in 2016, Northern Kentucky's overall landscape and population has changed dramatically. Once a sparsely populated, rugged wilderness, with beautiful creeks, broad rivers, and fertile valleys, the region has, for the most part, been transformed into a sprawling urban metropolis, a home to hundreds of thousands. Instead of the occasional explorer, the rivers are now filled with recreational boaters mixed with heavy commercial traffic, and a good portion of the once fertile rolling hills and valleys has all but been erased, replaced with continually expanding industrial parks and subdivisions.

Early settlers, such as James Taylor Jr., Jacob Fowler, William Cave, and Thomas Kennedy knew well the potential of the incredibly beautiful territory they had discovered at the mouth of the Licking River; and, through their efforts and those of their many descendants, as well as later-arriving immigrants, Northern Kentucky has grown into one of the most desirable places in the country for both new business and home ownership.

Certainly the region has its challenges, as do many regions of similar size and population across the entire United States. Continuing signs of economic prosperity and recovery mix with continuing signs of poverty in the urban core. While some see great accomplishment with the building of magnificent high-rises, condos, and factories, others see only the disheartening fact that the once beautiful rural landscape is being taken over in the name of progress.

That being said, the entire Northern Kentucky region is on a steady uphill climb, though it remains a work in progress. For many decades, Kentucky's northernmost counties have been considered the state's "stepchild" region. Just as relevant, most Cincinnatians have viewed Boone, Kenton, and Campbell counties as part of their own city, referring to that region as nothing more than their southern suburb. However, with the incredible success of the Greater Cincinnati–Northern Kentucky International Airport, Newport on the Levee, recent rehabilitation projects in Covington's inner core, and the explosion in residential construction and industrial expansion in the outlying cities, this wonderful region now lives as a true partner to its northern neighbor. In fact, many believe wholeheartedly that the "Greater" in Greater Cincinnati most certainly refers to Northern Kentucky.

Appendix A

Northern Kentucky Civil War Fortifications

Kenton County

J. L. Kirby Smith Battery—located at what is now Laurel and Lake streets in southwestern Ludlow, this battery was named for Colonel Joseph L. Kirby Smith, 43rd Ohio Infantry, who was mortally wounded at the Second Battle of Corinth, October 1862.

Coombs Battery—believed to be named for Leslie Coombs, a member of Major General Lew Wallace's staff. What few remains are still visible are located within Covington's Devou Park.

Bates Battery—named for Brigadier General Joshua Hall Bates, chairman of the Cincinnati Committee for Public Safety. This battery was also in Devou Park; any remnants now lie north of the Devou Village Apartments along Sleepy Hollow Road.

Perry Battery—named for Cincinnati attorney Aaron F. Perry. Some traces remain but are on private property, on the south side of Redwood Court, between Elder Court and Chestnut Road, Fort Wright.

Rich Battery—named for Stephen Rich, landowner of the site. Built in 1861, it is referred to as "Old Battery" on military maps. Completely destroyed by residential construction, it was located in the area of present-day Tartan Drive, Fort Wright.

Fort Mitchel—constructed in 1861 and named for Major General Ormsby M. Mitchel, who originally directed the construction of Cincinnati's defenses in 1861. Situated at present-day Summit Lane in Fort Mitchell, little remains. The driveway leading to the home at the end of Summit Lane follows the old military road, and a few shallow rifle pits can be seen in the front yard. The city of Fort Mitchell derives its name from the general and the fort, though the city's name was misspelled and never corrected.

Kyle Battery—located immediately northeast of Fort Mitchel on a farm owned by Robert S. Kyle. The site was destroyed by the construction of Interstate 75 at Kyle's Lane.

McRae Battery—named for Captain Alexander McRae, 3rd United States Calvary, who was killed at the Battle of Valverde, New Mexico Territory, 1862. It was located in the area of present-day East Henry Clay Avenue and Christine Court, Fort Wright.

Fort Wright—was left uncompleted in 1864. Designed for thirteen heavy guns, Fort Wright could cover all the ground from the front of Kyle's Battery eastward to the Licking River. It was named for Major General Horatio Wright, commander of the Department of the Ohio. Located just west of the Fort Wright City Building, the city of Fort Wright gets its name from this officer and fort.

Hooper Battery—Originally designated Kyle Battery, it was along the same ridge as McRae. The site was completely covered over with dirt to make a level yard for a private residence, which later became the James A. Ramage Civil War Museum. The site is situated along Highland Avenue in Fort Wright, between the Bluegrass Swim Club and the Covington city limits. Entrance to the site is made from the church lot.

Carlisle Battery—named for local attorney and politician John G. Carlisle. It was located on the hillside between Hooper and Burbank batteries.

Burbank Battery—named for Lieutenant Colonel Sidney Burbank, military commander of Cincinnati. It was located on the hillside above Kuhr's Lane, across from Mother of God Cemetery, Covington.

Hatch Battery—also known as Brickyard Battery, it was named for Cincinnati Mayor George H. Hatch.

Bufford Battery—constructed in 1863 and named for half-brothers and generals Napoleon Bufford and John Bufford. This position was selected to command the ground from Fort Wright to Holt Battery in Campbell County.

Burnet Battery—first known as Quarry Battery, it was renamed for Robert W. Burnet, commander of a local militia. It was located on the hill southwest of the present-day intersection of Warren and West Twenty-Sixth Street, Covington.

Anderson Battery—first known as Tunnel Battery due to its being located directly over a railroad tunnel (still in use), it was named for Larz Anderson II, a Cincinnati businessman and brother to Brevet Major General Robert Anderson. Minor traces and a few rifle pits can still be seen on the hillside southeast of the Boy's and Girl's Club on West Twenty-Sixth Street—overtop the railroad tunnel, Covington.

Campbell County

Wiggins Battery—named for Samuel Wiggins, a Cincinnati banker and realtor. Also referred to as John's Hill Battery, this position overlooked the Licking River Valley.

Holt Battery—Originally known as Three Mile Creek Battery, it was named for Major General Joseph Holt, Judge Advocate General of the Army. This property is owned by Vista Pointe Apartments in Wilder; construction has destroyed much of the original battery. The site lies on the hill behind the United Dairy Farmers at Moock Road and Licking Pike, Wilder.

McLean Battery—also known as Locust Hill Battery, it was named for Major Nathaniel H. McLean, Chief of Staff for the Department of the Ohio. Destroyed by residential development in 1994, it was located along the ridge parallel to Licking Pike south of Beech Woods (Kearney) Battery.

Harrison Battery—believed to be named for Montgomery Pike Harrison, an Indiana officer killed in Texas in 1849. Its location has never been determined precisely, but was just southwest of Shaler Battery.

Shaler Battery—named for the owner of the property, Dr. Nathaniel B. Shaler, chief surgeon of the Newport Barracks. The Evergreen Cemetery now occupies the entire Shaler property, and this earthwork is the most easily accessible of all the remaining defensive positions. A gazebo within the cemetery, at the highest ground, marks the site of the original battery.

Groesbeck Batteries—referred to as Batteries 1 and 2, these two small positions were built in 1864 to guard approaches to Fort Burnside and were named for William S. Groesbeck, a Cincinnati lawyer and politician. They were located on the hill overlooking Alexandria Pike, on the site of what became the Beverly Hills Supper Club, Southgate.

Phil Kearney Battery—originally named Beech Woods Battery, it was renamed for Major General Philip Kearney, who was killed at the Battle of Chantilly in 1862. It was located in the area of Cannon Ridge Drive, Southgate.

Fort Burnside—constructed in 1863, this elaborate earthwork fort commanded the area from Shaler Battery to Fort Whittlesey. It was named for Major General Ambrose Burnside, commander of the Department of the Ohio in 1863–1864. It was situated to the east of the Grosebeck Batteries.

Fort Whittlesey—named for Colonel Charles Whittlesey, who had retired a few months before the threat to Cincinnati and was called back into service by Lew Wallace, his former division commander. The fort was located on the high ground across North Fort Thomas Avenue from Tower Park.

Battery Lee—was constructed in 1863 to overlook the Ohio River Valley to the east and named for R. W. Lee, whose full identity remains unknown. The site was leveled in 1890 to create a parade ground for

Fort Thomas. Alexander Road, which lies east of the Fort Thomas Mess Hall at Tower Park, loops around the site of the original battery.

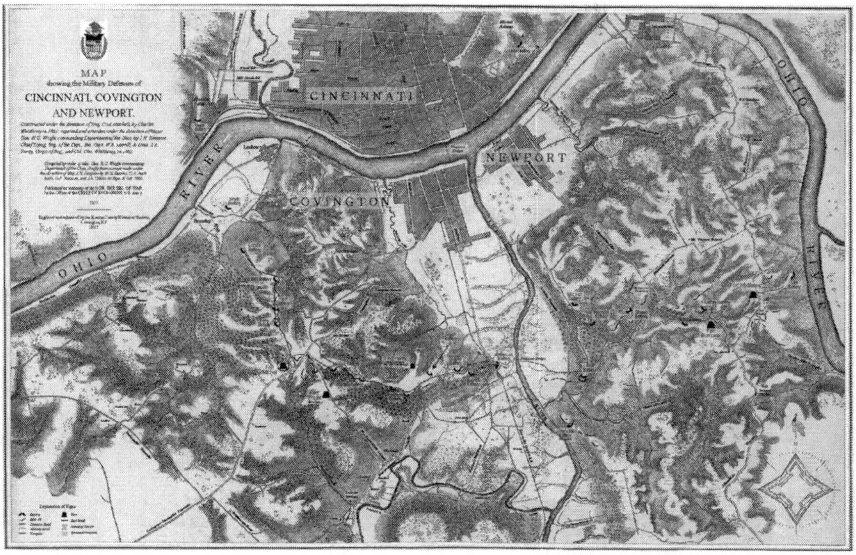

Map of Northern Kentucky Civil War fortifications. Kenton County Historical Society.

Several training camps were also established throughout the region, including Camp Kenton Station and Camp Lee, near Maysville; Camp Collins at Warsaw; Camp Frazer at Cynthiana (destroyed by John Hunt Morgan's men in 1862); Camp Covington; and Camp King (near present-day Menken Field), Covington. Civil War hospitals were also important in the region, and six were located here: five at Covington and one at Newport. The most important was likely the 218-bed, Seminary United States General Hospital, located on Eleventh Street near Madison, in Covington, on property owned by the Western Baptist Theological Institute. After the war, in 1867, Henrietta Ester Scott Cleveland established Saint Elizabeth Hospital at that location, relocating the facility from East Seventh Street.[1]

Appendix B

Population of Selected Northern Kentucky Cities, 1950–2017

CITY	1950	1960	1970	1980	1990	2000	2017*
Alexandria	536	1,318	3,844	4,735	5,592	8,286	9,340
Augusta	1,599	1,458	1,443	1,455	1,336	1,204	1,175
Bellevue	9,040	9,336	8,847	7,678	6,997	6,480	5,845
Bromley	980	998	1,069	844	1,137	838	804
Brooksville	622	601	609	680	670	589	643
Carrollton	3,226	3,218	3,884	3,967	3,715	3,846	3,874
Covington	64,452	60,376	52,535	49,585	43,264	40,640	40,797
Dayton	8,977	9,050	8,751	6,979	6,576	5,966	5,413
Dry Ridge	640	802	1,100	1,250	1,601	2,191	2,219
Erlanger	3,694	7,072	12,676	14,466	15,979	16,676	18,813
Falmouth	2,186	2,568	2,593	2,482	2,378	2,169	2,139
Flemingsburg	1,502	2,067	2,483	2,835	3,071	2,658	2,864
Florence	1,325	5,837	11,661	15,586	18,624	23,551	32,460
Highland Heights	1,569	3,491	4,543	4,435	4,223	5,153	7,155
Independence	285	309	1,751	7,998	10,444	14,982	27,024
Ludlow	6,374	6,233	5,815	4,959	4,736	4,409	4,524
Maysville	8,632	8,484	7,411	7,983	7,169	9,011	8,866
Newport	31,044	30,070	25,998	21,587	18,871	17,048	15,241
Owenton	1,429	1,376	1,280	1,341	1,306	1,327	1,539
Southgate	1,903	2,070	3,212	2,833	3,266	3,472	3,845
Union	150	185	233	601	1,001	2,893	5,807

Population of Selected Northern Kentucky Cities, 1950–2017

CITY	1950	1960	1970	1980	1990	2000	2017*
Walton	1,358	1,530	1,801	1,651	2,034	2,450	3,927
Warsaw	829	981	1,232	1,328	1,202	1,615	1,688
Wilder	204	239	823	633	691	2,624	3,071
Williamstown	1,466	1,,611	2,063	2,502	3,203	3,925	3,965

Statewide rankings by population. As of 2019, Covington ranks 5th overall; Florence, 8th; Independence, 16th; Erlanger, 21st; Fort Thomas, 24th; Newport, 26th; and Maysville, 40th.

Source: "Population of Kentucky Cities Ranked by Size," www.togetherweteach.com, retrieved November 15, 2016.

*Population in 2017 is estimated. All information in the population chart was gathered at www.wikipedia.com under the topic of each individual city listed.

Notes

1. Northern Kentucky's Prehistory

1. According to the *American Heritage Dictionary,* "prehistory" is defined as human history in the period before recorded events: before human habitation and often before the written word, where historical discoveries and documentation have been made through archaeological examination, study, and research at a much later time. With regard to North America and, more precisely, Northern Kentucky, the term is used by historians to refer to the time period prior to the year 1492.

2. "When Did Dinosaurs Live?" National History Museum, London, http://www.nhm.ac.uk/discover/when-did-dinosaurs-live.html, retrieved November 20, 2014.

3. Ibid.

4. Stanley Hedeen, *Big Bone Lick: The Cradle of American Paleontology* (Lexington: University Press of Kentucky, 2008), 20.

5. June Krants, "A Brief Pre-history of Northern Kentucky," *Northern Kentucky Heritage* 3, no. 1 (Fall–Winter 1995): 45–48.

6. 2014 ICS geologic time scale, http://www.stratigraphy.org/index.php/ics-chart-timescale, retrieved July 5, 2014.

7. "Pliocene Epoch," https://www.britannica.com/science/Pliocene-Epoch, retrieved November 18, 2014.

8. Jeannine Kreinbrink, "Glaciers," in *The Encyclopedia of Northern Kentucky,* ed. Paul A. Tenkotte and James C. Claypool (Lexington: University Press of Kentucky, 2009), 403.

9. Hedeen, *Big Bone Lick,* 22.

10. Ibid.

11. Walter Sullivan, "A Great Lost River Gets Its Due," *New York Times,* Science Section, November 29, 1983, 1.

12. Ibid.

13. Ibid.

14. Ibid.

15. Kreinbrink, "Glaciers."

16. William Drew Andrews, Rick Bullard, and John Rockaway, *Geology of Northern Kentucky and The Ohio River Valley,* Report at the American Institute of Professional Geologists event April 23, 2005, ky.aipg.org/NEWSLETTERS/2005SummerNL.pdf, retrieved November 16, 2014.

17. Kreinbrink, "Glaciers."

18. L. S. Brand, "Some Notes of the Pleistocene History of the Cincinnati Region," *Ohio Journal of Science,* March 1934.

19. *Where the River Bends,* a documentary on Northern Kentucky created by KET and narrated by Nick Clooney, 2011.

20. Ibid.

21. Krants, "Brief Pre-history of Northern Kentucky."

22. Andrews, Bullard, and Rockaway, *Geology of Northern Kentucky and The Ohio River Valley.*

23. Joseph F. Gastright, "Buffalo Traces," in *The Encyclopedia of Northern Kentucky,* 128.

24. Ibid.

25. Ibid.

2. Ancient Civilizations and Historic Peoples

1. John E. Burns, *History of Covington, Kentucky, through 1865,* ed. Karl Lietzenmayer (Covington, KY: Kenton County Historical Society, 1986), 5.

2. Ibid.

3. Andrew Curry, "How Did People Reach the Americas?" www.usnews.com/science/articles/2008/07/24, retrieved August 19, 2015.

4. Jeannine Kreinbrink, "American Indians," in *The Encyclopedia of Northern Kentucky,* ed. Paul A. Tenkotte and James C. Claypool (Lexington: University Press of Kentucky, 2009), 20–23.

5. Ibid.

6. Ibid.

7. Ibid.

8. Ibid.

9. Ibid.

10. *Early Kentucky: Historical Background,* Program I of a WKET Kentucky history series for schools, ket.org/kentuckystory/program1.htm, retrieved November 16, 2014.

11. "Woodland Technology and Weapons," Illinois State Museum, www.museum.state.il.us., retrieved June 1, 2016.

12. Kreinbrink, "American Indians."

13. *Early Kentucky: Historical Background.*

14. W. D. Funkhouser and W. S. Webb, *Reports in Archeology and Anthropology,* vol. 2 (Lexington: University of Kentucky, 1932).

15. Jerry E. Clark, "Shawnees," in *The Tennessee Encyclopedia of History and Culture,* https://tennesseeencyclopedia.net/entries/shawnees/, retrieved November 16, 2014.

16. Kreinbrink, "American Indians."

17. Richard J. Dewhurst, *The Ancient Giants That Ruled America* (Rochester, VT: Bear and Co., 2013), 68–69.

18. Burns, *History of Covington,* 7.

19. Ibid., 7–8.

20. Funkhouser and Webb, *Reports in Archeology.*

21. "History of the Fort Ancient," www.ftancient.org, retrieved June 20, 2016.

22. David Walbert, "Disease and Catastrophe," https://www.ncpedia.org/anchor/fate-north-carolinas-native, retrieved June 1, 2016.

23. www.ftancient.org.

24. "Mound Builders: Why Did They Disappear?" touringohio.com/history/mound-builders-disappear.html, retrieved June 20, 2016.

25. Clark, "Shawnees."

26. Kenneth Barnett Tankersley, of the North American Studies and Anthropology Programs at Northern Kentucky University, states in "Kentucky's Native Past," an excerpt from his book in progress, *Kentucky Cherokee: People of the Cave,* that many nations of American Indians have lived in Kentucky. He believes the Cherokee, or "cave people," for instance, dwelled in the many caves in the state, especially those in the Eastern Kentucky hills. Etchings on a sandstone outcrop overlooking Panther Branch—3.5 miles southwest from present-day Campton, Wolfe County—are clearly the traditional sign of the Bird Clan of the Cherokee, along with a date of 1717. However, there is no way of determining if these two markings were made at the same time; and, even if they were, there is no proof this was an actual settlement. Historians do agree that various Indians *roamed* through all parts of Kentucky. Tankersley also states that the Cherokee "boundaries" extended north to the Ohio River, but again offers no documentation of any actual settlement anywhere in the future state. Information at the Cherokee Nation's website, www.cherokee.org, as well as at "Cherokee Indians," www.indians.org, states that the Cherokee tribe had no settlements within the borders of what is now Kentucky.

27. Jeannine Kreinbrink, 2008 research report on Native Americans in Northern Kentucky, white paper for private client, on file with the author.

28. "Historic American Indian Tribes of Ohio," www.ohiorivertrail.org, retrieved July 6, 2104.

29. "The Name Kentucky," *A History of the Daniel Boone National Forest, 1770–1970,* www.foresthistory.org, retrieved June 20, 2105.

30. Ibid.

3. Early Northern Kentucky Explorers

1. "Timeline of Quebec History (1663–1759)," https://en.wikipedia.org/wiki/Timeline_of_Quebec_history, retrieved August 30, 2016, and "Demographic History of the United States," www.u-s-history.com, retrieved August 30, 2016.

2. William Elsey Connelley, *History of Kentucky,* vol. 1 (New York: American Historical Society, 1922), 13.

3. John Filson, *The Discovery, Settlement and Present State of Kentucke,* 1784 (Lincoln, NE: Zea Books, 2017), 7.

4. Frank E. Ross, "The Fur Trade of the Ohio Valley," *Indiana Magazine of History,* www.indiana.edu, retrieved October 5, 2013.

5. Isaac Joslin Cox, *The Journeys of Rene Robert Cavalier Sieur de La Salle* (New York: Allerton Book Company, 1905).

6. John E. Burns, *History of Covington, Kentucky, through 1865,* ed. Karl Lietzenmayer (Covington, KY: Kenton County Historical Society, 1986), 9.

7. Thomas D. Clark, "Kentucky: A Historical Overview," in *The Kentucky Encyclopedia,* ed. John E. Kleber (Lexington: University Press of Kentucky, 1992), xvii.

8. "Kentucky Conquest Trails," www.floridahistory.com/Kentucky.html, retrieved May 14, 2014.

9. River to Rail: The Rise and Fall of River and Rail Transportation in Madison, Indiana, Madison-Jefferson County Public Library, www.mjcpl.org, retrieved June 26, 2014.

10. Burns, *History of Covington.*

11. "Big Bone Lick," brochure, Kentucky State Parks, https://parks.ky.gov/parks/historicsites/big-bone-lick/, retrieved May 24, 2014.

12. Stoddard Johnston, *First Explorations of Kentucky* (Louisville, KY: Filson Club, 1898).

13. "Big Bone Lick."

14. Ibid.

15. George Thornton Fleming, *History of Pittsburgh and Environs,* vol. 1 (New York: American Historical Society, 1922), 178.

16. http://familytreemaker.genealogy.com/users/1/i/t/James-Aitcheson/GENE1–0014.html, retrieved June 1, 2014.

17. Ibid.

18. Charles C. Hall, "Colonel Washington's Frontier Forts," in *Prelude to the French and Indian War, Part II,* 2003, www.frontierforts.org, retrieved May 24, 2014.

19. "Dr. Thomas Walker History," http://parks.ky.gov/parks/historical sites/thomas-walker/history.aspx, retrieved May 20, 2014.

4. Christopher Gist: Separating Fact from Fiction

1. Lawrence A. Orrill, *Christopher Gist and His Sons,* Pennsylvania State University Archives, http://journals.psu/index.php/whp/article/download, retrieved June 4, 2014.

2. For a more detailed summary of Christopher Gist's expedition, see *Northern Kentucky Heritage* 22, no. 2 (Spring–Summer 2015).

3. William M. Darlington, *Christopher Gist's Journals, with Historical, Genealogical and Ethnological Notes* (Pittsburgh, PA: J. R. Weldin and Co., 1893), 127–129.

4. My scenario for Gist's Kentucky expedition is not new. Other researchers, including Willard Rouse Jillson in his *Pioneer Kentucky* (Frankfort, KY: State Journal Co., 1934), clearly indicate that Gist made it as far west as Salt River and never journeyed further north than approximately present-day Falmouth. However, John Mitchell's *British and French Dominions* map of 1755 may hold the best clue to Christopher Gist's true route, as the famed expedition is actually detailed within that famous drawing. See John Mitchell, "A Map of the British and French Dominions in North America with the Roads, Distances, Limits, and Extent of the Settlements" (London: Andrew Millar, 1755). While Mitchell's river names are not completely accurate and some rivers are not named at all, his rough estimate of Gist's route—the only mapped version of the excursion from that time period—mimics almost exactly the scenario described in the text.

5. Allen Webb Smith, *Beginning at The Point: A Documented History of Northern Kentucky and Environs, the Town of Covington in Particular, 1751–1834,* (Park Hills, KY: Self-published, 1977), 1.

6. John E. Burns, *History of Covington, Kentucky, through 1865,* ed. Karl Lietzenmayer (Covington, KY: Kenton County Historical Society, 1986), 10.

7. Carl Waldman, Alan Wexler, and Jon Cunningham, "John Finley," in *Encyclopedia of Exploration,* vol. 1 (London: Aldus Books, 1971).

8. "Eskippathiki," www.kyatlas.com/ky-eskippathiki.html, retrieved August 11, 2016

5. The French and Indian War, and Daniel Boone Visits Kentucky

1. http://familytreemaker.genealogy.com/users/1/i/t/James-Aitcheson/GENE1–0014.html, retrieved April 15, 2014.

2. SparkNotes Editors, "SparkNote on The French and Indian War (1754–1763)," SparkNotes LLC (n.d.), http://www.sparknotes.com/history/american/frenchindian/, retrieved July 17, 2014.

3. Caroline Cox and Ken Albala, *Opening Up North America, 1497–1800* (New York: Infobase Publishing, 2009), 98–102.

4. Lowell H. Harrison and James C. Klotter, *A New History of Kentucky* (Lexington: University Press of Kentucky, 1977), 17.

5. "Big Bone Lick," brochure, Kentucky State Parks, https://parks.ky.gov/parks/historicsites/big-bone-lick/, retrieved on May 24, 2014.

6. Ibid.

7. Jared Sparks, ed., *The Works of Benjamin Franklin,* vol. 6 (Philadelphia: Childs and Peterson, 1840), 275–276.

8. Ibid.

9. Cox and Albala, *Opening Up North America.*

10. Nathan Boone, *My Father, Daniel Boone: The Draper Interviews with Nathan Boone,* ed. N. O. Hammon (Lexington: University Press of Kentucky, 1999), 30–31.

11. Ibid.

12. From Filson's history, presented in the article "Daniel Boone Opens Up the West, 1769–71," www.eyewitnesstohistory.com, retrieved December 5, 2014.

13. Carl Waldman, Alan Wexler, and Jon Cunningham, "Kenton, Simon," in *Encyclopedia of Exploration,* vol. 1 (London: Aldus Books, 1971).

14. Lewis Collins and Richard H. Collins, *Collins' Historical Sketches of Kentucky, History of Kentucky,* vol. 2 (Covington, KY: Collins and Co., 1878), 451–457.

15. Ibid., 16–19.

16. Ibid.

17. Mary Keturah Jones, "The History of Campbell County, Kentucky," a presentation at the Centennial Celebration at the Campbell County Public Library, July 4, 1876.

18. Neal O. Hammon, "Captain Thomas Bullitt," in *Early Kentucky Land Owners, 1773–1780,* http://genealogytrails.com/vir/fincastle/fincastleland_intro.html, retrieved July 4, 2015.

19. Virgil A. Lewis, *History of the Battle of Point Pleasant,* 1909 (Charleston, SC: Nabu Press, 2010).

6. James Harrod, Richard Henderson, and the Revolutionary War

1. Lewis Collins and Richard H. Collins, *Collins' Historical Sketches of Kentucky, History of Kentucky,* vol. 2 (Covington, KY: Collins and Co., 1878), 16–19.

2. Constance Lindsey Skinner, *Pioneers of the Old Southwest: A Chronicle of the Dark and Bloody Ground* (Ann Arbor: University of Michigan Library, 1919).

3. Sword Wiley, *President Washington's Indian War: The Struggle for the Old Northwest, 1790–1795* (Norman: University of Oklahoma Press, 1985).

4. Sherryl Line, "The Revolutionary War in the West," www.HistoryBuff.com, retrieved June 26, 2014.

5. Ibid.

6. Diane Stewart Powels, "John Stuart/Stewart: The Longhunter and Companion of Daniel Boone," www.familysearch.org, retrieved June 26, 2014.

7. "Felix Walker's Narrative," in George W. Ranck's "Boonesborough," reprinted in Neal O. Hammon, *Early Kentucky Land Records, 1773–1780*, Filson Club Publications, no. 5 (Louisville: Filson Club, 1993).

8. George W. Ranck, "How Kentucky Became a State," *Harpers New Monthly Magazine,* June 1892, 48.

9. A History of the Daniel Boone National Forest, Chapter 13, p. 2, www.foresthistory.org., retrieved June 28, 2014.

10. John Boh, "Simon Kenton and the Licking River Valley," *Bulletin of the Kenton County Historical Society,* June 2009.

11. Register of the Kentucky Historical Society, vols. 64–65 (Frankfort: Kentucky Historical Society, 1966), 91.

12. Camille Wells, *Survey of Historic Sites in Kentucky: Fleming County* (Frankfort: Kentucky Heritage Commission, 1979).

13. A History of the Daniel Boone National Forest, Chapter 13, p. 2.

7. Kentucky under Siege

1. John Mack Faragher, *Daniel Boone: The Life and Legend of an American Pioneer* (New York: Holt, 1992), 130.

2. A History of the Daniel Boone National Forest, Chapter 14, p. 3, www.foresthistory.org., retrieved June 28, 2014.

3. Chief Blackfish, https://en.wikipedia.org/wiki/Blackfish_(Shawnee_leader), retrieved June 28, 2014.

4. Faragher, *Daniel Boone.* 147–149.

5. Running the gauntlet was a punishment in which the victim was forced to run between two rows of Indians who would strike him with switches and other weapons as he passed through. Usually the victim was set free if he lived through the torture, but often he was forced to turn around and repeat the procedure.

6. A. M. Yealey, "History of Boone County, Kentucky," http://boonecountykyhistory.org/pages/—a.-m.-yealey-history-of-boone-county-ky.php, page 5, retrieved April 15, 2014.

7. John Sugden, "Blackfish," in *American National Biography* (New York: Oxford University Press, 1999).

8. Theodore Roosevelt, *The Winning of the West,* vol. 2 (Gloucester, UK: Dodo Press), 97.

9. John E. Burns, *History of Covington, Kentucky, through 1865*, ed. Karl Lietzenmayer (Covington, KY: Kenton County Historical Society, 1986), 15.

10. Ibid.

11. Jack Wessling, "Rogers' Defeat," in *The Encyclopedia of Northern Kentucky,* ed. Paul A. Tenkotte and James C. Claypool (Lexington: University Press of Kentucky, 2009), 768.

12. Ibid.

13. Henry Don Lee, "Revolutionary War Battle Commemorated, Survivors' Descendants Meet," *Northern Kentucky Heritage* 7, no. 1 (Fall–Winter 1999): 24.

14. Maude Ward Lafferty, "Destruction of Ruddle's and Martin's Forts in the Revolutionary War," *Register of the Kentucky Historical Society* 54, no. 189 (October 1956).

15. R. E. Banta, *The Ohio* (Lexington: University Press of Kentucky), 157.

16. "Historic Martin's Station," www.martinsstation.com, retrieved May 14, 2012.

17. Lafferty, "Destruction of Ruddle's and Martin's Forts."

18. Ibid.

19. "Battle of Piqua," https://en.wikipedia.org/wiki/Battle_of_Piqua, retrieved November 5, 2014.

20. Jack Wessling, "Lt. Colonel George Muse," in The *Encyclopedia of Northern Kentucky,* 639.

21. "The City of Covington, Kentucky," *Covington Journal,* April 12, 1873, 1.

22. "Early History of Covington," leaflet presented in 1957 and archived at the Kenton County Public Library, featured on the website www.nkyviews.com, retrieved December 1, 2014.

23. Doris Riley, "Sparta," in The *Encyclopedia of Northern Kentucky,* 847.

24. Burns, *History of Covington,* 16.

25. Ibid., 18.

26. Kandie Adkinson, "The Kentucky Land Grant System," *Historical Confederation of Kentucky* 13, no. 3, https://www.familysearch.org/wiki/en/Kentucky_Land_and_Property, retrieved September 15, 2014.

27. Caroline R. Miller, "Bracken County," in The *Encyclopedia of Northern Kentucky*, 43–44.

28. Neal O. Hammon, *Daniel Boone and the Defeat at Blue Licks* (Cedar Park, TX: Boone Society, 2005), 16.

29. Robert Spencer Coterill, *History of Pioneer Kentucky* (Cincinnati: Johnson and Hardin, 1917), 184.

30. Personal interview with Anne Crabb, author of various Kentucky pioneer history books, June 14–16, 2016.

31. Draper Manuscripts, vols. 11CC, 12CC, 21S, and 22SS (now available online at Familysearch.org); email interviews with Fleming County historian

and news writer Charles Mattox, June 2016. There appears to be some confusion regarding the participation of these three men in this skirmish. Some histories mention a similar event dated 1791: the kidnapping of children from a nearby station followed by a skirmish at Battle Run. However, it is extremely unlikely that there were two such similar incidents. Details of the 1782 event are widely documented, and this is clearly the only such occurrence. Some historian some years ago probably placed an incorrect date in his or her account, and that misinformation has been passed along inadvertently.

32. "The Heroines of Bryan Station Fort," https://sites.google.com/site/bryanstationdar/the-heroines-of-bryan-station-fort, retrieved April 21, 2016.

8. The Battle of Blue Licks

1. Neal O. Hammon, *Daniel Boone and the Defeat at Blue Licks,* (Cedar Park, TX: Boone Society, 2005), 45–46.

2. Ibid., 51–53.

3. Ibid., 53–54.

4. "Battle of Blue Licks," https://en.wikipedia.org/wiki/Battle_of_Blue_Licks, retrieved August 18, 2014.

5. Ibid.

6. Hammon, *Daniel Boone and the Defeat at Blue Licks,* 64.

7. Ibid.

8. John E. Burns, *History of Covington, Kentucky, through 1865,* ed. Karl Lietzenmayer (Covington, KY: Kenton County Historical Society, 1986), 18.

9. James Fischer, "A Forgotten Hero Remembered, Revered, and Revised: The Legacy and Ordeal of George Rogers Clark," *Indiana Magazine of History* 92, no. 2 (June 1996), https://scholarworks.iu.edu/journals/index.php/imh/article/view/11522/16754, retrieved October 5, 2017.

9. Permanent Northern Kentucky Settlers

1. Mary Keturah Jones, "The History of Campbell County, Kentucky," presentation at the Centennial Celebration at the Campbell County Public Library, Newport, Kentucky, on July 4, 1876, 3.

2. Various descriptions of his cabin site state that the location is "1/4 mile below Three Mile Ripple," which is opposite present-day Summit Drive, Latonia. One-quarter mile south of that creek would place his homestead at approximately the eleventh green of the golf course.

3. Lula Reed Boss, "Old Fort Being Restored," www.nkyviews.com/masoncounty, retrieved August 28, 2014.

4. Patricia Shadwick, paper posted on Ancestry.com for the Ellswoth-

Davis families, http://freepages.genealogy.rootsweb.ancestry.com/~mather/Ellswrth/Prettyman.shtml, retrieved May 1, 2015.

5. Margaret Strebel Hartman, "History of Grant and Company Salt Works," www.nkyviews.com, retrieved May 2, 2016.

6. www.findagrave.com/coljohngrant/kentucky, retrieved August 26, 2014.

7. Information found on the Kentucky Historical marker found at Grant's Lick in 2017.

8. John E. Burns, *History of Covington, Kentucky, through 1865,* ed. Karl Lietzenmayer (Covington, KY: Kenton County Historical Society, 1986), 42.

9. Letter to John May from Samuel Beall at Williamsburg, December 9, 1782, Beall-Booth Family Papers (Manuscript Department of the Filson Club, Louisville), reprinted in Neal O. Hammon's *Early Kentucky Land Records, 1773–1780,* http://genealogytrails.com/vir/fincastle/fincastleland_intro.html, retrieved August 30, 2014.

10. John Klee, "John May," in *The Encyclopedia of Northern Kentucky,* ed. Paul A. Tenkotte and James C. Claypool (Lexington: University Press of Kentucky, 2009), 593.

11. John Klee, "Maysville," in *The Encyclopedia of Northern Kentucky,* 595.

12. "The Kentucky Migration," www.freepages.genealogy.rootsweb.ancestry.com/~slhessick/peakes04.htm, retrieved April 1, 2014.

13. http://familytreemaker.com/genealogy.comusers/e/d/w/Dena-a-edwards/GENES-0002.html, retrieved August 28, 2014.

14. Ibid.

15. Mike Cunningham, "Vignettes of History from The Villa Hills Millennium Project," *Bulletin of the Kenton County Historical Society,* August 2000: 2–3.

16. "Kyle family," www.ftwright.com., retrieved July 24, 2015.

17. "Crescent Springs," in *The Encyclopedia of Northern Kentucky,* 248–249.

18. Leitch was also granted land that became the city of Leitchfield, Kentucky.

19. www.rootsweb.ancestry.com/~kycampbe/jacobfowler.htm., retrieved September 4, 2014.

20. "Thomas and Rebecca Lindsey, Sr.," www.rootsweb.com, retrieved May 31, 2016.

21. Thomas Ward, "Dover," in *The Encyclopedia of Northern Kentucky,* 279.

22. "Edward Strode," www.frontierfolk.net, retrieved May 2, 2016.

23. Sabrina Alcorn Baron, "Glencoe," in *The Encyclopedia of Northern Kentucky,* 404.

24. Gypsy M. Gray, "History of Gallatin County, Kentucky" (Gallatin County, Kentucky, 1954), 15.

25. www.cityofwalton.org, retrieved September 23, 2016.

26. Robert M. Rennick, "Flemingsburg," in *Kentucky Place Names* (Lexington: University Press of Kentucky, 1984), 103.

27. Ellen Eslinger, *Citizens of Zion: The Social Origins of Camp Meeting Revivalism* (Knoxville: University of Tennessee Press, 1999), 112.

28. Camille Wells, *Survey of Historic Sites in Kentucky: Fleming County* (Frankfort: Kentucky Heritage Commission, 1979.

10. Northwest Territory and Fort Washington

1. "Cincinnati," www.wikipedia.com., retrieved April 29, 2016.

2. John Klee, "George Mason," in *The Encyclopedia of Northern Kentucky,* ed. Paul A. Tenkotte and James C. Claypool (Lexington: University Press of Kentucky, 2009), 583.

3. Paul Tenkotte, "Daniel Drake," in *The Encyclopedia of Northern Kentucky,* 280.

4. Margaret Strebel Hartman, "Thomas Kennedy (1741–1821)," www.nkyviews.com, retrieved September 11, 2013. (Thomas Kennedy was Francis's brother.)

5. Ibid.

6. Gary Tanner, "Reverend Tanner Was One of Kentucky's First Baptist Preachers," www.baptisthistoryhomepage.com, retrieved April 29, 2016.

7. "Petersburg, Kentucky," www.nkyviews.com, retrieved July 18, 2014.

8. Tanner, "Reverend Tanner."

9. Ann Lutes, "A Brief History of Boone County, Kentucky," www.nkyviews.com, retrieved July 22, 2014.

10. John E. Burns, *History of Covington, Kentucky, through 1865,* ed. Karl Lietzenmayer (Covington, KY: Kenton County Historical Society, 1986), 18.

11. Helen B. Lindsey, "Leitch's Station in Campbell County," www.nkyviews.com, retrieved April 26, 2016.

12. Jack Wessling, "Benjamin Beall," in *The Encyclopedia of Northern Kentucky,* 69.

13. http://genforum.genealogy.com/peachey/messages/243.html, retrieved August 2, 2014.

14. Doris Riley, "New Columbus," in *The Encyclopedia of Northern Kentucky,* 649.

15. Hartman, "Thomas Kennedy (1741–1821)."

16. John Boh, "Thomas Kennedy," in *The Encyclopedia of Northern Kentucky,* 502.

17. Robert C. Dorsey, "Thomas Kennedy, Founder of Covington," a Gist Historical Society Paper from August 24, 1954, wwwnkyviews.com, retrieved July 17, 2015.

18. Mildred Belew, "A Brief Look at Pendleton County, Kentucky: In Celebration of Their Bicentennial," *Northern Kentucky Heritage* 6, no. 1 (Fall–Winter 1998): 40.

19. Thomas Fleming, "Fallen Timbers, Broken Alliance," http://www.historynet.com/fallen-timbers-broken-alliance.htmpages, retrieved October 10, 2015.

20. "General Charles Scott," www.nkyviews, retrieved July 20, 2014.

21. Allan W. Eckert, *That Dark and Bloody River* (New York: Bantam Books, 1995).

11. Kentucky Becomes a State

1. Laurie J. Blakely, "History of Covington," *Commercial Tribune,* August 23, 1914, www.nkyviews, retrieved May 16, 2016.

2. For information on the Sandford Family, see http://familytreemaker.genealogy.com/users/g/a/s/Chaun-Leslie-Glass/WEBSITE-0001/UHP-0012.html, retrieved September 1, 2014.

3. "General Thomas Sandford," in *The Encyclopedia of Northern Kentucky,* ed. Paul A. Tenkotte and James C. Claypool (Lexington: University Press of Kentucky, 2009), 802–803.

4. The 1883 Atlas of the region clearly shows B. F. Sanford (no "d") and his descendants, and Sanfordtown (also with no "d").

5. Allen Webb Smith, *Beginning at The Point: A Documented History of Northern Kentucky and Environs, the Town of Covington in Particular, 1751–1834* (Park Hills, KY: self-published, 1977), 136.

6. Atlas of Boone, Kenton, and Campbell Counties, 1883, published by the Campbell County Historical and Genealogy Society, Alexandria, Kentucky, 1998.

7. Sandford Family, http://familytreemaker.genealogy.com/users/g/a/s/Chaun-Leslie-Glass/WEBSITE-0001/UHP-0012.html.

8. Ibid.

9. John E. Burns, *History of Covington, Kentucky, through 1865,* ed. Karl Lietzenmayer (Covington, KY: Kenton County Historical Society, 1986), 183.

10. "Colston Family," in *The Encyclopedia of Northern Kentucky,* 210.

11. John Klee, "Joseph Desha," in *The Encyclopedia of Northern Kentucky,* 265.

12. Diane Perrine Coon, "Miles Withers Conway," in *The Encyclopedia of Northern Kentucky,* 223–224.

13. Thomas Boyd, *"Mad" Anthony Wayne* (New York: Scribner and Sons, 1929.

14. Margaret Strebel Hartman, *Glimpses of Covington through 1839 and 1840* (Covington, KY: Christopher Gist Historical Society, 1965).

15. "Battle of Fallen Timbers," www.OhioHistoryCentral.com, retrieved July 29, 2014.

16. Ibid.

17. Burns, *History of Covington,* 22.

18. W. Julian Fessler, "Jacob Fowler's Journal," *Chronicles of Oklahoma* 8, no. 2 (June 1930), http://www.okhistory.org/publications/enc/entry.php?entry=GL006, retrieved June 15, 2014.

19. "Ellison Williams," in *The Encyclopedia of Northern Kentucky,* 959.

20. Burns, *History of Covington,* 31.

21. Jennifer S. Warner, "*Boone County: From Mastodons to Millennium*" (Florence, KY: Boone County Historical Society, 1999), 33.

22. www.booonecountyky.org, retrieved July 19, 2014.

23. "William Decoursey," Rootsweb.ancestry.com/~kycampbe/Williamdecoursey.htm, retrieved August 26, 2014.

24. John Boh, "Kenton County," in *The Encyclopedia of Northern Kentucky,* 505–506.

25. "William Decoursey."

26. www.alexandriaky.org, retrieved May 2, 2016.

27. Jack Wessling, "Francis Spilman," in *The Encyclopedia of Northern Kentucky,* 849.

28. www.alexandriaky.org, retrieved May 2, 2016.

29. Margaret S. Hartman, "Captain John Bartle," *Falmouth Outlook,* August 11, 1978, 10.

30. Paul John Schewene, "Berlin," in *The Encyclopedia of Northern Kentucky,* 81.

31. Descriptions of the location of his settlement vary. Some state that it was on the "western side of the Licking opposite Leitch's Station" (Blakely, *History of Covington*), which would place Martin's cabin along the Decoursey Pike at the mouth of Decoursey Creek, about one mile south of Interstate 275. Others say that it was "about a mile above Rittenhouse" and "just below Buena Vista" (Burns, *History of Covington,* 42), which would place the site at present-day Meinken Field.

32. "Benjamin Craig, Sr., (March 30, 1751–December 5, 1822)," http://familytreemaker.genealogy.com., retrieved August 8, 2014.

33. Mary Ann Gentry, "A History of Carroll County," *Northern Kentucky Heritage* 2, no. 1 (Fall–Winter 1994).

34. Diane Perrine Coon, "English," in *The Encyclopedia of Northern Kentucky,* 304.

35. Robert M. Rennick, *Kentucky Place Names* (Lexington: University Press of Kentucky, 1984), 325.

36. "Wilmington," in *The Encyclopedia of Northern Kentucky,* 964.

12. Newport Established

1. Jack Wessling, "Lt. Colonel George Muse," in *The Encyclopedia of Northern Kentucky,* ed. Paul A. Tenkotte and James C. Claypool (Lexington: University Press of Kentucky, 2009), 639.

2. Ibid.

3. Michael Whitehead, "Newport," in *The Encyclopedia of Northern Kentucky,* 651.

4. John Conrad, "Crittenden," in *The Encyclopedia of Northern Kentucky,* 251.

5. "Kentontown," in *The Encyclopedia of Northern Kentucky,* 511.

6. Jack Wessling, "Richard Southgate," in *The Encyclopedia of Northern Kentucky,* 843.

7. Jack Wessling, "Grant Family," in *The Encyclopedia of Northern Kentucky,* 416–417.

8. Mary Wade Duff, "Searching for Senoirs: the French Connection," *Bulletin of the Kenton County Historical Society,* January 1998: 2. (Note: Senour is the common spelling as of 2019.)

9. John Boh, "People Named Rich in Present-Day Kenton County," *Bulletin of the Kenton County Historical Society,* October 1993.

10. Ibid.

11. John E. Leming, "A Bicentennial History of Bracken County," *Northern Kentucky Heritage* 4, no. 2 (Spring–Summer 1997): 44.

12. Rebecca Mitchell Turney, "William Bracken," in *The Encyclopedia of Northern Kentucky,* 109.

13. Caroline R. Miller, "Bracken County," in *The Encyclopedia of Northern Kentucky,* 43–44.

14. Ibid.

15. www.flemingcounty.org, retrieved August 18, 2014.

16. Nancy Capace, "John Finley," in *The Encyclopedia of Kentucky,* 3rd ed., vol. 1 (St. Clair Shores, MI: Somerset Publishers, 1999), 29.

17. Evelyn Welch, "Percival P. Butler" and "William Orlando Butler," in *The Encyclopedia of Northern Kentucky,* 136–137.

18. Mildred Bowen Belew, "Boston Station," in *The Encyclopedia of Northern Kentucky,* 105.

19. Mildred Bowen Belew, "Pendleton County," in *The Encyclopedia of Northern Kentucky,* 140–141.

20. John Boh, "Thomas Kennedy—Pioneer," *Bulletin of the Kenton County Historical Society,* July–August 2007: 5.

21. Dan Moore, "John H. Moore Home," in *The Encyclopedia of Northern Kentucky,* 493.

22. Mary Ann Gentry, *A Bicentennial Look at Carroll County* (Carrolton, KY: Carroll County Historical Society, 1999), 23.

23. Bill Davis, "Benjamin Craig," in *The Encyclopedia of Northern Kentucky,* 247.

24. Bill Davis, "Ghent," in *The Encyclopedia of Northern Kentucky,* 397–398.

25. www.boonecountyky.org, retrieved August 1, 2014.

26. William Conrad, *The Early History of Union, Kentucky,* www.nkyviews.com, retrieved June 19, 2015.

27. Ibid.

28. Jeannine Kreinbrink, "Mountain Island," in *The Encyclopedia of Northern Kentucky,* 632.

29. Barbara Loomis Brown, "William Arnold," in *The Encyclopedia of Northern Kentucky,* 37.

30. Ann Lutes, *A Brief History of Boone County, Kentucky,* www.nkyviews.com, retrieved July 22, 2014.

31. Robert Rankin and Margaret Blakely, "The Piatt Family," *Northern Kentucky Heritage* 6, no. 1 (Fall–Winter 1998): 55–58.

32. Glenn Clift, *History of Maysville and Mason County,* vol. 1 (Maysville, KY: Mason County Historical Society, 1985).

33. "Edward Canby," www.wikipedia.com, retrieved August 21, 2106.

34. "The Piatt Family."

35. Paul Anderson and Laurie Wilcox, "Anderson Ferry," in *The Encyclopedia of Northern Kentucky,* 26.

36. "Eagle Tavern," in *The Encyclopedia of Northern Kentucky,* 288.

37. Nancy Tretter, "Beaverlick," in *The Encyclopedia of Northern Kentucky,* 650.

38. Ruth Wade Cox Brunnings, "Richwood," in *The Encyclopedia of Northern Kentucky,* 756–757.

13. Northern Kentucky in the Early 1800s

1. US Census, http://lwd.dol.state.nj.us/labor/lpa/census/1990/poptrd1.htm, retrieved August 24, 2016.

2. "A Short History of the Newport Barracks," www.rootsweb.com/~kycampbe/newportbarracks.htm, retrieved August 24, 2016.

3. "Big Bone Lick History," www.parks.gov, retrieved September 20, 2016.

4. "Big Bone Lick, Kentucky," www.monticello.org, retrieved September 21, 2016.

5. "Covington's Sesquicentennial Year," *Kentucky Post and Times Star Special Edition,* August 21, 1965, page 29K.

6. Ibid.

7. Ibid.

8. Joy Higgins, "Napoleon," in *The Encyclopedia of Northern Kentucky,* ed. Paul A. Tenkotte and James C. Claypool (Lexington: University Press of Kentucky, 2009), 643.

9. Ruth Wade Cox Brunnings, "Bedinger Family History and Genealogy," www.bedinger.org, retrieved September 6, 2014.

10. Ibid.

11. Ruth Wade Cox Brunnings, "Major George Michael Bedinger," in *The Encyclopedia of Northern Kentucky,* 73.

12. Margaret Warminski and Matthew Becher, "Petersburg," in *The Encyclopedia of Northern Kentucky,* 713.

13. Robert M. Rennick, *Kentucky Place Names* (Lexington: University Press of Kentucky, 1984), 329.

14. Ibid., 208.

15. Elissa Plattner, "Camp Springs," in *The Encyclopedia of Northern Kentucky,* 149.

16. Ibid.

17. John Conrad, "Grant County," in *The Encyclopedia of Northern Kentucky,* 413.

18. Margaret Strebel Hartman, *Glimpses of Covington through 1839 and 1840* (Covington, KY: Christopher Gist Historical Society, 1965).

19. "General Leonard Stephens," in *The Encyclopedia of Northern Kentucky,* 853.

20. Bill Davis, "Benjamin Craig," in *The Encyclopedia of Northern Kentucky,* 247.

14. Earthquakes and the War of 1812

1. Robert D. Webster, "Earthquakes and Northern Kentucky," *Northern Kentucky Heritage* 15, no. 2 (Spring–Summer 2008): 14.

2. Ibid.

3. Ibid.

4. Quoted in ibid.

5. John H. B. Latrobe, "1871 Address to the Maryland Historical Society," *Northern Kentucky Heritage* 11, no. 2 (Spring–Summer 2014): 36–43.

6. Karl Lietzenmayer, "The War of 1812 in Kentucky," *Northern Kentucky Heritage* 20, no. 2 (Spring–Summer 2013): 20.

7. "Prelude to the War of 1812," www.themarinersmuseum.com., retrieved April 18, 2016.

8. Ibid.

9. John E. Burns, *History of Covington, Kentucky, through 1865,* ed. Karl Lietzenmayer (Covington, KY: Kenton County Historical Society, 1986), 56.

10. Lietzenmayer, "The War of 1812 in Kentucky," 21.

11. www.ket.org/history/the-war-of-1812-and-kentucky's-role/, retrieved September 8, 2016.

12. Ibid.

13. "Who Killed Tecumseh?" www.americanindianhistory.blogspot.com, retrieved September 12, 2016.

14. Colonel Joseph L. Donnelly, *Newport Barracks: Kentucky's Forgotten Military Installation* (Covington, KY: Kenton County Historical Society, 1999).

15. Ibid.

16. "Causes of the War of 1812," www.thehistorychannel.com, retrieved August 19, 2016.

17. www.ket.org/history/the-war-of-1812-and-kentucky's-role/, retrieved September 8, 2016.

18. Lietzenmayer, "The War of 1812 in Kentucky," 22–23.

19. "John Adair," www.wikipedia.com, retrieved September 12, 2016.

20. Lietzenmayer, "The War of 1812 in Kentucky," 24.

21. "The Battle of New Orleans," https://www.history.com/topics/battle-of-new-orleans, retrieved June 1, 2016. Various sources fail to indicate an exact number of American deaths, citing as few as 13 and as many as 43.

22. Ibid.

23. Christopher Klein, "Six Myths about the Battle of New Orleans," www.history.com, retrieved September 1, 2016.

24. Ibid.

25. "The War of 1812," www.themarinersmuseum.com, retrieved April 25, 2016.

26. Tom Eble, "Crumbling Landmark Tells a Challenging Story. Now, Choctaw Academy Will Be Saved," *Lexington Herald Leader,* June 21, 2018, 1.

15. Covington Is Established, and Roads Become Turnpikes

1. "For Sale," *Western Spy,* December 25, 1812.

2. Margaret Strebel Hartman, "Glimpses of Covington through 1839 and 1840," Christopher Gist Historical Society, Covington, Kentucky, January 26, 1965.

3. Lewis Collins and Richard H. Collins, *Collins' Historical Sketches of Kentucky, History of Kentucky,* vol. 2 (Covington, KY: Collins and Co., 1878), 423–426.

4. Joseph F. Gastright, "Covington," in *The Encyclopedia of Northern Kentucky,* ed. Paul A. Tenkotte and James C. Claypool (Lexington: University Press of Kentucky, 2009), 233.

5. Steve Culbertson and Carol Culbertson, "DeCoursey and Culbertson Railway Stations," in *The Encyclopedia of Northern Kentucky,* 260.

6. Greg Perkins, "Oak Ridge," in *The Encyclopedia of Northern Kentucky,* 684.

7. Arthur L. Dirks, *Woods and Pettegrew Family History* (Taunton, MA: Dirks Designs, 2015), 42–46.

8. "Kleete Family," http://www.colonial-settlers-md-va.us/, retrieved January 15, 2015.

9. According to the official Fort Wright website (https://www.fortwright.com), Kyle's Lane is named for Robert Samuel Kyle. The 1883 Atlas shows "Jacob Kyle's Orchard" at what is now Interstate 71/Interstate 75 and Kyles Lane.

10. "Bromley—Landmark House," www.kentonlibrary.org/regional-history/bromley/landmarkhouse, retrieved June 9, 2015.

11. Jennifer S. Warner, *Boone County: From Mastodons to Millennium* (Florence, KY: Boone County Bicentennial Book Committee, 1999), 82.

12. A. Gwynne Henderson and Nancy O'Malley, "The Maysville–Lexington Road," www.transportation.ky.org, retrieved October 4, 2016.

13. "US 27," in *The Encyclopedia of Northern Kentucky,* 909.

14. Carl R. Bogardus, Sr., *The Story of Gallatin County* (Gallatin County, KY: , 1994), 49.

15. www.cityofwalton.org, retrieved September 26, 2016.

16. Henderson and O'Malley, "The Maysville–Lexington Road."

17. John Klee, "Covered Bridges, Mason County," in *The Encyclopedia of Northern Kentucky,* 233–234.

18. Charles Bogart, "Dover Covered Bridge," in *The Encyclopedia of Northern Kentucky,* 279–280.

19. "Northern Kentucky Had Covered Bridges, Too," *Northern Kentucky Heritage* 2, no. 1 (Fall–Winter 1994): 6–9.

20. Robert M. Rennick, *Kentucky Place Names* (Lexington: University Press of Kentucky, 1984), 138.

21. Doris Riley, "New Liberty," in *The Encyclopedia of Northern Kentucky,* 650.

22. www.rootsweb.ancestry.com/~kycampbe/jacobfowler.htm., retrieved September 4, 2014.

23. Patrick Snadon, "William Bullock," in *The Encyclopedia of Northern Kentucky,* 131–132.

24. "Florence," in *The Kentucky Encyclopedia,* ed. John E. Kleber (Lexington: University Press of Kentucky, 1992), 329.

25. John Boh, "Linden Grove Cemetery," in *The Encyclopedia of Northern Kentucky,* 554.

26. Ibid.

16. Northern Kentucky Welcomes Industry

1. John Boh, "Iron Industry," in *The Encyclopedia of Northern Kentucky,* ed. Paul A. Tenkotte and James C. Claypool (Lexington: University Press of Kentucky, 2009), 480–482.

2. "Covington, Kentucky," www.wikipedia.com, retrieved September 16, 2016.

3. John E. Burns, *History of Covington, Kentucky, through 1865,* ed. Karl Lietzenmayer (Covington, KY: Kenton County Historical Society, 1986).

4. Joseph Gastright, "The Latonia Springs," *Northern Kentucky Heritage* 9, no. 1 (Fall–Winter 2001): 36–38.

5. Drake's article was published in the *Transylvania Journal of Medicine and Associate Sciences*, referenced and detailed in James A. Ramage and Andrea S. Watkins, *Kentucky Rising* (Lexington: University Press of Kentucky, 2011), 224.

6. "Big Bone Lick History," www.parks.ky.gov, retrieved September 22, 2016.

7. Winston Coleman, Jr., and James C. Kelly, "Old Kentucky Watering Places," *Northern Kentucky Heritage* 8, no. 2 (Spring–Summer 2001): 54–58.

8. James C. Claypool, "Latonia Racecourse," in *The Encyclopedia of Northern Kentucky,* 538.

9. Arnold Taylor, "King Cholera in Covington, Kentucky 1832–1873," *Northern Kentucky Heritage* 24, no. 1 (Fall–Winter 2016): 14–24.

10. Ibid.

11. Ibid.

12. Jean Calvert and John Klee, *Maysville, Kentucky: From Past to Present in Pictures* (Maysville, KY: Mason County Museum, 1983), 27.

13. Newspaper reprint located under "Pendleton County," www.nkyviews.com, retrieved October 23, 2016.

14. Don Clare, "Rabbit Hash," in *The Encyclopedia of Northern Kentucky,* 742–743.

15. Ibid.

16. Charles D. Hockensmith, "January and Wood Company," in *The Encyclopedia of Northern Kentucky,* 485–486.

17. Karl Lietzenmayer, "Colonel Buckner, His Family, and the Beechwood Home," *Bulletin of the Kenton County Historical Society,* July–August 2010: 8–10.

18. Karen L. Leek, "Verona," in *The Encyclopedia of Northern Kentucky,* 911–912.

19. Robert Rennick, "Post Offices," in *The Encyclopedia of Northern Kentucky,* 728.

20. "Covington, Kentucky," www.wikipedia.com, retrieved September 16, 2016.

21. Gail Chastang, "Dinsmore Homestead," *Northern Kentucky Heritage* 5, no. 1 (Autumn–Winter 1997–1998): 17; William S. Bryant, "Dinsmore Homestead," in *The Encyclopedia of Northern Kentucky,* 270.

22. Michael R. Sweeney, "Meatpacking," in *The Encyclopedia of Northern Kentucky,* 608.

23. Ibid.

24. Ibid.

25. Ibid., 609.

26. "Brewing Industry," in *The Encyclopedia of Northern Kentucky,* 117.

27. Dave Schroeder, "Our Rich History: Whatever You Want to Call It, Beer and Covington Have Gone Hand-In-Hand since 1859," www.*NKy.Tribune,* retrieved July 6, 2015.

28. "Brewing Industry."

17. German and Irish Immigration, and Another War

1. Statistics for each city found at www.wikipedia.org.

2. Don Heinrich Tolzmann, "German Immigrants," in *The Encyclopedia of Northern Kentucky,* ed. Paul A. Tenkotte and James C. Claypool (Lexington: University Press of Kentucky, 2009), 394.

3. Paul Tenkotte, "Irish Americans," in *The Encyclopedia of Northern Kentucky,* 479.

4. Ibid.

5. Tolzmann, "German Immigrants."

6. "The Famous Frontiersman Daniel Boone Dies in Missouri," www.history.com, retrieved April 28, 2016.

7. "Removal of the Remains of a Pioneer," *Cincinnati Daily Press,* May 24, 1860.

8. "Descendants of Ellison Williams," www.familytreemaker.genealogy.com/users/e/d/w/Dena-A-Edwards.GEN., found at https://www.genealogy.com/ftm/e/d/w/Dena-A-Edwards/index.html, retrieved November 24, 2013.

9. Karl Lietzenmayer, "Stephen Collins Foster," in *The Encyclopedia of Northern Kentucky,* 366–367.

10. "The Alamo," www.history.com, retrieved September 22, 2016.

11. Tim Herrmann, "Mexican War," in *The Encyclopedia of Northern Kentucky,* 617.

12. "Mexican War: 1846–48," www.explorekyhistory.ky.gov, retrieved September 23, 2016.

13. Herrmann, "Mexican War."

18. Northern Kentucky in the Mid-1800s

1. John Boh, "Iron Industry," in *The Encyclopedia of Northern Kentucky,* ed. Paul A. Tenkotte and James C. Claypool (Lexington: University Press of Kentucky, 2009), 911–912.

2. www.stewartironworks.com, retrieved November 4, 2016.

3. Ibid.

4. Ibid.

5. Glenn Drummond, "Hemingray Glass Company," in *The Encyclopedia of Northern Kentucky,* 442.

6. Charles R. Tharp, "Dayton, Kentucky: A Brief History of its 150 Years," *Northern Kentucky Heritage* 7, no. 1 (Fall–Winter 1999): 37.

7. Robert D. Webster, "Godfrey Frankenstein: Scenic Artist," *Northern Kentucky Heritage* 22, no. 1 (Fall–Winter 2014): 24.

8. "Diabolical Outrage," *New York Times,* Monday, August 14, 1854.

9. "Covington and Lexington Railroad," www.lexhistory.org, retrieved October 1, 2016.

10. John E. Burns, *History of Covington, Kentucky, through 1865,* ed. Karl Lietzenmayer (Covington, KY: Kenton County Historical Society, 1986), 154. Covington's Greer Street is named for this early entrepreneur.

11. "Covington and Lexington Railroad."

12. Burns, *History of Covington.*

13. "Covington, Kentucky," www.wikipedia.com, retrieved September 16, 2016.

14. Karl Lietzenmayer, "M. C. Motch, Jewelers: A Kentucky Centennial Company," *Bulletin of the Kenton County Historical Society,* May–June 2011: 2–5.

15. Charles H. Bogart, "Railroad Depots," in *The Encyclopedia of Northern Kentucky,* 745–746.

16. Ibid.

17. Burns, *History of Covington.*

18. Ibid., 153–154.

19. Ibid.

20. Ibid.

19. Slavery and the Underground Railroad

1. Diane Perrine Coon, "Slavery," in *The Encyclopedia of Northern Kentucky,* ed. Paul A. Tenkotte and James C. Claypool (Lexington: University Press of Kentucky, 2009), 834–835.

2. Ibid.

3. Ibid.

4. Garry Aldeman with Mary Bays Woodside, "A House Divided: Civil War in Kentucky," *Hallowed Ground Magazine,* Spring 2000, https://www.battlefields.org/learn/articles/house-divided-civil-war-kentucky, retrieved October 10, 2016.

5. Alice Allison Dunnigan, *The Fascinating Story of Black Kentuckians: Their Heritage and Traditions,* (Washington, DC: Associated Publishing, 1982), 15.

6. Coon, "Slavery."

7. Adelman with Woodside, "A House Divided."

8. Coon, "Slavery."

9. Details presented are derived from various sources, including several entries by Diane Perrine Coon from *The Encyclopedia of Northern Kentucky*: "Slavery"; "Underground Railroad, Boone, Carroll, and Gallatin Counties," 899;

"John Pavy," 704; "Fuller Brothers," 373–374; and "Alexander Sebastian," 813–814. See also Eliza Harris, "Henry Bibb," www.wikipedia.com, retrieved October 5, 2016; Thomas L. Purvis, ed., *Newport, Kentucky: A Bicentennial History* (Newport, KY: Otto Zimmerman & Son, 1996); Caroline R. Miller, "Underground Railroad, Bracken County," in *The Encyclopedia of Northern Kentucky,* 902; Theodore H. H. Harris, "Underground Railroad, Campbell and Kenton Counties," in *The Encyclopedia of Northern Kentucky,* 903; and Jean Calvert and John Klee, *Maysville, Kentucky: From Past to Present in Pictures* (Maysville, KY: Mason County Museum, 1983), 35.

10. "Addison White," www.ohiohistorycentral.org/anndisonwhite, retrieved May 13, 2017.

11. "National Underground Railroad Museum of Maysville," in *The Encyclopedia of Northern Kentucky,* 645.

12. Joseph Gastright, "Daniel Henry Holmes," in *The Encyclopedia of Northern Kentucky,* 454.

13. Steven Weisenburger, *Modern Medea: A Family Story of Slavery and Child-Murder in the Old South* (New York: Hill and Wang, 1999), 20.

14. "John Pollard Gaines," in *The Encyclopedia of Northern Kentucky,* 378.

15. Weisenburger, *Modern Medea.* 20.

16. Ibid., 36–37.

17. Ibid., 20.

18. Ibid., 62.

19. "Margaret Garner," in *The Encyclopedia of Northern Kentucky,* 387.

20. Weisenburger, *Modern Medea.*

21. "Margaret Garner."

22. Ruth Wade Cox Brunnings, "Margaret Garner," at www.richwoodpresbyterian.org, retrieved October 12, 2016.

23. Ibid.

20. The American Civil War in Northern Kentucky

1. Garry Adelman with Mary Bays Woodside, "A House Divided: Civil War in Kentucky," *Hallowed Ground Magazine,* Spring 2000, https://www.battlefields.org/learn/articles/house-divided-civil-war-kentucky, retrieved October 10, 2016.

2. Ibid.

3. Ibid.

4. "Kentucky in the American Civil War," www.wikipedia.com, retrieved October 16, 2016.

5. Ibid.

6. Ibid.

7. Paul L Whalen, "Jesse Root Grant," in *The Encyclopedia of Northern*

Kentucky, ed. Paul A. Tenkotte and James C. Claypool (Lexington: University Press of Kentucky, 2009), 412–413.

8. Adelman with Woodside, "A House Divided."

9. John E. Burns, *History of Covington, Kentucky, through 1865,* ed. Karl Lietzenmayer (Covington, KY: Kenton County Historical Society, 1986), 324.

10. Ibid., 322.

11. "Black Brigade of Cincinnati," www.cityofftwright.com, retrieved October 21, 2016.

12. Burns, *History of Covington,* 330.

13. "Defense of Cincinnati," www.wikipedia.com, retrieved October 21, 2016.

14. Burns, *History of Covington,* 327.

15. Ibid., 332.

16. Ibid., 329.

17. Ibid., 324.

18. Ibid.

19. "John Hunt Morgan," www.wikipedia.com, retrieved October 22, 2016.

20. Several articles have been written about minor skirmishes in the region, especially those in Boone County. Even today, however, there is much confusion as to the exact details. Some have written about two separate encounters, on September 17 and 25, 1862, while others have determined that both skirmishes occurred on a single day, September 17. The reported number of prisoners taken ranges from 40 to more than 60. Some report that a Union camp was attacked, while others say it was a Rebel camp. Two historical markers have been erected at the two locations, but even those have conflicting details. The text here provides the best information available, gathered from various sources and believed to be the most accurate.

21. Daniel F. Dixon, *Snow's Pond: The Forgotten Civil War Skirmish in Boone County, Kentucky's Past,* (Mr. Vernon, IN: Windmill Publishing, 1999), https://www.bcpl.org/cbc/doku.php/skirmish_at_snow_s_pond, retrieved October 23, 2015.

22. Burns, *History of Covington,* 339

23. Kentucky Historical Marker no. 550, located on the southwest corner at the intersection of US 25 and US 42 in Florence, Kentucky.

24. Laurie Wilcox, "Florence," in *The Encyclopedia of Northern Kentucky,* 350.

25. Dixon, *Snow's Pond.*

26. Burns, *History of Covington,* 341.

27. James A. Ramage, "Augusta Civil War Raid," in *The Encyclopedia of Northern Kentucky,* 44–45.

28. Burns, *History of Covington,* 342.

29. Ibid., 343.

30. Jean Calvert and John Klee, *Maysville, Kentucky: From Past to Present in Pictures* (Maysville, KY: Mason County Museum, 1983), 29.

31. www.americancivilwar.com, retrieved October 1, 2016.

32. Burns, *History of Covington,* 346.

33. Ibid., 347.

34. Michael E. Beecher, "John Hunt Morgan's Escape through Boone County," *Union (KY) Community Recorder,* January 31, 2013.

35. Ibid.

36. Stephen T. McMurtry, "Bruce, Henry, Jr.," in *The Encyclopedia of Northern Kentucky,* 125–126.

37. Burns, *History of Covington,* 324.

38. www.americancivilwar.com, retrieved October 1, 2016.

39. Burns, *History of Covington,* 347.

21. Northern Kentucky after the Civil War

1. Jim Embry, "Segregation," in *The Encyclopedia of Northern Kentucky,* ed. Paul A. Tenkotte and James C. Claypool (Lexington: University Press of Kentucky, 2009), 816–817.

2. "Jim Crow Laws of Kentucky," http://classroomhelp.com/till/jimcrow-laws/Jimcrowkentucky.html, retrieved October 20, 2017.

3. Eric R. Jackson, *Northern Kentucky—Black America Series* (Charleston, SC: Arcadia Publishing, 2005), 33.

4. Theodore H. H. Harris, "Jacob Price," in *The Encyclopedia of Northern Kentucky,* 735–736.

5. Ibid.

6. Embry, "Segregation."

7. Ibid.

8. Ibid.

9. Theodore H .H. Harris, "African Americans," in *The Encyclopedia of Northern Kentucky,* 6.

10. Ralph Wolff, "John A. Roebling Bridge," in *The Encyclopedia of Northern Kentucky,* 490–492.

11. Phil Taliaferro, in "Daniel Carter Beard," *The Encyclopedia of Northern Kentucky,* 70

12. "Cherry Grove," in *The Encyclopedia of Northern Kentucky,* 174.

13. Mary Ann Gentry, *A Bicentennial Look at Carroll County* (Carrollton, KY: Carroll County Historical Society, 1999), 34.

14. "Frank Duveneck," in *The Encyclopedia of Northern Kentucky,* 286–287.

15. Terry W. Lehman, in "Streetcars," *The Encyclopedia of Northern Kentucky,* 856–857

16. Ibid.

17. Karl Lietzenmayer, "Coppin's Department Store," in *The Encyclopedia of Northern Kentucky,* 225.

18. Ibid.

19. John Boh, "Fritz Mineral Water Company," in *The Encyclopedia of Northern Kentucky,* 373.

20. "Newport Mineral Water Company," in *The Encyclopedia of Northern Kentucky,* 658.

22. Northern Kentucky in the Late 1800s

1. Robert D. Webster, *The Balcony Is Closed* (Covington, KY: Kenton County Historical Society, 2006), 5.

2. Ibid., 7.

3. Pamela Ciafardini Casebolt, "Italian Americans," in *The Encyclopedia of Northern Kentucky,* ed. Paul A. Tenkotte and James C. Claypool (Lexington: University Press of Kentucky, 2009), 482.

4. Ibid., 483.

5. Philip G. Ciafardini, *Italians of Newport and Northern Kentucky* (Charleston, SC: Images of America, 2007), 29.

6. Ibid., 67.

7. Mary Ann Gentry, *A Bicentennial Look at Carroll County* (Carrollton, KY: Carroll County Historical Society, 1999), 11.

8. Ibid., 33.

9. Diane Perrine Coon, "Carrollton Furniture Company," in *The Encyclopedia of Northern Kentucky,* 163.

10. Denny Kelley-Warnick, "Warsaw Furniture Factory," in *The Encyclopedia of Northern Kentucky,* 933.

11. Mary Jo Hardcorn, "Hatfield Coal Company," in *The Encyclopedia of Northern Kentucky,* 205.

12. Ibid.

13. Campbell County, Kentucky—200 Years (1794–1994) (Newport, KY: Campbell County Historical Society), 21.

14. James C. Claypool, "Latonia Racecourse," in *The Encyclopedia of Northern Kentucky,* 537–538.

15. Ibid.

16. Robert D. Webster, "Origin of the LLL Highway," *Bulletin of the Kenton County Historical Society,* May–June 2010: 5.

17. Betty Maddox Daniels, "Fort Thomas Military Reservation," in *The Encyclopedia of Northern Kentucky,* 361.

18. Betty Maddox Daniels, "Fort Thomas," in *The Encyclopedia of Northern Kentucky,* 360–361.

19. See John E. Burns, *History of Covington, Kentucky, through 1865,* ed.

Karl Lietzenmayer (Covington, KY: Kenton County Historical Society, 1986), 24; and Thomas L. Purvis, ed., *Newport, Kentucky: A Bicentennial History* (Newport, KY: Otto Zimmerman & Son, 1996).

20. "Distilleries," in *The Encyclopedia of Northern Kentucky,* 272–273.

21. Chuck Eilerman, "Eilerman and Sons, Men's Clothiers," in *The Encyclopedia of Northern Kentucky*, 296.

22. "Cohen Shoe Stores," in *The Encyclopedia of Northern Kentucky,* 206.

23. Gentry, " A Bicentennial Look at Carroll County," 35.

24. Terry W. Lehmann, "Green Line Company," in *The Encyclopedia of Northern Kentucky,* 422–423.

25. Ibid.

23. Lagoon Amusement Park and the Start of the Twentieth Century

1. David E. Schroeder, "Lagoon Amusement Park," in *The Encyclopedia of Northern Kentucky,* ed. Paul A. Tenkotte and James C. Claypool (Lexington: University Press of Kentucky, 2009), 528–529.

2. Ibid.

3. Thomas L. Purvis, ed., *Newport, Kentucky: A Bicentennial History* (Newport, KY: Otto Zimmerman & Son, 1996), 113.

4. Michael R. Sweeney, "Hospitals," in *The Encyclopedia of Northern Kentucky,* 462–463.

5. Ibid.

6. Jim Reis, "Pearl Bryan," in *The Encyclopedia of Northern Kentucky,* 126.

7. Charles K. Wolfe, *Kentucky Country: Folk and Country Music of Kentucky* (Lexington: University Press of Kentucky, 1982), 3.

8. Sharon McGee, "George Lee Wainscott," in *The Encyclopedia of Northern Kentucky,* 923.

9. Nancy J. Tretter, "Remke Markets," in *The Encyclopedia of Northern Kentucky,* 751.

10. Purvis, *Newport, Kentucky,* 163.

11. Ibid., 113.

12. Ibid., 167.

13. James C. Klotter, "William Goebel," in *The Encyclopedia of Northern Kentucky,* 405–406.

14. Ibid.

15. Michael R. Sweeney, "Donaldson Lithographic Company," in *The Encyclopedia of Northern Kentucky,* 277–278.

16. John Boh, "An International Edge: the Kelley-Koett Company (1903–1956)," *Northern Kentucky Heritage* 3, no. 2 (Spring–Summer 1996): 43.

17. Robert D. Webster, *The Balcony Is Closed* (Covington, KY: Kenton County Historical Society, 2006), 9–11.

18. Mary Jo Hardcorn, "Icehouses," in *The Encyclopedia of Northern Kentucky,* 472.

19. Ibid.

20. Bernie Spencer, "Night Riders," in *The Encyclopedia of Northern Kentucky,* 666.

21. Ibid.

24. The Basilica, World War I, and Prohibition

1. David E. Schroeder, "Devou Park," in *The Encyclopedia of Northern Kentucky,* ed. Paul A. Tenkotte and James C. Claypool (Lexington: University Press of Kentucky, 2009), 266–267.

2. Ibid.

3. Ibid.

4. "R. A. Jones and Company, Inc.," in *The Encyclopedia of Northern Kentucky,* 747.

5. Ibid.

6. Ibid.

7. Michael J. Poehner, "YMCA," in *The Encyclopedia of Northern Kentucky,* 982–983.

8. Ibid.

9. Ibid.

10. Melissa Reinert, "YMCA Expansion to Serve as 'Beacon of Health,'" *Boone Community Recorder,* July 20, 2017, 1.

11. Winston Coleman, Jr., and James C. Kelly, "Old Kentucky Watering Places," *Northern Kentucky Heritage* 8, no. 2 (Spring–Summer 2001): 57–58.

12. Patricia Hahn, "History of the Boone-Kenton Lumber Company," unpublished paper, Erlanger Historical Society, Erlanger, Kentucky, 2014.

13. "Tacoma Park," in *The Encyclopedia of Northern Kentucky,* 865.

14. Ibid.

15. Chris Meiman, "Pleasure Isle Swim Club," in *The Encyclopedia of Northern Kentucky,* 718–719.

16. David E. Schroeder, "World War I," in *The Encyclopedia of Northern Kentucky,* 975–976.

17. Ibid.

18. Don Heinrich Tolzmann, "German Americans," in *The Encyclopedia of Northern Kentucky,* 395.

19. Schroeder, "World War I," 976.

20. Ibid.

21. Robert Gioielli, "Gambling," in *The Encyclopedia of Northern Kentucky,* 738.

25. Northern Kentucky in the 1920s and 1930s

1. "The Roaring Twenties," www.history.com, retrieved March 15, 2017.

2. Leah Konicki, "A Look at Sears Houses in Northern Kentucky," *Northern Kentucky Heritage* 2, no. 2 (Spring–Summer 1995): 35.

3. For additional information on the suburb of Fort Mitchell, see Paul A. Tenkotte, *A Home of Our Own: The Suburb of Fort Mitchell, Kentucky, 1910–2010* (Cincinnati: Black Tie Press, 2011).

4. Robert D. Webster, *The Balcony Is Closed* (Covington, KY: Kenton County Historical Society, 2006

5. Thomas L. Purvis, ed., *Newport, Kentucky: A Bicentennial History* (Newport, KY: Otto Zimmerman & Son, 1996), 169.

6. Ibid.

7. Gabrielle Summe, "Dairies," in *The Encyclopedia of Northern Kentucky,* ed. Paul A. Tenkotte and James C. Claypool (Lexington: University Press of Kentucky, 2009), 254.

8. Ibid.

9. Ibid.

10. Ibid.

11. Robert D. Webster, "John Henry Tewes, Jr. and the Tewes Poultry Farm," *Bulletin of the Kenton County Historical Society,* November–December 2010: 1–10.

12. Robert D. Webster, "Fires," in *The Encyclopedia of Northern Kentucky,* 332–333.

13. William S. Bryant, "George Speri Sperti," in *The Encyclopedia of Northern Kentucky,* 848.

14. Michael R. Sweeney, "Dixie Chili," in *The Encyclopedia of Northern Kentucky,* 275.

15. Ibid.

16. John E. Leming, Jr., "Radio," in *The Encyclopedia of Northern Kentucky,* 743.

17. Ibid.

18. Ibid.

19. "WCVG," 940; John E. Leming, "WNOP,"968–969; and Chuck Eilerman, "WZIP," 980, all in *The Encyclopedia of Northern Kentucky.*

20. Robert D. Webster, *The Beverly Hills Supper Club: The Untold Story behind Kentucky's Worst Tragedy* (Dayton, KY: Saratoga Press, 2012), 8–29.

21. Ibid.

22. "John Thompson," in *The Encyclopedia of Northern Kentucky,* 878.

23. Noelle Higdon Grimes and Matthew J. Grimes, "Colonial Cottage," in *The Encyclopedia of Northern Kentucky,* 209–210.

24. Don Heinrich Tolzmann, "The Story of Goetta," *Bulletin of the Kenton County Historical Society,* March–April 2007: 5.

25. "Redlining," www.Blackpast.org, retrieved October 20, 2017.

26. The 1937 Flood and World War II

1. Jennifer Gregory, "Flood of 1937," in *The Encyclopedia of Northern Kentucky,* ed. Paul A. Tenkotte and James C. Claypool (Lexington: University Press of Kentucky, 2009), 345–347.

2. Ibid.

3. Ibid.

4. Ibid.

5. Ibid.

6. Ibid.

7. Ibid.

8. James C. Claypool, "Edward 'Eddie' Acaro," in *The Encyclopedia of Northern Kentucky,* 34–35.

9. Robert B. Snow, "World War II," in *The Encyclopedia of Northern Kentucky,* 976–978.

10. Ibid.

11. Ibid.

12. Ibid.

13. Ibid.

14. James C. Claypool, "Alvin C. Poweleit," in *The Encyclopedia of Northern Kentucky,* 731.

15. Snow, "World War II."

16. Ibid.

17. Ibid.

18. Ibid.

19. Ibid.

20. Verna L. Bond-Broderick, "Patricia 'Pat' Scott," in *The Encyclopedia of Northern Kentucky,* 812.

21. Joe Feiertag, Nicole Ropp, and Richard Rawe, "Cincinnati/Northern Kentucky International Airport," in *The Encyclopedia of Northern Kentucky,* 179–181.

22. Ibid.

23. Ibid.

24. Robert Schrage, *Carl Kiger: The Man beyond the Murder* (Covington, KY: Merlot Group, 2011), 94–95.

25. Various newspaper accounts in the *Kentucky Post* and the *Times-Star,* in August and December 1943.

26. Mildred Belew, "Griffin Industries," in *The Encyclopedia of Northern Kentucky,* 424.

27. Robert D. Webster, *The Balcony Is Closed* (Covington, KY: Kenton County Historical Society, 2006).

28. Lori Haller, "Green Derby Restaurant," in *The Encyclopedia of Northern Kentucky,* 421–422.

29. Terry W. Lehmann, "Green Line Company," in *The Encyclopedia of Northern Kentucky,* 422–423.

30. Ibid.

27. The Gourmet Strip, Civil Rights, and Urban Flight

1. Paul A. Tenkotte, "Gourmet Strip," in *The Encyclopedia of Northern Kentucky,* ed. Paul A. Tenkotte and James C. Claypool (Lexington: University Press of Kentucky, 2009), 410–411.

2. Robert D. Webster, "Fires," in *The Encyclopedia of Northern Kentucky,* 332–333.

3. Robert B. Snow, "Korean War," in *The Encyclopedia of Northern Kentucky,* 524–525.

4. "Duro Bag Manufacturing Company," in *The Encyclopedia of Northern Kentucky,* 285.

5. "The Civil Rights Movement," www.history.com/topics/black-history/civil-rights-movement, retrieved June 24, 2018.

6. Jeffrey Hampton, *Leaving Children Behind: Black Education in Covington, Kentucky* (Covington, KY: Kenton County Historical Society, 2011), 90.

7. Ibid., 90–91.

8. Ibid., 86.

9. Ibid., 94.

10. Ibid., 98.

11. Ted Van Dyk, "School Busing Didn't Work and to Say So Isn't Racist," *Politico Magazine,* August 6, 2015, https://www.politico.com/magazine/story/2015/08/school-busing-civil-rights-121077, retrieved October 20, 2017.

12. Tanner Colby, "The Massive Liberal Failure on Race," *Slate Magazine,* February 3, 2014, https://www.bunkhistory.org/resources/255?related=881&relationship_name=RELATED, retrieved October 20, 2017.

13. Van Dyk, "School Busing Didn't Work."

14. Ibid.

15. Colby, "The Massive Liberal Failure."

16. "White Flight," www.wikipedia.com, retrieved November 18, 2016.

17. "The 1950s," www.history.com, retrieved March 15, 2017.

18. Thomas L. Purvis, ed., *Newport, Kentucky: A Bicentennial History* (Newport, KY: Otto Zimmerman & Son, 1996), 266.

19. Robert D. Webster, "The Garden of Hope," *Bulletin of the Kenton County Historical Society,* September–October 2006: 6–8.

20. Robert D. Webster, *The Beverly Hills Supper Club: The Untold Story behind Kentucky's Worst Tragedy* (Dayton, KY: Saratoga Press, 2012), 26.

21. Michael L. Williams, "Sin City Kentucky: Newport Kentucky's Vice Heritage and Its Legal Extinction, 1920–1991," PhD diss., ir.library.louisville.edu/cgi/viewcontent.cgi?article=2573&context=etd,

21–22, retrieved September 15, 2016.

22. James C. Claypool, "Turfway Park," in *The Encyclopedia of Northern Kentucky,* 894–895.

23. Ibid.

28. Interstates and Higher Education

1. "Expressways," in *The Encyclopedia of Northern Kentucky,* ed. Paul A. Tenkotte and James C. Claypool (Lexington: University Press of Kentucky, 2009), 314–315.

2. Ibid.

3. John Schlipp, "Skeeter Davis," in *The Encyclopedia of Northern Kentucky,* 257.

4. John Schlipp, "Kenny Price," in *The Encyclopedia of Northern Kentucky,* 736–737.

5. www.mediabase.com/mmrweb/allaboutcountry/Charts.arp.format=C1R, retrieved November 13, 2017.

6. Jack Wessling, "Skating Rinks," in *The Encyclopedia of Northern Kentucky,* 833–834.

7. Robert D. Webster, "Bowling in Northern Kentucky," *Northern Kentucky Heritage Magazine* 20, no. 2 (Spring–Summer 2013): 28–38.

8. Ibid.

9. J. S. Brooking, "Vent Haven Museum," in *The Encyclopedia of Northern Kentucky,* 911.

10. Robert D. Webster, *The Beverly Hills Supper Club: The Untold Story behind Kentucky's Worst Tragedy* (Dayton, KY: Saratoga Press, 2012), 141.

11. Ibid.

12. Jim O'Brien, "Tornadoes," in *The Encyclopedia of Northern Kentucky,* 881–882.

13. http://www.dowcorning.de/de_DE/content/about/aboutcomm/cton_homepage.aspx, retrieved November 26, 2016.

14. John Miller and Paul Kiernan, "Nucor to Buy Gallatin Steel for $770 Million," https://www.wsj.com/articles/nucor-to-buy-gallatin-steel-for-770-million-1410813837, retrieved November 26, 2016.

15. David E. Schroeder, "Thomas More College," in *The Encyclopedia of Northern Kentucky,* 876–877.

16. Ibid.

17. James C. Claypool and Elizabeth Comer Williams, "Northern Kentucky University," in *The Encyclopedia of Northern Kentucky,* 676–679.

18. Ibid.

19. www.nky.edu, retrieved November 3, 2016.

29. Inner-City Decay, Poverty, and the Region's Worst Disaster

1. Paul A. Tenkotte, "Our Rich History: Poverty, Homelessness, a Challenge throughout Our Region's History That Persists Today," special to www.*NKyTribune,* June 11, 2018, retrieved June 12, 2018.

2. Ibid.

3. www.rosedalegreen.org, retrieved June 12, 2018.

4. Tenkotte, "Our Rich History."

5. Thomas L. Purvis, ed., *Newport, Kentucky: A Bicentennial History* (Newport, KY: Otto Zimmerman & Son, 1996), 268.

6. John Boh, "Main Strasse German Village," in *The Encyclopedia of Northern Kentucky,* ed. Paul A. Tenkotte and James C. Claypool (Lexington: University Press of Kentucky, 2009), 576–577.

7. Mike Williams, "Newport's Second Cleanup," in *The Encyclopedia of Northern Kentucky,* 619.

8. Ibid.

9. "Newport, Kentucky," www.wikipedia.com,retrieved November 5, 2016.

10. Robert D. Webster, "Fires," in *The Encyclopedia of Northern Kentucky,* 332–333.

11. For more information, see Robert D. Webster, *The Beverly Hills Supper Club: The Untold Story behind Kentucky's Worst Tragedy* (Dayton, KY: Saratoga Press, 2012).

12. Ibid.

30. Local Sports Figures, and Hollywood Comes to the Midwest

1. James C. Claypool, "Steven Cauthen," in *The Encyclopedia of Northern Kentucky,* ed. Paul A. Tenkotte and James C. Claypool (Lexington: University Press of Kentucky, 2009), 169–170.

2. John Schlipp, "Films and Filmmaking," in *The Encyclopedia of Northern Kentucky,* 328–329.

3. Nina Clooney, "George Clooney/Nick Clooney," in *The Encyclopedia of Northern Kentucky,* 202–203, and John Schlipp, "Rosemary Clooney," in *The Encyclopedia of Northern Kentucky,* 203–204.

4. Schlipp, "Films and Filmmaking."

5. Jennifer S. Warner, *Boone County: From Mastodons to the Millennium* (Burlington, KY: Boone County Historical Society, 1998), 378.

6. Paul A. Tenkotte and Nancy J. Tretter, "Earthquakes," in *The Encyclopedia of Northern Kentucky,* 289–290.

7. Robert D. Webster, "Fires," in *The Encyclopedia of Northern Kentucky,* 332–333.

8. Ibid.

9. Robert D. Webster, "How Well Do You Know Your Neighbor?" *Bulletin of the Kenton County Historical Society,* September–October 2006: 5–7.

10. http://www.kywoolfest.org/, retrieved June, 15 2017.

11. Diane Perrine Coon, "Rich Ladder Company," in *The Encyclopedia of Northern Kentucky,* 756.

12. "Carrollton Bus Crash," www.wikipedia.com, retrieved January 8, 2018.

31. Revitalization Explodes in Covington and Newport

1. "Covington, Kentucky," www.wikipedia.com, retrieved November 4, 2016.

2. Lou Settle, "Roebling Murals," in *The Encyclopedia of Northern Kentucky,* ed. Paul A. Tenkotte and James C. Claypool (Lexington: University Press of Kentucky, 2009), 768.

3. Thomas Ward, "Newport on the Levee," in *The Encyclopedia of Northern Kentucky,* 659.

4. James C. Claypool, "Millennium Monument World Peace Bell," in *The Encyclopedia of Northern Kentucky,* 619.

5. Michael Whitehead, "L&N Purple People Bridge," in *The Encyclopedia of Northern Kentucky,* 527.

6. http://www.newportky.gov/City-Government/Planning-and-Development.aspx, retrieved October 20, 2017.

7. John Iceland and Erik Hernandez, *Understanding Trends in Concentrated Poverty: 1980 to 2014,* https://pennstate.pure.elsevier.com/en/publications/understanding-trends-in-concentrated-poverty-19802014, retrieved November 15, 2017.

8. www.neighborhoodfoundation.com, retrieved November 1, 2017.

9. US Census Bureau, "American FactFinder—Results," http://factfinder2.census.gov., retrieved November 2, 2017.

10. US Census Bureau, 2016 estimated, https://www.census.gov/data/tables/2016/demo/popest/nation-total.html, retrieved November 3, 2017.

11. Ibid.

12. http://www.covingtonky.gov/government/departments/department-of-development/programs-strategic-projects/housing-development, retrieved November 2, 2017.

13. Colin Woodward, "How Cincinnati Salvaged the Nation's Most Dangerous Neighborhood," *Politico,* June 16, 2016.

14. Boris Ladwig, "New Poll: Heroin Epidemic Hits Louisville and Northern Kentucky Hard," *Insider Louisville,* May 9, 2017, 1.

15. Terry DeMilo, "Overdose Count 51 in 3 Days in NKY, 70 in Hamilton County," *Cincinnati Enquirer,* March 20, 2017, 1.

16. Kenton County Health Department Statistics, https://nkyhealth.org/, retrieved March 18, 2017.

32. Some River-Town Charm Remains

1. "BPB Celotex Opens New Plant in Carrollton," Bizjournals.com/Louisville, Nov 2, 2000, retrieved November 26, 2016.

2. http://www.kentuckytourism.com/historic-masterson-house/2051/, retrieved November 5, 2016.

3. "Kentucky Speedway," in *The Encyclopedia of Northern Kentucky,* ed. Paul A. Tenkotte and James C. Claypool (Lexington: University Press of Kentucky, 2009), 516.

4. http://bellevueky.org/about/historic-preservation/, retrieved December 8, 2016.

5. Michael R. Sweeney, "Phillip Allen Sharp," in *The Encyclopedia of Northern Kentucky,* 822.

6. Ibid.

7. Melissa J. Wickelhaus, "Flood of 1997, Licking River," in *The Encyclopedia of Northern Kentucky,* 347–348.

8. Ibid.

9. www.arkencounter.com, retrieved November 5, 2016.

10. Tom Loitus, "Ark Park Tax Incentives Worth Up to $18M Approved," *Louisville Courier-Journal,* April 4, 2016, retrieved October 31, 2017.

11. Ibid.

12. "Ark Encounter," www.wikipedia.com, retrieved November 5, 2016.

Appendix A

1. For additional information on St. Elizabeth Hospital, see Brian Hackett and Paul A. Tenkotte, *For the Centuries: St. Elizabeth Healthcare and Northern Kentucky, 1861–2011* (Edgewood, KY: St. Elizabeth Healthcare, 2011).

Selected Bibliography

Baugher, Ruby Dell, and Sarah Hendricks Claypool. *Kentucky: Yesterday and Today.* Evansville, IN: Kinkaid Publishing House, 1964.

Bogardus, Carl R., Sr. *Story of Gallatin County.* Edited by James C. Claypool. Gallatin County, KY: Sue M. Bogardus, 1994.

Burns, John E. *History of Covington, Kentucky, through 1865.* Edited by Karl Lietzenmayer. Covington, KY: Kenton County Historical Society, 1986.

Clark, Thomas D. *History of Kentucky.* Ashland, KY: Jesse Stuart Foundation, 1988.

Conrad, John B., ed. *History of Grant County, Kentucky.* Williamstown, KY: Grant County Historical Society, 1992.

Davis, S. "Interesting Historical Facts—City of Covington." *Covington Journal,* April 12, 1873: 1.

Dorsey, Robert C. "Thomas Kennedy: Founder of Covington, Kentucky." *Gist Historical Society Papers,* Box 4, Folder 24, August 24, 1954. Archived at the main branch of the Kenton County Public Library, Covington, Kentucky.

Encyclopedia of Northern Kentucky, The. Edited by Paul A. Tenkotte and James C. Claypool. Lexington: University Press of Kentucky, 2009.

Foster, Judith Ann. *History of Bracken County—Bicentennial Edition.* Brooksville, KY: Bracken County Extension Homemakers, 1996.

Gateway City, Covington, Kentucky, 1815–2015. Edited by James Claypool and Paul Tenkotte. Covington, KY: Clerisy Press, 2015.

Gentry, Mary Ann. *History of Carroll County, Kentucky.* Madison, IN: Coleman Printing, 1984.

Hampton, Jeffrey. *Leaving Children Behind: Black Education in Covington, Kentucky.* Covington, KY: Kenton County Historical Society, 2011.

Harrison, Lowell H., and James C. Klotter. *A New History of Kentucky.* Lexington: University Press of Kentucky, 1997.

Historical Dictionary of the Civil Rights Movement. Edited by Ralph E. Luker and Christopher M. Richardson. Lanham, MD: Rowman & Littlefield, 2014.

Houchens, Marian Sidebottom. *History of Owen County.* Owenton, KY: Owen County Historical Society, 1976.

Kentucky Encyclopedia. Edited by John E. Kleber. Lexington: University Press of Kentucky, 1992.

Klotter, James C., and Freda C. Klotter. *A Concise History of Kentucky.* Lexington: University Press of Kentucky, 2008.

MacKoy, William. "William MacKoy Remembers Covington." *Cincinnati Commercial,* October 15, 1876.

Onkst, Wayne A. *A Centennial History of Erlanger, Kentucky.* Erlanger: Erlanger Historical Society, 1996.

Penn, William A. *Kentucky Rebel Town: The Civil War in Cynthiana and Harrison County.* Lexington: University Press of Kentucky, 2016.

Purvis, Thomas L., ed. *Newport, Kentucky: A Bicentennial History.* Newport, KY: Otto Zimmerman & Son, 1996.

Rankins, Walter. *Historical Augusta and Augusta College.* Augusta, KY: Self-published, 1949.

Schrage, Robert. *Legendary Locals of Covington.* Mount Pleasant, SC: Arcadia Press, 2014.

Smith, Allen Webb. *Beginning at The Point: A Documented History of Northern Kentucky and Environs, the Town of Covington in Particular, 1751–1834.* Park Hills, KY: Self-published, 1977.

Tenkotte, Paul. "Rival Cities to Suburbs: Covington and Newport, Kentucky, 1790–1890." Ann Arbor, MI: UMI Dissertation Information Service, 1989.

Warner, Jennifer S. *Boone County: From Mastodons to the Millennium.* Burlington, KY: Boone County Bicentennial Book Committee, 1998.

Index

Page numbers in italics refer to illustrations.